African American Women in Congress

Forming

and

Transforming

History

LaVerne McCain Gill

Rutgers University Press
New Brunswick, New Jersey

All photographs in this book were supplied by the
offices of the congressional representative or senator.

Library of Congress Cataloging-in-Publication Data

Gill, LaVerne McCain, 1947–
    African American women in Congress : forming and transforming history / LaVerne
McCain Gill.
        p.   cm.
    Includes bibliographical references and index.
    ISBN 0-8135-2352-4 (cloth : alk. paper). — ISBN 0-8135-2353-2 (pbk. : alk. paper)
    1. Afro-American women legislators—Biography.   2. United States. Congress—
Biography.   I. Title.
E.840.6.G55   1997
328.73'092'2—dc20
[B]
                               96-29294
                                    CIP

British Cataloging-in-Publication information available

Manufactured in the United States of America

For my mother, Mary Willette McCain Williams
my stepfather, Clement R. Williams
my husband, Dr. Tepper L. Gill
my sons, Dylan and Tepper
my brothers, Paul and John

In memory of my brother, Frederick Sterling McCain

Contents

Acknowledgments

This book grew from a public radio program entitled "The Talented Ten: African American Women in the 103rd Congress," an independent production that I wrote and produced and that aired in 1994. Underwritten by General Motors and distributed by American Public Radio (now International Public Radio), the program aired on more than one hundred stations in the United States and Canada. A number of people participated in providing support for both the audio and this written account of the fifteen African American women who have served or are serving in the U.S. Congress. Any number of people deserve thanks for their support and encouragement in getting this book completed. At the risk of leaving someone out, I will attempt to recall as many as possible who have been with me throughout this ordeal. Any omissions are of the head and not the heart.

With a deep and abiding faith, I owe the greatest thanks to God for giving me the gifts that I needed to complete this endeavor. Secondly, I want to thank my immediate family. My husband, Dr. Tepper L. Gill, has made it possible for me to write without worry or distraction. He has allowed me to travel with him to Kiev, Ukraine, and southern Italy, where he made certain that I had an opportunity to write while accompanying him on his mathematical research and speaking engagements. His partnership has been invaluable in helping me to sustain a peace of mind that I hope is reflected in this book.

I have been blessed with two sons, Tepper and Dylan, who have both encouraged me and provided me with the inspiration and love to go forward so that their generation might benefit from the knowledge herein. Dylan also helped arrange the initial interviews with the congresswomen and was a production assistant for the "Talented Ten" public radio program.

My mother, Mary Williams, and my stepfather, Clement Williams, had to forgo precious moments of companionship because of my long hours writing. I appreciate their unconditional support and encouragement with all of my endeavors. Although those moments cannot be recaptured, perhaps they will find in this book another level of satisfaction.

Paul and John McCain, my brothers, have been constantly supportive and vigilant and have taken up some of my responsibilities with our parents when I was unavailable.

Theirs has been a quiet kind of love that sometimes goes unnoticed. As always, the abiding spirit of my late brother, Frederick McCain, is present.

From a technical standpoint, I am indebted to George Wilson, Capitol Hill correspondent for American Urban Radio Network, for his assistance in interviewing Carol Moseley-Braun, Maxine Waters, Carrie Meek, Eddie Bernice Johnson, and Shirley Chisholm for the radio program. I am also indebted to him for his institutional memory, emanating from more than two decades as one of a handful of African American correspondents in the congressional press galleries. To the many press secretaries of the congresswomen interviewed for this book, a note of appreciation is extended for their time and commitment to fitting these interviews into the members' busy schedules. Of course, to the congresswomen themselves for taking time out to participate in the interviews, a special debt of gratitude is owed, for without their political courage, this book would not be. Photographs of Shirley Chisholm, Barbara Jordan, Yvonne Burke, Cardiss Collins, and Katie Hall appear courtesy of the U.S. House of Representatives. Photographs of Eleanor Norton, Maxine Waters, Barbara-Rose Collins, Carol Moseley-Braun, Corrine Brown, Carrie Meek, Cynthia McKinney, Eva Clayton, Eddie Bernice Johnson, and Sheila Jackson-Lee appear courtesy of their respective congressional offices.

Accessible research facilities also deserve mention, because without them a lot of material would have been unavailable through normal sources. They are Howard University's Founders Library, the U.S. Senate Library, and the Center for the American Woman and Politics at Rutgers University. Having been a publisher of an African American newspaper, I must also recognize and thank those members of the black press who record history that cannot be found in the mainstream media. So a special note of thanks to the publishers of *Ebony, Jet,* and the Afro-American newspaper chain.

There are those who have provided valuable input and considerable criticism—sometimes brutal critiques—that have been accepted with love and humility. They include Theodore Jones, Irving McDuffie, Adrienne Daniels, and Thelma Calbert. My appreciation to them and my hope that they will feel that I have adequately responded to their suggestions. Special thanks to my two stepdaughters, Dorian McDuffie and Jennette Hardy, for their support and encouragement.

There are others who have been supportive without even knowing that they have contributed, but their encouragement and prayers have been duly felt and recorded. While I cannot name them all, they include my many colleagues at Princeton Theological Seminary and particularly the Association of Black Seminarians, my friends Irene Bush, Florence and Charles Tate, Harold and Shiela Bradshaw, Dr. Evans Crawford and his wife, Elizabeth, and Tom Porter, Lynn Rosario, Oggi Ogburn, and artist Vivian McDuffie. In Kiev, I owe a special thanks to Dr. Wilhelm Fushchich and Dr. Olga Fushchich and the Ukrainian Academy of Sciences; in Italy, to Dr. Ruggero Santilli and Carla Santilli of the Institute for Basic Research for making special writing accommodations for me while in Europe.

Professionally, I want to extend a special note of gratitude to my agent Natasha Kern and her colleague Oriana, who have had the faith that this project would reach fruition and took the care and precision to craft a relationship with the publisher that enabled me to work without excessive pressure.

To my acquiring editor, Leslie Mitchner, who has been critical but caring with a new writer: I thank you. I also want to acknowledge my lawyer, Eric Steele.

There is also a special unknown core of people who deserve acknowledgment. They include the cafeteria staff of Princeton Seminary and the staffs of Barnes & Noble's Starbucks coffee shop in Princeton Market Fair and the Hyatt Regency Coffee Shop in Reston Town Center in Virginia. They have allowed me to spend untold hours, writing, correcting, and reading research material, while supplying me with endless cups of coffee. Included also in this group is a special relationship developed during the past year with the inmates at the Garden State Correctional Facility in New Jersey, where I served as a chaplain along with the Reverend Ray Dubois. I cannot close without mentioning them.

Finally, I hope that this book begins a new inquiry into the political history of African American women and that some enterprising writer will capture the lives of each of these fifteen women, since each deserves a book dedicated to her particular political odyssey. I hope this book will be only the primer for those extensive biographies.

African American Women in Congress

Chapter 1 **Introduction**

I think, anyone looking at the floor of Congress from the gallery will
see a distinctive change in the make-up of this Congress. You have
African American women who have come in with decidedly different
styles and approaches to doing business in this Congress. Just to look
down and see Cynthia McKinney in her vibrant colors and her golden
tennis shoes and her hair in braids, to see Carrie Meek talking in a
different language and using some of the very colorful and wonderful
language of people from the South and from Florida that you haven't
heard in this Congress before. I mean . . . Eddie Bernice Johnson, from
Texas, who comes with a wealth of experience, certainly stands out.
Not only the different styles and colors and way we talk and the way
we handle ourselves, but our commitment to our people in ways that
allow us to challenge some of the traditions of this House and to
challenge someone who would get on the floor and talk about
African Americans in a demeaning way. . . . I think people know that
we're all here. And, certainly this new group of women has added to
our presence in a profound way.

—Maxine Waters (D-Calif.) commenting on the African
American women of the 103d Congress, 1993–1994[1]

The fifteen African American women who served in Congress were
paradoxical political figures. They represented social change and reform while also upholding political tradition. On the one hand, they were well-established Democrats with the
requisite political acumen to get elected and remain in office. On the other hand, they were
the heirs apparent to the centuries of struggle waged by black women for almost four hundred years, and they owed something to that legacy. Theirs had been the struggle within
the struggle. Active in the major reform movements of the country, African American women
played an integral part in the abolitionist, suffrage, and civil rights movements. The fruits
of their centuries of labor would be late in coming.

Not only would their efforts not be rewarded, but their invisibility would result from
a country that viewed African American progress as male and feminist progress as white.
The foreshadowing of this dilemma was brought out in the late nineteenth century by Ellen
Carol Dubois: "In her classic study of the rupture during Reconstruction, Ellen Dubois
reminds us how different the alignments would have been had feminists campaigned for
the vote for women white and black. Their failure to do so, along with the Republicans'
abandonment of their cause, gave birth to an enduring syllogism of American political understanding: if the 'Negro' was male, then the 'woman' was white."[2]

Certainly what followed was the result of that syllogism. From a political and gender perspective, research on women in Congress reveals that of the 172 women who have served in Congress, only fifteen have been African American. Seventy-nine black men have served in Congress, beginning in 1870.

The first African American woman elected to Congress was Shirley Chisholm, who was sworn in in 1969. It was certainly a historic moment and the result of centuries of labor, but it was also nearly a century after the first black man, Hiram Revels (R-Miss.), was sworn into the Senate in 1870. Because of the compromises made by white women suffragettes with white southern politicians, it was also more than fifty years after the first woman, Jeannette Rankin, began her term in 1917. Although she entered three years before the adoption of the Nineteenth Amendment, the suffragettes had already begun to execute their strategy of expediency. It was a strategy that would include white women compromising away the rights of African American women and immigrants in exchange for the voting franchise.

Unfortunately, the white women's suffrage movement was a part of the racism and classism that plagued the country during this time, and the result tainted the relationships between the feminist movement and the African American womanist movement up through the present time.

In addressing this issue, Christine Stansell writes:

> In 1865, the radicals of the Republican Party, the party of black emancipation and women's rights, began to break away from their commitment to universal suffrage to push through the Fifteenth Amendment, which gave the vote to the freedmen. In abandoning women's suffrage they reasoned that such a radical measure would only compromise any amendment for wider enfranchisement, and that the needs of the freedmen were more urgent. . . . Some leaders of the women's movement—Lucy Stone, for example—followed the Republican leadership, believing that their own demands could wait until the bloody revanche in the South was stilled and the crisis of black male citizenship resolved. Others—most notably, Elizabeth Cady Stanton and Susan B. Anthony—broke ranks to form their own uncompromising movement for "woman suffrage" in the process abnegating their commitment to black freedom. In the postwar movement they helped to found, black women would be excluded for decades and black men would long be disdained.[3]

Thus, the road to Capitol Hill for African American women had been long and arduous—strewn with aborted strategies and unreliable allies. From the historic "Ain't I a Woman" address of Sojourner Truth to Fannie Lou Hamer's unforgettable lament, "I'm sick and tired of being sick and tired," in the 1960s, black women have confronted racism and sexism, taken leadership roles, risked their lives, and gained ground for black men and white women.

Through it all, the triumph far outweighed the tribulations, and the fifteen African American women who served between 1969 and 1996 have not only made history but have transformed it. It is an epoch framed by the election of the first black woman, Shirley

Chisholm (D-N.Y.) in 1969 and the 1996 retirement of Cardiss Collins (D-Ill.), a twenty-three year veteran of the House of Representatives and the longest serving African American woman in history. Of equal significance is the fact that the fifteen women who served during this time were prepared and poised to take on the leadership that had been denied them for so long.

A composite profile of the fifteen reveals the following: a third of them are lawyers; one had been a nurse, two had been college administrators; the rest were former schoolteachers and social workers. Eighty percent were also former state legislators. Of those, more than half had actually served on the committees that carved out their congressional districts amid heated state reapportionment battles. They were well educated: 87 percent had bachelors' degrees, and two-thirds had additional graduate or professional degrees. All but two had been married, divorced, or widowed. Thirteen were mothers—some with school-aged children while serving in Congress—others were grandmothers by the time they reached Washington. Their average age when first sworn in to Congress was forty-six, and ages ranged from thirty-six to sixty-eight as they began their first terms.

Individually and politically they were distinctly different legislators. While all were Democrats, their scope ranged from local machine politicians to mavericks who functioned better as challengers to the status quo. Still others could be considered to have been less parochial, identified more as Democratic National Committee standard bearers, than as local politicians. Their voting patterns were equally as unpredictable. They could easily have been labeled liberal legislators. However, key issues such as capital punishment, trade agreements, various crime provisions, and budget priorities produced divergent views and some conservative voting records. Primarily, the African American women in Congress were womanist politicians with interests in issues that dealt with the eradication of sexism, racism, and classism. Such concerns invariably translated into more legislation, with the areas of education, health care, economic development, job development, and job training being the major focus. International issues received less of their attention, though Haiti and South Africa were exceptions, as well as Vietnam during the Chisholm years.

Historical Perspective

I believe that black women have a very special gift of leadership, because we have been called upon to lead in very trying times. And history has recorded the fact that black women rose to the forefront in times of struggle during periods of conflict about civil rights. But we don't have to go that far forward to recall that there was also leadership even in the days of slavery in this country.
—Congresswoman Barbara Jordan, commenting on African American women in Congress[4]

While men reaped the benefits of enfranchisement that were bestowed upon African Americans following Reconstruction, black women, though qualified, were left out. In 1870, after the Fourteenth[5] and Fifteenth[6] Amendments to the Constitution were adopted, Revels led a cadre of black men who served in Congress for nearly three decades, ending in 1901 with the departure of George White (R-N.C.). It would be nearly three decades before another black man would enter Congress. In 1928 Oscar DePriest (R-Ill.)—with assistance from journalist and suffragette, Ida B. Wells-Barnett—was elected to a segregated House of Representatives.

Eight years earlier in 1920, white women had gained the voting franchise with the adoption of the Nineteenth[7] Amendment. Prior to its adoption, Jeannette Rankin had been elected to the House of Representatives. The white women's suffrage movement came at great expense to African American women. Despite the efforts of black women suffragettes such as Mary Church Terrell, Ida B. Wells-Barnett, and Nannie Helen Burroughs, white women continued to choose a narrow path for gaining the vote by refusing to integrate their movement and negotiating with white men to maintain European-American hegemony over American politics.

Angela Davis writes:

> The nineteenth-century women's movement was also plagued by classism. Susan B. Anthony wondered why her outreach to working-class women on the issue of the ballot was so frequently met with indifference. She wondered why these women seemed to be much more concerned with improving their economic situation than with achieving the right to vote. As essential as political equality may have been to the larger campaign for women's rights, in the eyes of Afro-American and White working-class women it was not synonymous with emancipation. That the conceptualization of strategies for struggle was based on the peculiar condition of White women of the privileged classes rendered those strategies discordant with working-class women's perceptions of empowerment.[8]

Davis provides the historical frame of reference for what would later constitute the distinction between African American women feminist and the white feminist movement. For the black woman in politics the issues were three: race, gender, and class. For white women the issue was gender, and class was assumed to imply privilege.

From the beginning of Reconstruction, white women berated enfranchised black men in order to gain favor and reconnect with white men who possessed the power to make a change. They embarked upon an approach after Reconstruction that they labeled their "expediency" strategy. In essence it would ensure that middle-class white women gained the franchise, but that black women and immigrants would not. It was a strategy that reinforced the already operative Jim Crow laws—laws that were legitimized by the Hayes-Tilden compromise that withdrew federal troops from the South. It also aligned white women with southern white men, who were determined to keep the franchise from blacks—men and women.

It would take the civil rights movement to bring black women into focus as viable political figures in their own right. Freed from seeking political activism through social clubs and associations, African American women took on leadership in the Student

Non-Violent Coordinating Committee, the Mississippi Freedom Democratic party, the voter registration and education projects, sit-ins, and freedom rides. They emerged from those movements with a renewed vigor and created political outlets on the local level, in which they became key participants, not just supportive bystanders. This time they would benefit from their efforts. They would not allow the impediments of racism and sexism to stand over the threshold of their political aspirations, darkening their horizons and preventing them from realizing political parity.

The key to the entrance of black women into Congress during this epoch was the 1965 Voting Rights Act. The act abolished literacy tests and other impediments to African American voters. In 1970, 1975, and 1982, the amendment was readopted, authorizing federal intervention to ensure the creation of minority districts where there was evidence of past discrimination. As these women entered state legislatures, they had an opportunity to establish congressional districts around their existing constituencies. More than half did. In 1968, three years after the Voting Rights Act paved the way for minority seats for state and congressional districts, Chisholm was elected to Congress. By 1972 she was running for president of the United States. The following year she was joined by three additional women, and the movement of black women into Congress, slow to arrive, was slowly gaining momentum.

About the Book

African American Women in Congress: Forming and Transforming History uses personal and political profiles to demonstrate how these fifteen women have been a significant part of the formation and transformation of American history during this first epoch. Through their stories, and in many instances in their own words, what evolves are not only portraits of individual women, but glimpses into the story of a nation. From segregated schools in their early years, through triumphs of the civil rights movement, to the Halls of Congress, these women's lives and narratives offer a window through which to view America. They are also products of that history, as well as agents of its transformation.

More than any other group, they are keenly aware that they stand on the shoulders of women such as Sojourner Truth, Ida B. Wells-Barnett, and Fannie Lou Hamer—fighters for the abolition of slavery, universal suffrage, and the two fundamental human rights of parity and human dignity.

This book benefits greatly from the public radio special from which it evolved. The program, written and produced by the author and entitled "The Talented Ten: African American Women in the 103rd Congress," was distributed by American Public Radio (now International Public Radio) in 1994 and included interviews with all of the women of the 103d Congress. It included background information on the trailblazers who preceded them. Not included in the program was Sheila Jackson-Lee (D-Tex.), who entered the 104th

Congress (1995–1996). This early audio special included taped interviews from each of the women serving in the 103d Congress. Aiding in the interviewing process as a part of the talent team was George Wilson, a veteran Capitol Hill radio correspondent working with the American Urban Radio Network. Subsequent follow-up interviews were conducted by the author, including one with Jackson-Lee.

African American Women in Congress is separated into four parts: the Trailblazers, the Urban Women of the 102d Congress, the U.S. Senate, and the Southern Women of the 103d and 104th Congress.

Part One: The Trailblazers. Five African American women paved the way in Congress, from the late 1960s into the early 1980s, for the ten who followed them in the 1990s. They were Shirley Anita Chisholm (D-N.Y.), the late Barbara Jordan (D-Tex.), Yvonne Brathwaite Burke (D-Calif.), Cardiss Collins (D-Ill.), and Katie Beatrice Hall (D-Ind.).

The women elected between 1969 and 1989 were distinctively different in their political profiles, yet similar in other ways. Chisholm, Jordan, and Burke achieved national recognition, each for different reasons. Chisholm was the maverick in the group. In addition to leading the way as the first black woman elected to Congress, she made history again in 1972 by running for the Democratic presidential nomination. A unique and gifted charismatic politician, she was joined in 1973 by three other black women.

One was Jordan, who represented the Eighteenth Congressional District of Texas. A strong defender of the Constitution, the late congresswoman is remembered most for her deliberative oratorical style during the Watergate hearings on the impeachment of President Richard Nixon. That speech alone conferred on her a reputation as a superb orator and a consummate statesman.

For six years, between 1973 and 1979, Yvonne Brathwaite Burke served as the representative from the Thirty-seventh Congressional District of California. She gained national recognition months before her election by her adept handling of the raucous Democratic National Convention of 1972—the year Chisholm commanded center stage with her history-making presidential quest. Burke went on to serve with distinction before deciding against reelection to a fourth term.

Seniority is the key to power in the U.S. House of Representatives, and no other black woman achieved the powerful status of Cardiss Collins, before her decision to retire in 1996. Her tenure of twenty-three years in the House was the longest of any black woman. She served as an unassuming colleague to all and a mentor to most of the fourteen other women.

Just as blacks were gaining power in Gary, Indiana, Katie Beatrice Hall began her political career. Her short tenure in the House of Representatives, from 1982 to 1984, will be remembered primarily for her introduction of the bill that declared Martin Luther King, Jr.'s birthday a holiday. The fifteen-year crusade ended when the bill she introduced and shepherded through the House and Senate was signed into law in 1983.

These women were the trailblazers. They entered Congress during a less genteel and socially conscious time in American history and survived to accomplish and set the pace and the tone for the women who would follow. Their experiences were instructive to those who currently serve in both houses.

Part Two: The Urban Women of the 102d Congress. In 1990, three women were elected to the House of Representatives, joining Collins, who had served for six years as the only black woman in Congress. These women, all still in office in 1996, were Maxine Waters (D-Calif.), Eleanor Holmes Norton (D-D.C.), and Barbara-Rose Collins (D-Mich.). They were not just colleagues of Collins's but shared the same type of constituency—urban, inner-city, and under-represented poor, predominantly black populations. Each had experience in national, state, or local politics.

Waters had fourteen years in the California state legislature and gained national exposure as a supporter of both the 1984 and 1988 presidential candidacies of Jesse Jackson. Norton, a national champion of civil rights, would now put her considerable skills to work in pursuit of statehood for her hometown, Washington, D.C. After years as a grassroots organizer in Detroit and a member of the Detroit School Board, Collins won a seat in the Michigan state assembly, then returned to Detroit as a member of the city council before launching her second bid for Congress.

Cardiss Collins publicly welcomed each of these women with open arms, sharing with them her hard-earned lessons in congressional effectiveness.

Part Three: The U.S. Senate. In 1992, the icon of the "Year of the Woman" turned out to be a little-known former black state legislator of the Illinois House of Representatives—Carol Moseley-Braun. The lawyer-turned-politician shocked the Democratic party leaders when she defeated a six-term incumbent during the primary. She followed that feat with a victory over a conservative Republican lawyer, becoming the first African American woman and the first black Democrat to be elected to the U.S. Senate.

Though Moseley-Braun entered under a cloud of controversy surrounding her campaign and personal finances, she later emerged as a skilled debater and a leader in some of the Senate's key legislative initiatives.

Part Four: The Southern Women of the 103d and 104th Congresses. The combination of reapportionment and the spectacle of the Clarence Thomas U.S. Supreme Court confirmation hearings paved the way for the significant number of black women who entered the House of Representatives in 1993. These women of the 103d Congress are aptly described by Maxine Waters in the opening of this chapter. All are from newly created congressional districts and remained in office in 1996. They are Eva Clayton (D-N.C.), Carrie Meek (D-Fla.), Corrine Brown (D-Fla.), Eddie Bernice Johnson (D-Tex.), and Cynthia McKinney (D-Ga.).

With the exception of Johnson, each was the first African American woman from her state to serve in Congress. Unfortunately, all would face, before their second terms, court challenges to their new districts. Landmark decisions would call for the redrawing of the districts of McKinney, Johnson, and Brown. Eva Clayton would narrowly miss such a

African American Women in Congress, 1969–1996

	Age at Swearing-in	Previous Political Elected Office	Occupation	Earned Degrees	Marital Status upon Entering Congress	Children	Religious Denom-ination
Shirley Chisholm *(chapter 2)*	44	state rep.	teacher	B.A.,M.A.	married	0	Methodist
Barbara Jordan *(chapter 3)*	36	state senator	lawyer	B.A.,LL.B.	single	0	Baptist
Yvonne Burke *(chapter 4)*	40	state rep.	lawyer	A.A.,B.A.,J.D.	married	2	Baptist
Cardiss Collins *(chapter 5)*	41	none	auditor	none	widowed	1	Baptist
Katie Beatrice Hall *(chapter 6)*	44	state senator	teacher	B.S.,M.S.	married	3	Baptist
Eleanor H. Norton *(chapter 7)*	53	none	lawyer	B.A.,M.A.,J.D.	separated	2	Episcop.
Maxine Waters *(chapter 8)*	52	state rep.	social worker	B.A.	married	2	Christian
Barbara-Rose Collins *(chapter 9)*	51	state rep., city council	purchas. clerk	none	widowed	2	Pan-African Orthodox
Carol Moseley-Braun *(chapter 10)*	45	state rep.	lawyer	B.A.,J.D.	divorced	1	Catholic
Corrine Brown *(chapter 11)*	46	state rep.	college adminis-trator	B.S.,M.S.	single	1	Baptist
Carrie Meek *(chapter 12)*	66	state senator, state rep.	college adminis-trator	B.S.,M.S.	divorced	3	Baptist
Cynthia McKinney *(chapter 13)*	37	state rep.	college lecturer	A.B.	divorced	1	Catholic
Eva Clayton *(chapter 14)*	58	none	consultant	B.S.,M.S.	married	4	Presbyter.
Eddie Bernice Johnson *(chapter 15)*	58	state senator, state rep.	nurse	B.S.,M.P.A.	divorced	1	Baptist
Sheila Jackson-Lee *(chapter 16)*	44	city council	lawyer	B.A.,J.D.	married	2	Seventh-Day Adventist

Source: Data compiled from *Biographical Directory of the United States Congress, 1774–1994* (Washington, D.C.: Government Printing Office, 1994).

fate. Chapters 11–15 include descriptions of the battles fought by these congresswomen to keep their seats.

Chapter 16 is a profile of the newest African American woman in the U.S. House of Representatives—Sheila Jackson-Lee (D-Tex.). Her David-and-Goliath victory over a favored incumbent would become part of Texas political lore. But she, too, would face the challenge of holding on to a district that was slated to be redrawn following a court order.

The epilogue addresses the transitions of 1996 and the projections into the future. By the end of 1996, the indomitable Barbara Jordan had died of leukemia; Cardiss Collins had ended twenty-three years, retiring at the close of the 104th Congress; and the new seats of all of the black women elected to the House during the 103d were in jeopardy. Three had already been eliminated.

The end of the 104th Congress was indeed an end of an epoch for African American women. With the retirement of Cardiss Collins at the end of the session, a generation of women leaders gave way to a new era, with its own opportunities for new "firsts." From the "unbought and unbossed" Shirley Chisholm to the "I don't have time to be nice" Maxine Waters, African American women in Congress have been a part of the formation and transformation of American history. More than any others in Congress, they have attempted to address the tridimensional problems of sexism, racism, and classism. Their inescapable heritage leaves very little choice but to continue the "struggle within the struggle."

Part One

The Trailblazers

Chapter 2 **Shirley Anita St. Hill Chisholm**

A Model of Courage and Commitment

We must turn away from the control of the prosaic, the privileged, and the old line, tired politicians to open our society to the energies and abilities of countless new groups of Americans—women, blacks, browns, Indians, Orientals and youth—so that they can develop their own full potential and thereby participate equally and enthusiastically in building a strong and just society, rich in its diversity and noble in its quality of life.[1]

Résumé

Shirley Anita St. Hill Chisholm

Personal

Born   November 30, 1924
Brooklyn, New York

Family   Married while in office to Conrad Chisholm (divorced 1977), then to Arthur Hardwick, Jr. (married 1978); no children

Religion   Methodist

Party   Democrat

Took office   Age 44, January 3, 1969

Education

B.A.   Brooklyn College, New York City, 1946

M.A.   Columbia University, New York City, 1952

Professional/Political Background

1946–1953   Nursery school teacher, Mt. Calvary Childcare Center, New York City

1953–1959   Director, Hamilton-Madison Child Care Center, New York City

1959–1964   Educational consultant, Division of Day Care, New York City

1964–1968   Assemblywoman, New York state legislature

1969–1982   U.S. House of Representatives

1983–1984   Lecturer, Mount Holyoke College, South Hadley, Massachusetts

1984–   Lecturer, teacher, political mentor

Selected Awards/Organizational Affiliations

Selected Honorary Degrees: Columbia University, Hampton University, LaSalle College, University of Maine, Pratt Institute, Coppin State College, North Carolina College, University of Cincinnati, Smith College.

Honorary member/Board of Directors: Cosmopolitan Young People's Symphony Orchestra, Fund for Research and Education in Sickle Cell Disease.

Awards: Alumna of Year, Brooklyn College, 1957; Outstanding Work in the Field of Child Welfare, Women's Council of Brooklyn, 1957; Key Woman of Year, 1963, Woman of Achievement, Key Women, Inc.; member, Delta Sigma Theta Sorority; member, National Association for the Advancement of Colored People.

Congressional Data

Twelfth Congressional District of New York: Brooklyn

Committees: Veterans' Affairs; Education and Labor; Rules; Committee on Organization Study and Review

91st Congress: 1969–1970
1968 general election results: 67 percent of the vote

92d Congress: 1971–1972
1970 general election results: 82 percent of the vote

93d Congress: 1973–1974
1972 general election results: 88 percent of the vote

94th Congress: 1975–1976
1974 general election results: 80 percent of the vote

95th Congress: 1977–1978
1976 general election results: 87 percent of the vote

96th Congress: 1979–1980
1978 general election results: 88 percent of the vote

97th Congress: 1981–1982
1980 general election results: 87 percent of the vote

Shirley Anita St. Hill Chisholm

*The First African American Woman
Elected to Congress*

Twelfth District, New York
Democrat
91st–97th Congresses, 1969–1982

I had to make a very, very difficult decision. And it was a personal decision I had to make. After I went in for the two-and-a-half weeks of training at the diplomatic seminars in Washington, D.C., I realized I'm
suffering from a kind of degeneration of the left eye, and I only have
peripheral vision. It would cause me not to be able to be as effective and to
do the kind of job that I would want to do. Because I'm a person that has
standards. So I made a decision to go in and tell the State Department that
at this point, with the possibility of a later operation looming on the horizon with respect to my eye, I think it would be better for me to withdraw
my name. I'm just about blind in that eye. And hopefully, going through a
major operation, I might be able to get some relief. That was my reason
for withdrawing from the position. Of course, I was sorry, because I grew
up in the islands, not in Jamaica, but in Barbados. My first husband was
Jamaican. I've traveled a great deal in those islands. And I had hoped to
complete my entire political career by going back to my original roots in
the Caribbean. That's where my heritage is. But it was not to be. What's to
be will be and what's not to be will not be.

Former congresswoman Shirley Chisholm's decision not to accept President Bill Clinton's 1993 nomination to become the ambassador to Jamaica dashed the hopes
of those who could still remember the excitement surrounding the fiery, outspoken, and
dynamic first African American woman elected to Congress. It also ended a political
career that had challenged, inspired, and enlisted a whole generation of women to run for
public office.

In the 1950s, a time when few women held political office at any level, Chisholm fought
her way through the labyrinth of New York's club politics. In the 1960s, she did battle with
the New York State Assembly. In the 1970s, she took on the U.S. Congress and presidential
politics, finally bowing out of politics gracefully in the 1980s. In all, it had been nothing
short of a spectacular career that awakened America to what it meant to be black, female,
and in Chisholm's own words, "unbought and unbossed," in the political arena.[2] She showed
that candor and political courage were possible even for black women, who were late to

arrive in congressional politics. By so doing, she set the tone and the pace for the women who would follow in her footsteps.

This black woman refused to be marginalized or constrained by the odds. Three years after her historic 1969 swearing-in ceremony as New York's Twelfth Congressional District representative, Shirley Chisholm launched an unprecedented bid for the United States presidency. Known for her uncompromising political stance on the Vietnam War, poverty, and women's rights, her rhetoric resonated with the refrains of the turbulent 1960s. She was symbolic of the "new politics" that introduced into mainstream political parties more women, blacks, and young people than ever before. That her presidential bid was thinkable in a racially sensitive, male-dominated America was a tribute to the era and her own unique place in it.

As a congresswoman, Chisholm was both nemesis and icon. She was a welcomed and treasured spokesperson for women, blacks, and young people who benefited from her outspoken, trenchant attacks on the white male power base and status quo, especially when she condemned them for waging an unjust war in Southeast Asia, penalizing the poor, and cheating women and minorities out of their birthrights of full citizenship. For those in power—who bore the brunt of her criticism—she was a constant and formidable agitator, persistent in her challenges, and caustic in her critiques.

Chisholm could not and did not take all of the credit for her political success, nor for the independence she was able to wield as a maverick. For almost three decades, her political activism was an integral part of the married life that she shared with Conrad Chisholm, her first husband. From her 1950s involvement with the New York Democratic clubs to her 1972 bid for the presidency, Shirley and Conrad Chisholm were a team. If she was the star, he was the producer who pulled the background pieces together to make the production complete. They struck a rare chord as partners, and most of her political career revolved around their married life. While not as much is known about Chisholm's second husband, Arthur Hardwick, Jr., their mutual respect and his admiration for her work surfaced when Chisholm decided in 1982 that she would leave politics. The accounts of these marriage partnerships are significant not only because they give a glimpse of a very human, very feminine 'other side' of the former congresswoman but also because they temper the strident style for which she is known. In a sense, Chisholm's tough persona masked a sensitivity that was readily apparent when she was under attack. For a nonconformist with a low level of tolerance for politics as usual, and no hesitation about singling out its practitioners, she often found it difficult to be on the other side of the critique. In both her books—*Unbought and Unbossed,* her autobiography, and *The Good Fight,* an account of her presidential campaign—she reveals the lasting wounds inflicted on her by her political opponents, many caused by those who questioned her tactics more than her abilities. Nowhere was Chisholm's sensitivity more evident than during the 1972 presidential campaign, when she defied the white feminist movement and the black congressional male leadership by forging ahead alone in a bid for the Democratic presidential nomination. Although she won a historic victory by garnering 151 convention delegate votes on the first ballot, even decades later the former congresswoman saw the experience in a bittersweet light.

> There was one basic thing which has always been, I guess, a very personal thing with me. And even today, as I'm moving ahead in years, I look back now, and I just could never understand why it was so difficult for men, who had worked with you and knew of your capabilities, your talents, and your versatility, to really push you for political office. And then you decide to make the move on your own, because you knew they would not do it, and then they would attack you, almost ferociously.
>
> That is something I've never really been quite able to understand. But I do understand it also, from the standpoint of a political history in this country for the feelings of such a long time, that it was time for the black woman to let the black man step forth. And therefore, any black woman who came forth in the early years when I was coming forth was seen as a pest, a hindrance, a woman who wanted to pay black men back, and all of that foolishness.

A quarter of a century later, Shirley Chisholm would still hold a passionate and painful recollection of the divisions that erupted in the Congressional Black Caucus and the women's movement as a consequence of her decision to run for president. Although the campaign was criticized at the time as quixotic, history shows something different. Shirley Chisholm had actually challenged a generation to seize the moment and push for change at a pivotal time in American history. And the fruits are clear today, as every black woman who has followed in her footsteps willingly pays homage to her as the congressional standard bearer, the trailblazer who not only opened doors, but made it possible to challenge as well as serve.

Generally credited as being one who had a penchant for being long on insight into the political system and short on patience with its operation, Chisholm endeared herself to some and alienated herself from others. Her fourteen years in the U.S. House of Representatives were nothing short of controversial and confrontational. On the one hand, she won kudos for being uncompromising and fiercely independent, and on the other she earned a reputation for being recalcitrant and arrogant.

The Early Years

What went into the makeup of this complex maverick and political enigma with the lilting accented English and the pedagogical style of a schoolteacher? Shirley Anita St. Hill was born to a poor, working-class immigrant couple in Brooklyn, New York, on November 30, 1924—the eldest of four girls. Chisholm's mother, Barbados-born Ruby Seale, and father, British Guiana–born Charles St. Hill, instilled a respect for education, a strong religious foundation, and a Marcus Garvey nationalism into the early lessons of their children.[3] "Become young ladies—poised, modest, accomplished, educated, and graceful and prepare to take your places in the world," Ruby Seale told her four daughters. It was the first part of the St. Hill family message. The second came from Charles St. Hill who cautioned that "strong people survive in this world" and that the girls should use the brain that God gave them to be strong.[4] These family values shaped Chisholm, providing her with a foundation steeped in the religious and moral teachings of her mother and accompanied by the political and black-consciousness-raising message of her father. The four daughters—Muriel, Odessa, Selma, and Shirley—attended church every Sunday with their mother and returned home to a father who preached the black nationalist message of Marcus Garvey at the kitchen table. Both messages would shape the political and moral agenda of the future congresswoman.

Getting established in pre-Depression New York was difficult for the St. Hills, who in 1927 decided to send their daughters to live with their maternal grandmother in Barbados. Shirley was just three years old at the time. It was to have been a short stay, while her parents established suitable living conditions in New York and saved enough money to support the family. However, with her mother working as a seamstress and her father as an unskilled laborer, it took longer than expected. Seven years passed before the children returned to New York to live with their parents. The sojourn in the West Indies was not without its benefits, according to Chisholm. In later life, she praised the early British school system of colonial Barbados, as well as the strict regimen of her grandmother. Both provided superior preparation for her stateside education and academic success. The often defiant Chisholm said that her grandmother was one of the few people whose authority she respected and would never defy.

In 1934 the girls moved back to Brooklyn to join their mother, father, and a new sister. Chisholm found herself in a four-room cold-water railroad flat. After the warm climate and beaches of Barbados, she was confronted with the cold winters and meandering streets of Brownsville. The adjustment was not easy. The family would move to a series of flats before the St. Hills saved enough money in 1945 to buy a house. In the meantime, the young girl was beginning to experience the difference between an island life, where almost all of her classmates and friends were of African descent, and an urban environment where diverse neighborhoods would shape the remainder of her formative years. "Most of our playmates and many of mother's and father's neighbors were of course, white and Jewish." About her mother, Chisholm adds, "Because she was English-speaking and could give advice about bills and other legal pitfalls of city life, she became a kind of neighborhood oracle and leader."[5] Chisholm's mother also established her leadership in the St. Hill household. She had to in order to manage a rebellious young daughter. Forbidden to date or enjoy popular music, Chisholm would test the limits by having boys walk her home from school, or she would play jazz on the piano—minor pranks by modern standards, but at the time enough to raise her mother's ire.

Her rebellion did not reach into the school, however. There she and her sisters excelled as honor students, satisfying another St. Hill requirement. Her academic achievements were such that when she graduated from Girls High School in Brooklyn in 1942, she received scholarship offers from several colleges. She remembers two offers in particular, one from Vassar and the other from Oberlin—neither of which her parents could afford. Instead, they encouraged her to take advantage of the free New York college system, a move that probably changed the course of Chisholm's life. Brooklyn College was the incubator for her political development. Neither Oberlin nor Vassar could have provided her with a similar experience.

The intellectual freedom she enjoyed in college was liberating, and she blossomed in the world of ideas and ideals. Her social freedoms, however, were still constrained by Ruby Seale St. Hill.

She was still required to attend church every Sunday as she always had. The girls and their mother attended a Quaker-style worship service at the English Brethren Church, an Anglican carryover from the British missionary work in the islands. Every Sunday they were required to attend and sit quietly for almost three hours while participating in silent praise and prayer—an order of worship Chisholm found difficult. The service was followed by Christian education and a third meeting that kept them in church the remainder of the day. Her mother's strict religious adherence carried over into Chisholm's personal life; even in college she was forbidden to date. Charles St. Hill, on the other hand, was less concerned with the girls' social life than he was with their understanding of the politics of being black in America. While all of the girls soaked up the words of their father, Shirley, his favorite, made use of them. Like other immigrants from the West Indies, Charles St. Hill was a staunch follower of the Marcus Garvey repatriation and economic-development movement. Thousands of blacks found meaning and a philosophy in the movement that helped them to endure the indignities of American racism through the cultural education provided by Garvey's Universal Negro Improvement Association (UNIA). Headquartered in New York during the 1920s and 1930s, Marcus Garvey, the Jamaica-born charismatic leader, held sway over thousands of followers, many of whom were immigrants and working-class poor. Garvey's message of self-help and nationalist pride in being of African descent was fed to the St. Hill girls along with their evening meal by their father, much to the dismay of their mother. What Chisholm received from the strong history message was her sense of what it meant to battle American racism. Remnants of her father's Garveyism would eventually become a part of her intellectual, political, and rhetorical arsenal as she grew in political consciousness at Brooklyn College.

The Garvey spirit of race empowerment was in effect when Chisholm joined other black college women to form an alternative social club when whites refused to admit them into theirs. Dinner table conversations may have brought racial awareness, and forming a club may have been liberating, but Chisholm would soon face the reality that racism and sexism also bracketed her life choices after college. There were few opportunities for black women college graduates, even bright ones who studied serious subjects—like

Chisholm, who majored in sociology and minored in Spanish. Teaching was one of the exceptions. Luckily for her, she felt called to teach. Her sister Muriel had tried to cross the safe line by majoring in physics, but after graduating magna cum laude, she could not find a job even as a technician. Chisholm's experience upon graduating cum laude from Brooklyn College in 1946 was not far from that of her sister, albeit for other reasons. Barely five feet tall and under one hundred pounds, Chisholm found it hard to convince any potential employer that she was anything other than a teenager, let alone a college graduate looking for employment. She eventually landed a job at the Mt. Calvary Childcare Center in Harlem, where she stayed for seven years, from 1946 until 1953.

As well as a job, Chisholm had something else new in her life. In her early twenties, she had just started dating. The first love of her life—whom she never named—was a Jamaican whose smooth style kept her in the dark about his marital status for three years. Just as she was about to defy her mother's warning about marrying him, she discovered that he was already married. That was the good news, considering the bad news— he was being sought for immigration fraud. The shock of the revelations was so great that she suffered a severe depression and had to retire to the home of a family friend to recuperate.

Vowing to never get involved again, after several months she returned to the daycare center and to Columbia University, where she was enrolled in a master's program. Although she declared herself a spinster for life, she had difficulty warding off the persistent advances from a short, stocky Jamaican actor-turned-private-investigator named Conrad Chisholm. He was more persistent than she was stubborn. A new phase of her life was about to begin. Unable to win her solitary war against romance, she gave in, and in 1949 they were married. It could not have been a more complementary match.

The Political Odyssey

Conrad and Shirley Chisholm enjoyed a long marriage that endured almost all of her thirty-year political career. The unassuming Conrad was a powerful force behind the soon-to-be dynamic politician. Between the 1950s and 1960s, Shirley Chisholm began her ascent into the limelight as a cigar box decorator at the Democratic Club in Brooklyn. Over the years she moved into its leadership before breaking off and forming a competing Democratic machine. The New York clubs were an integral part of the political power system in Brooklyn, functioning in a manner not dissimilar from the Chicago ward politics—each kept the same white men in power while holding blacks and other minorities in check. Shirley Chisholm challenged the system immediately.

Blacks and Hispanics sat outside the monthly meetings waiting to ask for a favor from the political leadership or just to ask for basic services such as trash collection. Of course, they were no different from the white groups who also waited for the assemblymen and borough party bosses to dispense basic services as though they were a privilege and not a right. The club system was supported in large measure by the proceeds received from weekly card games organized by women, most of whom were wives of the white leaders. Chisholm's decorated cigar boxes were used to collect the money, which yielded as much as $8,000 annually, providing the major portion of the club's budget. Yet, even though the women were responsible for a major financial contribution, they had limited power and had to finance the parties out of their own pockets. It was one of Chisholm's first lessons in politics—minorities provided the votes and women voted and did the work. Neither shared in the power. Chisholm intended to change that model. She first urged the women to ask for an annual budget from the men who were in control, since the women's card parties were the financial backbone of the clubs. The men finally agreed to an initial yearly budget of $500, and Chisholm, the only black in the women's group, became an overnight "leader" among the women.

This was not lost on the male leadership, who hoped to neutralize her. They put her on the governing body of the club, hoping that it would quiet her and bring her into line, but she saw through their ploy. "On the old 17th A. D. Club board, it had been just a game they were playing with me and I had known it and played it for what it was worth," Chisholm recalled.[6] It was also too late to bridle her vision of what could be. She had already aligned herself with some of the radical blacks who wanted to move toward dismantling the all-white leadership in the club and in elective office. Wesley M. Holder was one of those people. Holder, a West Indian from Guiana had embarked upon a mission to get a black elected to office from the Brooklyn Democratic Club. His first attempt failed. But now he had Shirley Chisholm as an ally, and the two broke away from the Seventeenth Assembly District Democratic Club and formed a black club—the Bedford-Stuyvesant Political League (BSPL). The BSPL was successful in getting the first black judge on the bench. In 1953 the club ran Lewis S. Flagg, Jr., for a seat on the municipal court bench and won. In 1958 Shirley Chisholm challenged Holder for the presidency of the BSPL. The bitter race created an adversary out of a friend. Holder considered her to be an ingrate—he had mentored her through the Brooklyn system, and now she turned around and attempted to displace him from his position at the head of the organization that he helped found. Of course, Chisholm saw it as fair game—she was as capable and qualified as he was to lead the club. After losing the election, she left politics temporarily and focused on her career. She had become an expert in the field of day care, and in 1959 she left the Hamilton-Madison Child Care Center in Manhattan to go to work for the city of New York as a consultant. The career challenges were exciting, but her first love—teaching—could not compete with politics. By 1960 Chisholm returned to the Brooklyn political club scene. This time she started her own club—the Unity Democratic Club. Holder's club had dissolved, and he was now a part of the old Seventeenth District club leadership. Chisholm's new group went up against the old Seventeenth again, this time to win. Teaming with another insurgent club, the Unity Democrats ran a candidate for committee member and lost. The unsuccessful candidacy was not in vain, however; with 42 percent of the vote, Unity was now looked upon as a formidable political force. In the meantime, Unity was becoming proficient in grassroots education and mobilization of black and Hispanic voters. By 1962 the club was ready to run a candidate for the General Assembly in Albany. With campaign literature that called for an end to "boss-ruled plantation politics," they ran Tom Jones, an African American attorney, and won. This time he even beat Chisholm's old nemesis, Holder.

Jones served in the assembly until 1964, when he decided to accept a judgeship. By this time the Unity Democrats had pretty much crushed the old system in a fashion that was being duplicated around the country. Political change was sweeping America, with new, previously disenfranchised groups gaining access to power and running what would have been considered nontraditional candidates for state and federal offices. Chisholm saw this as a perfect time for a black woman to seek a state assembly seat. While she would not be the first black woman to run, she would be the first to come in with a black political machine behind her. She entered the primary with token opposition, won easily, but faced an uphill battle in the general election. As an outside candidate, her biggest handicap was lack of access to club financing. In the end she bankrolled her own campaign with $4,000 in personal savings. Not only did she have to fight to raise money on her own, she soon discovered she would also have to wage a fight against sexism.

> I met with hostility because of my sex from the start of my first campaign. Even some women would greet me, "You ought to be home, not out here." Once, while I was collecting nominating petition signatures in the big Albany housing project—where Conrad and I had been captains for several years—one man about seventy lit into me. "Young woman, what are you doing out here in this cold? Did you get your husband's breakfast this morning? Did you straighten up your house? What are you doing running for office? That is something for men."[7]

Chisholm, however, was not deterred by such comments because her biggest obstacle was still race. As such, she, along with other blacks had been helped by the Supreme Court's "one man, one vote" decision, which after redistricting resulted in a number of minority districts around the country. She won the general election and joined seven other blacks as a member of the largest African American contingent to enter the New York legislature. Her first decade in elected politics began when a new political fervor was emerging in America. The era was infused with social and political upheavals characterized by political assassinations and their aftermath, including the killing of President John F. Kennedy in 1963 and black Muslim leader Malcolm X in 1965. These were followed by the murders in 1968 of presidential candidate Robert Kennedy and civil rights leader Martin Luther King, Jr. All of this violence was being broadcast on television and brought into American homes along with the daily carnage of the Vietnam War. In 1968, the year Chisholm was elected to Congress, a previously apathetic electorate woke up to the devastation brought by the inner-city riots and the violence against antiwar demonstrators outside the Democratic National Convention in Chicago. Chisholm served in the New

York General Assembly from 1964 to 1968. During that time, her legislative accomplishments, while not numerous, were nevertheless significant. She opposed a bill that became law to provide state funding for private religious schools; proposed legislation to provide state aid to day-care centers; and voted to increase funding for schools based on a per-pupil basis. The state legislature was a dry run for Chisholm's congressional tenure, but it was not one about which she felt good. If anything, she became politically disillusioned by witnessing the legislative process—one in which too many compromises, too many bad votes based on political expediency, and too little respect for women characterized assembly life. In essence, Chisholm was still fighting the system, the consummate outsider on the inside.

In 1968, a more sanguine Shirley Chisholm began a campaign that would lead her out of the state legislature and into the national limelight. Redistricting in New York resulted in a new Twelfth Congressional District, and Chisholm decided that she would stake claim to it. The district would for the first time create an opportunity for Brooklyn's black and Puerto Rican population to elect a person of color to represent them in Congress. Before the 1960s, gerrymandering was used to disenfranchise blacks, but by the end of the decade, two events changed the way congressional districts were formed—the Voting Rights Act of 1965 and the U.S. Supreme Court decision that required congressional districts to be compact and contiguous. It was the latter that forced the New York state legislature to create the Twelfth Congressional District.

By 1967 the Democratic machine had recognized the reality of black representation in club politics and in political office. When more than a half-dozen black candidates, including Chisholm, appeared on the party list of hopefuls, for the new seat, the machine feigned neutrality. In the formation process, it stated, it would leave the choice to "the people." Machine neutrality did not last long, however. After a newly formed citizens committee endorsed Chisholm, the machine privately began pushing the nomination of one of her opponents—black city councilman William C. Thompson.

"The county machine never did endorse a candidate," said Chisholm, "but every action of its people showed, to the most unsophisticated resident of Bedford-Stuyvesant that William C. Thompson was their man. White people think black people are stupid, but it came through to the community that the organization could not bring itself to endorse me because I would not submit to being bossed by any of them. It was interesting that, even among themselves, they never questioned my competence or dedication. What they said was always that I was hard to handle."[8] As Chisholm moved toward the primaries, she was favored by only one of the political organizations in Brooklyn—her own, the Unity Democratic Club. Her other two opponents, Thompson and Dolly Robinson, a labor organizer, received endorsements from the predominantly white party organizations.

Calling her the easiest product to sell, Holder entered into Chisholm's political life again. After years of bad blood, he had decided to team up with her as they had done in the past. The call surprised but pleased her. Holder had been a formidable opponent and would be an invaluable partner in putting together her campaign. There was no doubt that between the two a concerted grassroots campaign against the machine would prove to be a winning ticket. As usual, Chisholm was bolstered by her husband, who not only provided the moral support but helped by laying some of the groundwork for the victory. Chisholm's campaign was centered around her previously established claim to fame as a renegade who rejected machine politics and white control over black and minority voters. Her campaign slogan said it all—"Fighting Shirley Chisholm—Unbought and Unbossed." She did not have to change her rhetoric at all, it had been her refrain all along. The slogan was put on shopping bags, posters, car caravans, and flyers and carried throughout Crown Heights, Williamsburg, and Bedford-Stuyvesant. "During the week I went to endless little house parties and teas given by women. In the black neighborhoods I ate chitlins, in the Jewish neighborhood bagels and lox, and in the Puerto Rican neighborhood arroyo con pollo. We contacted every neighborhood woman leader we could find. 'Bring your women,' I would urge them."[9] Chisholm knew something about women in political campaigns—they were workers—but what she wanted to do was something more. She wanted to make them a part of the important governance in the campaign, to politicize and empower them beyond the norm. Her cigar-decorating days paid off in heightened awareness of the limited role that women usually played in politics.

Chisholm and Holder's hard work was rewarded. She outdistanced both Thompson and Dolly Robinson and headed for the general election against a noted civil rights leader, but as far as Brooklyn politics were concerned, a carpetbagger. James Farmer, the former head of the Congress of Racial Equality, was a Manhattan resident put forth by the Republicans to run against Chisholm. It was done in the hope that national name recognition would overcome Democratic party loyalty and cost her the election. The law did not require the nominee to live in the district, just to live in the state. "Farmer's campaign was well-oiled; it had money dripping all over it. He toured the district with sound trucks manned by young dudes with Afros, beating tom-toms; the big, black, male image. He drew the television cameramen like flies, a big national figure, winding up to become New York City's second black Congressman (after Adam Clayton Powell)," Chisholm recalled.[10]

She was certainly ready to fight, but when the general-election campaign began moving into high gear, she found herself handicapped by illness. In July she was admitted to the hospital for abdominal surgery, an operation that kept her bedridden for four weeks in the final months of the campaign. In August, when she discovered that Farmer had made headway by asking accusingly, "Where's Mrs. Chisholm?" she could not take it any longer. She called her doctor, told him that the stitches were not in her mouth and that she was going to go out and campaign. With that, the once thin and now frail Chisholm wrapped a towel around her waist and hips to prevent her clothes from falling off and she walked down three flights of stairs. Mounting a sound truck, she proclaimed her return to the campaign trail. "Ladies and gentlemen," she said on the loud speaker, "this is fighting Shirley Chisholm and I'm up and around in spite of what people are saying."[11]

Holder, Chisholm's campaign manager, was her most valuable campaign supporter, next to Conrad Chisholm. Beyond his organizational skills, he had a keen political insight. He made her aware of the internal sabotage by white machine volunteers who destroyed mailing labels. Most of all, he made her aware of the black male chauvinism within the party. Holder's assessment of the situation was that black male Democrats were meeting with Farmer to undermine Chisholm, because she was an aggressive black woman. Rather than seeing it as a stumbling block, Holder turned the situation into a stepping stone by strategizing and restructuring the campaign to appeal to women. A statistician by profession, he knew that among black voters, for every male vote there were more than two female votes. He used that information to recast Chisholm's campaign, pointing up her gender rather than ignoring it.

Although she did not want to use what she called "woman power" to get elected, Chisholm did it anyway. She used everything she had to beat Farmer, including campaigning in Spanish in the Puerto Rican community, her knowledge and experience of twenty years in the district, and what she calls her "messianic" transformation once in open debate. She won the election with thirty-four thousand votes against Farmer's approximately thirteen thousand, a two-and-a-half-to-one margin.

The Congressional Years and Beyond

Shirley Chisholm won more than the opportunity to represent the Twelfth Congressional District. As the first African American woman elected to Congress, she was a symbol of a new era. By March of her first year, she received more than three thousand invitations to speak or lecture.[12] Her prominence was due in part to her stand against defense spending for the Vietnam War. She was also becoming known as a pro-abortion congresswoman, giving her high visibility in the women's movement. Chisholm was claimed by the civil rights, feminist, and antiwar movements. Headlines similar to the now-defunct Washington, D.C., *Evening Star* newspaper were typical; "First Negro Woman in Congress" read its November 6, 1968, issue. Chisholm joined eight African American congressmen, who, when their ranks expanded to thirteen, went on to form the Congressional Black Caucus in 1970. There was no doubt, however, that Shirley Chisholm, was the most visible and nationally known black member of Congress, except for Adam Clayton Powell, Jr., who had been returned to Congress in 1969. Indeed, some people referred to her as the female Adam Clayton Powell because she refused to be bound by congressional protocol if it interfered with her getting the job done. She was determined that she would be there to fight for the people who had been denied the opportunity to have their viewpoints authentically represented in Washington—even if it meant ignoring the rules from time to time.[13] Committee assignments were the first real political test for incoming members. Assignments were made by the party in control, and preference was given based on seniority and predilection. When she sought her committee assignments, Chisholm made it known that she wanted to get on the Education and Labor Committee because of her background in child care and education. Besides, it was beneficial for her constituency. However, the conservative chairman of the House Ways and Means Committee, Wilbur Mills of Arkansas, a powerful member of the Democratic leadership, placed her on the Agriculture Committee instead—a committee that, obviously, had nothing to do with Brooklyn and that would diminish her voice. In response to this and other tactics, Chisholm lashed out at the congressional status quo. The seniority system, she renamed the "senility system," since it was run based on time served as opposed to competence. Rather than take the assignment offered, she decided to go to the "well" (the front of the House of Representatives, where debates and statements are made) and offer an amendment nullifying her assignment to the Agriculture Committee. Although it was out of the ordinary, she succeeded, but not without a warning from her colleagues that she had just signed a suicide pact by making enemies of the major Democratic party leadership. Chisholm was once again up against white male bosses. It was a condition that would typify her tenure in Congress.

On another score, however, Chisholm broke new ground. Finding that the Capitol Hill staff was almost totally white-male dominated, she decided to hire a staff that was composed of all women, half of them white and half black. It was a stance that no other woman on the Hill had ever taken. Nor has any taken it since. While she did hire males eventually, the congresswoman stood firm in bringing in hard-working women who would have had opportunities denied them in other Congressional offices. It was a continuation of her efforts to bring women out of the background and into the foreground of politics.

Unfortunately, it did not take long before Congresswoman Chisholm ran into the same disappointments in the House of Representatives that she had encountered in the New York state legislature. Not only did she see conservative white men as her congressional adversaries, but she had problems with liberals who would not stand up for what they believed. As she put it, "When it comes time to put the heat on in committee and on the floor, and to do something, like passing an amendment or increasing an appropriation, too many of these white knights turn up missing. . . . Give me a Southern conservative everytime. I know who he is and where he's coming from. It's all out there in the open and I can deal with him."[14]

Reelected to a second term in 1970, she was finding her way around Capitol Hill and the country. Speaking out against the war, for women's rights, abortion rights, and the poor, her visibility had become such that the country saw her as one of its premiere leaders, while others saw her as definite presidential material. As a matter of fact, one poll conducted by *Nation* magazine and Johnson Publications, the publishers of *Ebony* and *Jet* magazines, placed Chisholm as one of three blacks who would likely be favored by black voters as a presidential candidate. The other two were Julian Bond, a Georgia state legislator at the time, and John Conyers, the congressman from Detroit.

Chisholm was, in fact, a lot more active outside Congress during the first three years than inside. She gave more than a hundred lectures on college campuses and was one of the founders of the National Organization for Women (NOW), which was formed to strengthen the political muscle of women.

Although she was a charter member of both NOW and the CBC, Chisholm was more radical than either organization. She sought to combine the goals of both in her own ambitions and refused to accept traditional roles and stereotypes. In contemporary parlance, Chisholm would be considered a womanist politician, meaning that for her, feminist politics were tridimensional. They were driven by the need to eradicate a sexism that was inextricably bound by racism and classism.

"Women in this country must become revolutionaries. We must refuse to accept the old, the traditional roles and stereotypes," she said.[15]

This view placed her outside of the immediate objectives of the feminist movement, which had as its paramount goal political empowerment for women—but not necessarily women of color or poor women. It also placed her outside of the immediate objectives of the CBC, for whom the issue of civil rights and equal rights was meant more for the advancement of men than women. She was bound to clash with both groups not only because of her message but also because of her style. It all came full circle when she announced her candidacy for president.

It was a winter day in her home district in Brooklyn. The short, wiry woman stood before the cameras to announce that she was running for the 1972 Democratic presidential nomination. It was nothing short of remarkable that the first African American woman elected to the U.S. Congress had reached a national standing that made this event thinkable. "I stand before you today as a candidate for the Democratic nomination for the Presidency of the United States. I am not the candidate of black America, although I am black and proud," announced Chisholm to a sea of cameras, constituents, and curious onlookers on January 25, 1972. She went on:

> I am not the candidate of the women's movement of this country, although I am a woman, and I am equally proud of that. I am not the candidate of any political bosses or special interests. . . . I am the candidate of the people.
>
> We must turn away from the control of the prosaic, the privileged, and the old line, tired politicians to open our society to the energies and abilities of countless new groups of Americans—women, blacks, browns, Indians, Orientals and youth—so that they can develop their own full potential and thereby participate equally and enthusiastically in building a strong and just society, rich in its diversity and noble in its quality of life. . . . I stand here without the endorsements of any big-name politicians or celebrities.[16]

This was a familiar and vintage Chisholm. The tough talk of rugged individualism came from a woman who had been forewarned that she could not count on her political allies for support. Neither the majority of the CBC nor her feminist allies in NOW had given her a definitive organizational endorsement. Yet she was determined to use the Democratic presidential primary to advocate systemic change in the country and expansion of opportunity in the party for women and blacks. A number of conditions made Chisholm's bid feasible. Her commitment to social change and the country's level of receptivity to reform had a lot to do with the 1960s. For the Democratic party as well as the country, 1968 was a watershed year. After the riot outside the national convention that year, the Democratic party opened its doors to reform, allowing for the influx of youth, the activist women's movement, and large numbers of blacks and other minorities. Their presence in the Democratic party in particular gave rise to the label "new politics" as they aggressively pushed to leverage their voting blocs. The "new politics" affected the Democratic party more than the Republican, which remained resistant to change that would have included more minorities, women, and youth in its membership. The Democrats, on the other hand, in an effort to reduce dissent and coalesce with emerging interest groups, adopted new convention rules to facilitate their participation. The rules called for, among other things, proportional representation within delegations to reflect population percentages. Consequently, the makeup of the 1972 Democratic convention would be the most diverse ever assembled, with age, gender, and race having proportional representation. The opportunity for Congresswoman Chisholm to have a significant political following was made all the more feasible by this potentiality.

Another issue that aided in making Chisholm's candidacy possible was the country's crisis in conscience—the Vietnam War. It dominated presidential politics in 1972, as it did in 1968. Congresswoman Chisholm was identified with opposition to the war and had also coauthored the legislation to end the military draft. Addressing this major divisive issue that still loomed over the country, Chisholm used her campaign announcement to aggressively challenge war policies of the current Republican administration of Richard Nixon and past Democratic administrations, thus reinforcing her reputation as a congressional dissenter.

Her position on the war and her forthright response to social issues gave her considerable credibility among the newly enfranchised eighteen-year-old voters. They, along with a nascent women's movement and racial minorities, were transforming the Democratic party. The bulk of that transformation came from two constitutional changes that were responsible for the youth and racial party newcomers. The Twenty-fourth Amendment adopted in 1964, commonly known as the Voting Rights Amendment, eliminated poll taxes and other impediments to minorities and poor people's enfranchisement, and the Twenty-sixth Amendment, adopted in 1971, gave eighteen-year-olds the voting franchise.

Chisholm had been cultivating the youth vote. By 1972 she was a familiar face on college campuses. She would instruct her staff to turn down other requests to speak in an effort to pick up the campus speaking engagements. Once on a campus she would hold informal and formal sessions discussing national politics with students. Students were not used to congressional attention at that level, and they revered Chisholm because of her defiance of politics-as-usual.

From the CBC Chisholm received support from Congressman Ronald Dellums

(D-Calif.) and Parren Mitchell (D-Md.), two mavericks by any standard at that time. They supported her to the end. However, the issue was not as cut and dry with the women's organization. Although Chisholm had been a founding member of NOW and the National Women's Political Caucus (NWPC), when it seemed she might seek the presidential nomination, the national leadership of both organizations refused to state their commitment either for or against her. Rather than allow them to skirt the issue, Chisholm came out front with her criticism and told the feminists that she wanted either a full endorsement or none at all.

They chose the latter. Chisholm's choice to run for president pushed the envelope too far. The women's movement had been pushing for equality but could not envision Chisholm's actions as furthering their cause. The novelty of a black woman presidential candidate, however, captured the imagination of the media. Occasional stories appeared speculating on what it would mean to have a black woman in the White House. Chisholm gave the feminist quest for power politics a human face and the imagination of the country was captured by the possibility, if not the probability that a black woman could someday become president. Her presence, however, created a problem for the male-dominated CBC, just as it had for the women of NOW and NWPC. The black male leadership, like the feminist movement, was on the threshold of achieving increased political power in presidential politics. Many had taken individual steps to ensure that their personal proximity to power was secure with the candidates of their party, while at the same time advocating a unified, noncommitted political organization that would barter the black vote. The idea was to leverage the collective black vote to achieve the maximum results from an electoral politics that otherwise dwarfed their numerical impact. A united effort and a focused agenda would provide a vehicle by which to achieve a consensus on strategic methods for extracting accountability from the presidential nominee.

The founding of the CBC in 1970 had been one of the most significant elements in executing this strategy, a move beyond post-Reconstruction black leadership that had historically belonged to civil rights organizations and churches—not elected national politicians. The CBC reflected the first major congressional leadership inside the political system, and it made the caucus the legitimate bargaining vehicle for the black vote. Many in the CBC viewed Chisholm—a junior congresswoman in terms of the congressional seniority system—as an upstart who jeopardized their nonconfrontational leadership of moderation.

As the 1972 election got into full swing, to further the call for unity, the CBC joined with the traditional black leadership and grassroots organizations in March 1972 to convene the National Black Political Convention in Gary, Indiana, or the "Gary Convention." According to Ronald Walters, noted Howard University political scientist, in his book, *Black Presidential Politics in America,* "The convention was attended by over 8,000 blacks, 3,000 of whom were delegates drawn from the ranks of constituencies of professional politicians to youthful black nationalist groups from cities around the country."[17] Chisholm had declared her candidacy in January 1972, but the leaders of the March 1972 Gary Convention ignored her campaign. Rather, the delegates to the convention focused on three objectives. The major one was to resolve the question as to whether they would come out and support one of the announced white presidential candidates or any one of the potential unannounced black contenders. Even in his recording of the event, Walters discounts Chisholm's campaign. Chisholm, for her part, chose not to attend the convention because she felt that she would be ignored or, even worse, considered a spoiler—a distraction from the organized agenda. The second issue was the creation of a black political party and the third was the passage of a platform of black issues to be presented to both major parties at national conventions. Although Chisholm did not attend, Walters reports that she had a "strong delegation lobbying" for her at the convention. The lobbying was of little consequence in terms of the CBC, because the fact was that most of the CBC members and many leaders of the convention had already committed themselves to a presidential candidate. Thus, while neutrality was assumed to be a prerequisite, in actuality it was not.

By the beginning of the Gary Convention, all the candidates had announced. Besides Chisholm, there were six other major primary candidates. South Dakota senator George McGovern had received endorsements from the Gary Convention leadership, including Congressman Walter Fauntroy (D-D.C.), Georgia state legislator Julian Bond, and Gary mayor Richard Hatcher. McGovern did not send a representative because he had already secured the support of most of the thirteen members of the CBC. Other declared candidates included Alabama governor George Wallace, who neither sought nor received support from the delegates. Senator Edmund Muskie, a moderate from Maine, was looked upon as a likely winner in white America, but he had no ties to black politics. Former New York mayor John Lindsay, who attempted to dissuade Chisholm from running, had a short-lived campaign, which ended in the early stages of the primaries. The longtime civil rights advocate, U.S. senator Hubert Humphrey (D-Minn.), was still suffering from the stigma of the Vietnam War and his vice presidency under Lyndon Johnson. Although he was an ardent supporter of civil rights, he had very little black support other than Congressman Louis Stokes of Ohio and Congressman Charles Diggs of Michigan. Augustus Hawkins of California remained uncommitted. Moderate Senator Henry "Scoop" Jackson from Washington state had a minuscule following among African Americans.

Theoretically, the Gary Convention delegates would approach each of these candidates and seek their support for the convention's platform. Three thousand delegates to the Gary Convention were significant in that they represented a seldom-seen political unity of blacks. In actuality, the real power to carry out the plan came from the CBC, which even though small in number, carried the leverage necessary to bargain with the Platform Committee at the Democratic National Convention on inclusion of the Gary Convention issues. When the convention adjourned, no presidential candidate had been endorsed by the body. Chisholm's candidacy was not given consideration, and the agenda was in the hands of the CBC, which had already endorsed other candidates. None of this kept Chisholm from the campaign trail. She hit it, with little funding, a staff full of young volunteers, and a stubborn resolve to see the primary through to the end. Her first stop was Florida.

There, guided by Gwendolyn Sawyer-Cherry, the first black woman elected to the Florida Senate, Chisholm made headlines and an impression on those who doubted her seriousness. Of all the candidates in the presidential race, the media turned much of its attention to Governor Wallace and Congresswoman Chisholm. Wallace and Chisholm were an odd match, indeed, as far as mutual admiration went. However, there was something similar about each of them. They were boundary pushers, outside of the mainstream of the acceptable but taking risks by speaking out about what they believed to be right and wrong. They just disagreed as to what was right and wrong. Wallace would later bring out one of the rare sides of Chisholm. Though feisty and opinionated, she could also be very caring and genuinely moved by individual encounters. On May 13, 1972, for the second time in as many decades, a presidential candidate was shot while campaigning. George Wallace, while leaving a campaign stop in Maryland, was hit and paralyzed by a would-be assassin. Chisholm was saddened by the attack but relieved that the assailant was not black—a situation that could have led to racial outbreaks in an already tense country. It was consistent for Chisholm, but surprising to others, that when she heard about the shooting, without press or notice she visited Wallace in the hospital. In an emotional exchange she told him of her concern for his well-being, and he tearfully acknowledged her visit. The rare encounter was one of the major human interest stories of the campaign.

Chisholm returned to the campaign trail, where she spent six months on the road carrying her message into eleven primaries that netted her twenty-eight delegates. What she did not receive from the feminist and black political leadership in Washington, D.C., on the national level, she made up for at the grassroots level. In California, her last stop before the Miami convention, she received support from the local chapters of the NOW and the NWPC, as well as the Black Panther party. In California, she came in a distant third with more than 150,000 votes, behind McGovern's 1.5 million and Humphrey's 1.4 million votes. Much of the credit for the grassroots support in California can be attributed to the campaign efforts of Congressman Ronald Dellums. Dellums shared Chisholm's vision and was philosophically bound to her campaign odyssey, but in the end he was urged by his advisers to move into the McGovern camp for political, not philosophical reasons.

The Democratic National Convention got under way in Miami in July, and its very convening was history making. Not only was Chisholm the first black to seriously contend for the nomination—black women held two of the highest positions at the convention. Even though Chisholm did not support their candidacies, Yvonne Brathwaite Burke was elected vice chair of the convention, and former ambassador Patricia Roberts Harris was elected chair of the Credentials Committee. Accounts of Chisholm's actions vary. From her perspective she was still fighting the system bosses. In this case, the Democratic National Committee chair Lawrence O'Brien had in her estimation selected moderate women who were not reformers. To Congressman William Clay (D-Mo.), one of Chisholm's major critics in the CBC, it was hypocritical for Chisholm to want support for her candidacy but not give the same kind of support for the two other black women. In his book, *Just Permanent Interests,* Clay describes Chisholm's presidential bid as divisive and leading toward a series of disputes within the CBC. The convention experience caused one of those disputes.

> As Chisholm's candidacy advanced, the public squabbles about her intentions escalated. Several weeks following the episode at the Conference of Black Elected Officials, the Democratic national chairman announced that Patricia Harris, the first black female ambassador in the history of the United States, would chair the Credentials Committee at the convention. Immediately, she was labeled an "Uncle Tom" by some black leaders and castigated as unqualified for the position. Joining the parade of attackers were Shirley Chisholm, John Conyers, and Julian Bond. They described Harris as the hand-picked tool of anti-reform elements in the Democrat party. Their preference for the chairmanship just happened to be a white male, Harold Hughes, U.S. Senator from Iowa.
>
> That same week, Carl Stokes launched an attack on Chisholm and others who supported Senator Hughes.[18]

The raucous 1972 Democratic National Convention proved to be the first major convention in which a black woman or any woman or any black received full consideration for the presidential nomination. A proud Percy Sutton, former Manhattan Borough president, placed Congresswoman Shirley Chisholm's name into nomination, putting himself in history along with her. Chisholm was able to garner 151 delegate votes on the first ballot. For her, just the idea that she had made it that far made the effort worthwhile. In addition, she had also been able to indirectly affect the rhetoric of the Democratic candidate, George McGovern.

Unfortunately, the aftermath of her campaign not only included strained relations with other members of the CBC, but political harassment from the Republican administration. Before it became known that the Nixon administration had targeted "enemies," Shirley Chisholm accused it of harassment for political reasons when a General Accounting Office (GAO) report was leaked to the press accusing her of wrongdoing. The report accused her of failure to keep accurate records, report receipts and corporate gifts, and to name a chair of her campaign committee. The charges carried the possible penalty of one year in prison for each count and a $1,000 fine for each charge. Chisholm was not intimidated by the claim.

"I do not fear an indictment, and I have no fear if I am indicted because I have nothing to hide. I don't need to use campaign funds. I earn $42,500 a year in Congress. I earn a great deal of money lecturing; I earn money writing and I thank God that I am a talented woman with many resources to make money," she told the press.[19] For two years, however, she endured the GAO scrutiny, only to be absolved of any wrongdoing in 1974. Later, other black members of Congress would undergo the same type of harassment.

Chisholm went on to serve in the House of Representatives until 1982, when she startled the country by declaring that she would not seek reelection. During her fourteen-year congressional career, she had proposed funding increases for federal day-care facilities; sponsored the Adequate Income Act of 1971, a guaranteed annual income program; and attempted to thwart the dismantling of the Office of Economic Opportunity under the Nixon administration. She was also an early supporter of anti-apartheid legislation and denounced British and American businesses for selling goods and arms to South Africa.

Disillusionment with the Congress was setting in as she strained to get her legislation through the House. Her personal life had changed as well. After almost thirty years of marriage, in February of 1978 her divorce from Conrad Chisholm was finalized. In November of that year she married her second husband, Arthur Hardwick, Jr. The congresswoman and Hardwick had not been married long before he was involved in a near-fatal automobile accident in April of 1979, which incapacitated him for months. She felt guilty about not being there for him and that added to her frustration. The personal side seemed, in the end, to have won out over the political. Her decision to retire from such a stellar and controversial career in Congress was greeted with mixed emotions, by a public that loved her bravado and a Congress that could never control her. She was indeed "unbought and unbossed," and leaving Capitol Hill earlier than most meant she would stay that way. Exiting from the House did not mean that she was leaving politics, however. She went on to cofound the National Political Congress of Black Women, Inc. (NPCBW), an organization that provides support, politically and economically, for black women from all walks of life. When the Reverend Jesse Jackson ran for president in 1984 and 1988, she was out front supporting his bid.

It would have been a fitting denouement to a phenomenal career if the former congresswoman could have accepted the 1993 offer of President Bill Clinton to become ambassador to Jamaica, but as Chisholm indicated, it was "not to be." Looking at the current political leadership of the 1990s, Chisholm toned down her critique, but did not dampen her expectations or her standards:

> My day has come and gone. I continue to be a mentor. I am helping a number of younger black men and women who are running for offices on the local level. I help to teach them how to prepare speeches. I'm a teacher. At heart, I have always been a teacher. . . . Something I am hearing. Something that really makes me feel very good. Both blacks and whites, old and young, rich and poor say over and over again, in their own way of putting it, they want the truth. Even if the truth hurts, they cannot stand to have hypocrisy and the double and triple standards that sometimes appear to emanate from Washington, D.C. out here to the people all over the country and then later find out that it was just a cover up. . . . I happen to feel that we do not have the same kind of concern, commitment, courage and resiliency in much of the black leadership today as we had in the days of old. There's something missing and it has nothing to do with ability. But there's a certain kind of courage that I do not see in black leaders today like I saw in the leaders of yore.[20]

If by that she means will there be another Shirley Chisholm, the answer is "not likely."

Chapter 3 **Barbara Charline Jordan**

The Conscience of the Constitution

I believe that black women have a very special gift of leadership.
Because we have been called upon to lead in very trying times. And
history has recorded the fact that black women rose to the forefront
in times of struggle during periods of civil rights. But we don't have to
go that far forward to recall that there was also leadership even in the
days of slavery in this country.

Résumé

Barbara Charline Jordan

Personal

Born February 21, 1936
Houston, Texas

Died January 17, 1996

Family Single; no children

Religion Baptist

Party Democrat

Took office Age 36, January 3, 1973

Education

B.A. Texas Southern University, 1956

LL.B. Boston University, 1959

Professional/Political Background

1959 Admitted to the Massachusetts and Texas bars

1960–1965 Attorney, Houston, Texas

1965–1966 Administrative assistant to County Judge, Harris County, Texas

1967–1972 Senator, Texas Senate

1973–1978 U.S. House of Representatives

1979–1996 Professor, Lyndon B. Johnson School of Public Affairs, University of Texas at Austin

1993–1996 Chair, Immigration Reform Commission

Selected Awards/Organizational Affiliations

Selected Honorary Degrees: Boston University, Harvard University, Tufts University.

Delegate, Texas State Democratic Convention 1967, 1969; delegate, Democratic National Convention 1968; voted one of the most influential women of the twentieth century, National Women's Hall of Fame, 1990; Eleanor Roosevelt Humanities Award, 1984; Spingarn Medal, National Association for the Advancement of Colored People, 1992; member, Delta Sigma Theta Sorority.

Congressional Data

Eighteenth Congressional District of Texas: Houston, Harris County

Committees: Judiciary; Public Works and Transportation; Appropriations

93d Congress: 1973–1974
1972 general election results: 81 percent of the vote

94th Congress: 1975–1976
1974 general election results: 85 percent of the vote

95th Congress: 1977–1978
1976 general election results: 86 percent of the vote

Barbara Charline Jordan

The First African American Woman
Elected to Congress from Texas

Eighteenth District, Texas
Democrat
93d–95th Congresses, 1973–1978

Former congresswoman Barbara Jordan's last major act of public service before her death was spirited, controversial, and as constitutionally engaging as her political life had been. In September 1994, Jordan, wheelchair-bound because of multiple sclerosis but more politically active than ever, entered the White House Executive Office Building to brief Chief of Staff Leon Panetta. Jordan had just completed the report and preliminary recommendations from the bipartisan Immigration Reform Commission, which she chaired.

Hearing that she was in the building, Vice President Al Gore, out of awe more than protocol, a Jordan aide recalls, hurried to greet the woman who two decades earlier rose overnight to national prominence as the voice of America's constitutional conscience. She had captured the patriotic imagination during one of the nation's worst political scandals—Watergate.

Since that time, she had become an American icon, sought after as a spokesperson for issues ranging from a return to traditional moral values to advocacy for the North American Free Trade Agreement (NAFTA). Jordan was the "integrity card." Awarded numerous honorary degrees, she was voted by the National Women's Hall of Fame in 1990 as one of the most influential women of the twentieth century. In 1994 she chaired the commission that would help shape immigration policies as the nation moved into the twenty-first century. However, Barbara Jordan would not see this project through. On January 17, 1996, she died in Austin, Texas, of pneumonia and complications from leukemia.

A consummate public servant, Barbara Jordan had responded to the call from President Bill Clinton to chair the U.S. Immigration Reform Commission, whose charge was to produce bipartisan recommendations for reforming the country's immigration laws, regulations, and policies. The assignment placed her once again at the precipice of a national divide—this time on the subject of immigration. In a time of fiscal austerity and economic transformation, immigration had become a volatile issue that challenged some of the nation's basic precepts and engaged a new generation of politicians in the debate over controlling the influx of undocumented workers into the American workplace.

Since retiring from Congress in 1978, Barbara Jordan had been a professor at the Lyndon B. Johnson School of Public Affairs at the University of Texas at Austin, where she said she received a certain amount of satisfaction from teaching a whole new generation of students about the rewards and responsibilities of public service. It was a reciprocal satisfaction, attested to by scores of her students upon her death. Teaching, however, did not take the place of real politics, and it lacked the spotlight of the political arena, which she relished with great gusto.

Investing her characteristic enthusiasm, verve, and energy into convening the eight-person panel—with its disparate political viewpoints on immigration and spanning the spectrum from conservative to liberal—Jordan was determined to create a unified and unifying voice for the nation. The strident tone in America around the issue of immigrants had already surfaced in California, where Proposition 187 was approved in 1994, forbidding the state from providing health, welfare, or educational benefits to illegal aliens, including children. One of its proponents sat on Jordan's committee and, to complicate matters further, her past opposition to the proposition had been vocal and public, for she had actively campaigned against its passage. Thus, it was indeed a challenge to gain a unanimous consensus from such a diverse group, but if anyone could do it, she could. And she did.

The White House chief of staff's briefing that September preceded the presentation of the committee report and recommendations to the press and the Congress. While in general, the measures mentioned were somewhat predictable, one was surrounded by controversy because it included a call for measures that some felt threatened the basic constitutional rights of citizens.

The commission supported the establishment of a national data bank to check Social Security numbers of employees. Some advocates of civil liberties equated the measure to the institution of national identification cards, usually associated with totalitarian states or regimes. In addition, advocates for immigrants were calling the measure insensitive to undocumented workers.

To compound matters, once the preliminary findings were out, there was some concern that the administration might be moving away from the commission's report. This position came to light when a White House source leaked to the press that not even the president could endorse his chairwoman's recommendations. That was a mistake. Too much was at stake for Jordan to allow the president to distance himself from the commission's work. Some behind-the-scenes maneuvering—which Jordan's admirers attribute to the power of her moral suasion and the quality of her political acumen—produced a firm statement from a characteristically wavering president. In his State of the Union Address in January of 1995, the president announced that his administration would support and implement the recommendations of the "Barbara Jordan" Commission.[1]

A rare statesmanship, a keen political acumen, and a public persona as a moral force in American politics best described the late Democratic congresswoman Barbara Jordan. It was a reputation earned during a twelve-year stint as an elected official—six years in the

Texas Senate and six years in the U.S. House of Representatives. The impression grew not just from her legislative accomplishments but from the quality of those twelve years. It lasted decades after her retirement from elected office, right through her death. More than two decades ago, when the nation listened transfixed to Barbara Jordan's superbly delivered speech before the House Judiciary Committee's hearings on the Watergate scandal. America bestowed upon her a reputation that would grow to heroic status. She began with this now famous opening salvo:

> Earlier today, we heard the beginning of the preamble to the Constitution of the United States, "We the people." It is a very eloquent beginning. But, when that document was completed on the 17th of September in 1787, I was not included in that "We the people." I felt somehow for many years that George Washington and Alexander Hamilton just left me out by mistake. But, through the process of amendment, interpretation, and court decision, I have finally been included in "We the people."
>
> Today, I am an inquisitor. I believe hyperbole would not be fictional and would not overstate the solemnness that I feel right now. My faith in the Constitution is whole, it is complete, it is total. I am not going to sit here and be an idle spectator to the diminution, the subversion, the destruction of the Constitution.[2]

It was July 25, 1974, and freshman congresswoman Barbara Jordan, a Democrat from Texas's Eighteenth Congressional District, spoke the words that mesmerized a nation. Thirty-five members of the House Judiciary Committee, chaired by New Jersey Democrat Peter Rodino, were charged with determining the extent to which the Republican president had knowledge of the break-in at the Democratic National Committee (DNC) headquarters in the Watergate office complex. Congresswoman Jordan, in her first term in the House of Representatives, was one of those deciding the fate of the thirty-seventh president of the United States, Richard Milhous Nixon.

The Watergate affair began two years earlier in Washington, D.C.—before she was elected—when Frank Wills, a black security guard working in the Watergate office building complex earned his footnote in history by calling the D.C. police to the scene of a burglary in progress. It was June 17, 1972.

In what would later be dismissed by a White House staff person as a "third-rate burglary," the D.C. police arrested five men who were breaking into the DNC headquarters. The five men were all tied to the Committee to Re-elect the President. Although the arrest did not influence the enormously successful reelection of the president—he defeated his Democratic opponent, Senator George McGovern, by one of the largest landslides in the nation's history, with a popular vote of 47,169,911 votes to 29,170,383 and an electoral college vote of 520 to 17—it did begin the revelation of one of the worst scandals in the history of the presidency. The arrest of two other men in the weeks that followed, a cascading from power of minor political operatives and eventually the political demise and imprisonment of key presidential advisers and cabinet members all came to be known as the Watergate scandal.[3]

The president's involvement in the scandal was uncovered by a combination of the dogged determination of the *Washington Post* team of Bob Woodward and Carl Bernstein; the Senate Select Committee on Watergate, chaired by North Carolina Democrat Sam Ervin; and a special prosecutor's office that petitioned the U.S. Supreme Court to force the president to comply with its subpoena for copies of tape-recorded sessions in the White House. Of course, the House Judiciary Committee's approval of three articles of impeachment that summer marked the death knell for the Nixon presidency.

The events that occurred from 1972 to 1974 were characterized by a shameless abuse of power. Evidence suggested that Nixon and his men had authorized the installation of eavesdropping devices inside the Democratic Committee headquarters, the funding of a dirty tricks squad whose job it was to sow dissension among Democrats, the payment of "hush money" to Watergate defendants to keep them from talking, and the funding of a White House "plumbers" unit created to plug leaks of classified information. In addition, an enemies list was compiled that included Congressman John Conyers (D-Mich.), CBS newsman Daniel Schorr, actress Carol Channing, and comedian Bill Cosby.[4]

Nixon compounded his problems by installing an elaborate tape recording device in the White House, which he wanted to use in writing his memoirs. Instead, it helped reveal the extent of his involvement in the Watergate scandal. It was the request for the tapes by Special Prosecutor Archibald Cox and Nixon's immediate firing of him for that request that prompted the House of Representatives to act.

Following the firing, Congress began impeachment proceedings. At the same time, a new prosecutor had been hired, Leon Jaworski, and he continued to pressure President Nixon for the tapes. After Nixon eventually turned over a portion of the tapes—one with an eighteen-and-a-half-minute gap—the special prosecutor was forced to petition the U.S. Supreme Court, which ruled that Nixon had to comply with the request for full disclosure.

Thus on the day of the hearings, when Barbara Jordan laid out charges to support her affirmative vote on the articles of impeachment against President Nixon, simultaneously other forces were converging on the administration—the judiciary and legislative branches of government as well as the press. The whole affair represented one of the most devastating challenges to contemporary American democracy in the twentieth century, and Jordan's poignant response was the single most memorable of that day.

As she continued, quiet came over the House Judiciary Committee room. Cameras clicked away at close range, showing a large-boned, deep-brown-skinned woman with carefully pressed hair and an oval face with eyes that peered over dark-rimmed eyeglasses. Her voice electrified the nation—distinctive, deep, and resonant. Her "r" rolled like thunder from her lips with unmistakable power. America had never heard such a rich and resonant voice coming from a woman in Congress. Of course, there were contralto singers, such as Marian Anderson, and women of color in the arts with extraordinary speaking styles, but commanding political oratory in the halls of Congress had remained the domain of white men. The presence of such a commanding and respected female voice would not be heard until the thirty-eight-year-old Jordan entered Congress using her unique stylistic elocution, coupled with a scholar's understanding of the Constitution, to make her case for the impeachment of the president:

> We know the nature of impeachment. We have been talking about it awhile now. It is chiefly designed for the President and his ministers to somehow be called into account. It is designed to bridle the Executive, if he engages in excesses. It is designed as a method of national inquisition into the conduct of public men. The framers confined in the Congress the power, if need be, to remove the President in order to strike a delicate balance between a President swollen with power and grown tyrannical and preservation of the independence of the Executive. The nature of impeachment is a narrowly channeled exception of the separation of powers maxim, the Federal Convention of 1787 said that. It limited impeachment to high crimes and misdemeanors and discounted and opposed the term "maladministration." It is to be used only for great misdemeanor.[5]

Jordan proceeded to lay out the articles that constituted impeachable conduct by the president and matched them with the evidence of Nixon's actions. The committee eventually and reluctantly approved three articles of impeachment: obstruction of justice, violation of the oath of office, and unconstitutional defiance of committee subpoenas. On August 9, 1974, faced with the near certainty of impeachment, President Richard Nixon resigned from office.[6]

The country, although shaken by the ominous prospects for the presidency, was invigorated by this newfound presence in the Congress. The heretofore little-known congresswoman from Texas was declared a national heroine, and the country would soon discover through the numerous articles and interviews that followed that she was also a national treasure, homemade in one of Houston, Texas's poorest wards.

The Early Years

Barbara Jordan may have inherited natural speaking abilities, but she was made into an outstanding orator by an admixture of family, teachers, and the zeitgeist of twentieth-century American society. Notwithstanding her persistent push for excellence and hard work, the ingredients included the unrealized oratorical skills of Arlyn Patten Jordan, the unrequited dreams of John Ed Patten, the rhythmic patterns of the Baptist Church, and the dedication of a college debate coach. All were undergirded by a strong and supportive family headed by the Reverend and Mrs. Benjamin Jordan.

On February 21, 1936, Benjamin and Arlyn Jordan of Houston, Texas, had their third daughter, Barbara Charline, delivered at home rather than in Houston's segregated hospital. It was a triumph of sorts because the child was delivered by a family member who had become a doctor. The baby girl would be their last child following Bennie Meredith (the middle daughter) and Rose Mary (the oldest). The three girls grew up under the stern hand of their father and the intense tutelage of their mother.

The Reverend Jordan lived a life of unrealized potential, stemming from the segregated society in Texas and the United States. Though college-educated at Tuskegee Institute, he worked as a full-time warehouseman and part-time Baptist minister. His wife, in the eyes of Barbara's maternal grandfather, John E. Patten, sublimated considerable oratorical talent to live a life as wife and mother—a fate the elder Patten counseled his favorite granddaughter, Barbara, to avoid.[7]

The Jordans lived on the brink of change, and through a solid family structure gave the world three daughters prepared to embrace the new and expanding world of opportunities of the late 1950s and 1960s. Barbara Jordan had added support in the form of her grandfather, John Patten. Patten lived a life that black men in the South feared: he was incarcerated in 1919 in one of Texas's worst prison systems for a crime he did not commit. Released almost six years later by the prison reforms of Governor Miriam Ferguson, he returned home, turning his efforts inward toward his family—investing time, dreams, and hope in his daughter Arlyn. At an early age, she was recognized as a skilled public speaker and was in demand at Baptist churches throughout Houston. Barbara Jordan would later comment that her mother "was the most eloquent, articulate person, I ever heard. If she had been a man, she would have been a preacher."[8]

Those limitations were probably equally obvious to Arlyn, affecting her decision to choose marriage and family over the elusive possibility of a profession. It was a choice, though, that John Patten objected to so much that he refused to attend her wedding. It was not until the birth of Barbara that Patten saw a glimmer of hope for influencing another mind. It was another chance to shape and mold a new talent. His efforts were not lost on Barbara, who continued to be appreciative of his contribution long after his death and her success.

She opened her 1979 autobiography, *Barbara Jordan: A Self-Portrait,* with a chapter dedicated to the impact of John Ed Patten on her life. She describes his doting and caring moments as he sat "by the light of a kerosene lantern" and read to her from a "worn volume of 'Songs for the Blood Washed' . . . the King James Bible, and Saalfield's *Standard Vest Pocket Webster's Pronouncing Dictionary.*"[9]

He spent hours with the young Barbara, teaching her how to speak and imparting words of wisdom about life and its possibilities, but although Patten was a tremendous influence on her, other familial forces also contributed to her development. The Jordans were an intergenerationally close-knit extended family. Similar to other black families in the 1940s and 1950s, they used education and religion to build a solid foundation as an outlet for their children. It was a nurturing environment that supplanted the potential devastation of substandard schools with the creation of an internal support system. Churches and families provided encouragement and protection against psychologically damaging images of black children's abilities.

This explains, in part, why Jordan found fertile ground for her burgeoning oratorical skills at Phillis Wheatley High School, where she carved out a niche in debate and public speaking. Eschewing the high school contests that called for teachers to select students based on favoritism (in too many instances that equated to shades of skin color), she refused to be trapped in the intraracial color consciousness of the time and moved in the direction of gaining recognition based on her abilities and merit.[10]

A memorable experience in her early life was her first trip to Chicago by train to compete in the National Ushers Convention Oratorical Contest. The trip followed her victory in the statewide competition, where the first prize was the all-expense-paid trip to the national contest. Sheltered and confined in Houston's Fifth Ward, Jordan received her first glimpse into the outside world. Benjamin Jordan had never let much of the outside into his house. The Jordan household had no television, and the three girls were forbidden to attend the movies or parties. But their closed world had its advantages; it created a place where positive reinforcement spurred children toward excellence. It was also a safe place for the dispensing of the maxims for success, which a generation of black children grew up learning, such as: "You have to be twice as good and more prepared than any white person in order to get ahead."

Jordan proved to be capable of meeting and exceeding expectations. She won the first-place prize in Chicago, and by the time she graduated from Phillis Wheatley High School in 1952, she had a collection of honors, including the much-coveted Girl of the Year Award presented by the Zeta Phi Beta Sorority. But most importantly, she earned a reputation throughout Houston and the Baptist Church in Texas as an excellent public speaker. She had taken up where Arlyn Patten Jordan left off, and that reputation followed her to Texas Southern University (TSU), where she studied from 1952 to 1956.

At the historically black TSU, Jordan came under the tutelage of the university's debate coach, Dr. Thomas Freeman, who included her in his retinue of up-and-coming orators in whom he invested personal financial resources and time. His was a commitment not unlike that of many black teachers and university professors during segregation, unsung heroes who gave students exposure to a world that was much broader than the Jim Crow South.

Freeman began teaching at TSU in 1949, straight out of the University of Chicago's doctoral program in theology. He was a young intellectual, incensed but not deterred by the system that robbed him and his students of the full benefit to be derived from their abilities. He is described by his students as a perfectionist who paid particular attention to grammar and enunciation as he pushed them to think "critically, analytically and conceptually."[11]

Jordan, his most popular student, attributed some of her success to his hard work and push for excellence. "I thought I had superb diction and that no one would need to correct anything," she told the audience at a tribute to Freeman in 1992. "Thomas Freeman found a flaw, and worked on it until it was corrected." She went on to say, "I cannot overestimate the impact and influence Dr. Freeman had on my life. . . . He stretches your mind. He places you on your own, teaches you to stand on your feet, think, and open your mouth and talk."[12] It had been a labor of love for Freeman, who would pack his students into his late-model car and travel to Chicago where, after 1954, they could compete in integrated regional debates. Even then, Freeman had to shield his students from discrimination on the way to debating sites. He packed lunches to keep from having to stop along the road and risk the humiliation of restaurants that would not serve them, and he contacted local ministers to ensure that they would have a place to stay once in town.[13]

His rule was to take only boys, but Jordan did not want to miss the adventure of riding with the team, so she gained weight and began wearing boxy suits, cut her hair, and in general made herself unattractive so that no one would worry about needing to chaperone her. It worked, and she got a chance to be a part of the Freeman entourage of debaters—the first female to go on tour.[14]

After winning one debate against a white team, Freeman recalled that the coach for the losing team confessed: "Thirty years ago I wrote a paper in which I argued that blacks were inherently inferior. After listening to the speeches tonight, I confess before this audience that I was wrong." Freeman remembers the remarks as having stunned the students, but he advised them as he had done in the past to "persevere, and to become somebody."[15]

Needless to say, the message was not lost on Jordan. It was after such a debate with the nationally recognized Harvard University team that she decided that she wanted to go to Harvard Law School. The TSU team tied with Harvard, and she took the tie to mean that TSU won, because she reasoned if Harvard had won, the judges would have said so. In her mind, it just meant that she was obviously good enough to go to Harvard.[16]

The year was 1956, and Harvard University Law School was not a likely possibility for the honor student from TSU. When she approached Freeman about her interest in applying there, he advised against it. Instead of trying to break the barriers that would have been necessary for her to attend Harvard, he encouraged her instead—as he had done with other students—to go to Boston University Law School, where the chances of getting in were better.[17]

Jordan followed his advice and applied to and was accepted by Boston, where she was one of six women and one of two blacks. The other African American student was Issie Shelton, another Texan. Shelton rode to Boston along with Jordan and classmate George Turner, whom Freeman had directed to Andover Newton Theological Seminary. The trip was her first move alone, beyond the protection of the Jordan household. Because the Boston University education was a financial sacrifice for the family, she was unable to come home during the holidays. It made the first year an especially hard and lonely one for her. She sought and found a place of solace on the campus—the chapel. Born and reared in the strict Baptist tradition of the South, Jordan marveled at the "freedom" expressed by the renowned black theologian, Howard Thurman, who at the time was dean of Boston University's Marsh Chapel.

The soft-spoken, contemplative Thurman differed significantly from the charismatic, God-fearing Texas Baptist tradition. The contrast was not just style—emphasis was also different. The Baptist upbringing had placed emphasis on the prohibitions of life, more so than the freedom of Christian faith. For Jordan, Thurman's theology was "liberating."[18]

So impressed was she that she claims to have saved every program from the chapel, to have gone back to her room and preached the sermons again to her disinterested roommates, and finally to have called her father to say that she might be interested in changing from studying law to studying theology. Benjamin Jordan, of course, was more than overjoyed that his daughter might follow in the footsteps of her paternal grandmother, who was a missionary. His mistaken assumption about missionary work—women's work—caused his daughter to change her mind. Barbara Jordan's vision was much broader than her father's, and if she were to choose theology, she wanted to lead and not to follow, so she quickly discarded the idea.[19]

But if her introduction to the famed Thurman was noteworthy and expanded her later understanding of Christianity, her contact with another soon-to-be famous African American would prove less welcoming and instructive.

Few black lawyers were available to give internships and guidance to Boston University's African American students, and white firms were unwilling. So when Jordan began to show promise as a law student, one of her professors suggested that she contact Edward Brooke—one of a few practicing black lawyers in the area—and seek his assistance in getting some legal experience. Jordan visited Brooke, but was neither impressed nor encouraged by him.[20]

Republican Edward Brooke would later represent Massachusetts in the U.S. Senate, making history as the first black to be elected to the Senate in the twentieth century. He served from 1967 to 1979, encompassing Jordan's term in the House of Representatives from 1973 to 1978. During the Watergate scandal, he was the first to call for the resignation of Richard Nixon.

The Brooke meeting was unfortunate because Jordan really needed a solid mentoring relationship while in law school. Boston was a challenge for her; she was not the top-notch student she had been at TSU. She attributed some of her difficulties to the lack of resources in black colleges at that time, which she felt inadequately prepared students for competition in Ivy League graduate and professional schools. Sweating through the first year resulted in anxiety on her first trip home as she awaited her grades. Racing to beat her parents to the mail, she felt the high expectations and pressure that an entire community, church, and family placed on her.

In this respect her story is an account of the hidden saga of the African American achiever—extended family support, high expectations for achievement, and the overall investment in the education and success of young people with potential. This is generally coupled with the hope that they will return home and work for the betterment of the community. In a very real sense, Jordan was a hometown celebrity who followed the rules and made it. She completed her first year with acceptable if not excellent grades, but went on to gain more confidence and better academic standing.

The Political Odyssey

A year after graduating from Boston University in 1959, she passed both the Massachusetts and Texas bar examinations. Returning to Houston after failing to get a job in the insurance industry in Boston, she set up a law practice in her parents' kitchen. During the summer she taught at Tuskegee Institute in order to make enough money to move from the kitchen into an office. Eventually, she was able to make the transition, and so, with used furniture and clerical help from a former classmate, Jordan opened a law office in the middle of the Fifth Ward, the black section of town.[21]

The slow process of building a law practice very quickly made the exciting world of politics look more appealing. After working as a volunteer in political campaigns and events, two years into her practice, in 1962, Jordan launched into her first political campaign. She ran for the Texas Senate but lost. Again in 1964, she ran unsuccessfully in the Harris County Democratic primaries.

Houston was much like other cities. White party operatives used black voters to win elections, but kept blacks out of elected office. In places such as Ohio, New York, Indiana, and Missouri, key blacks were used to get out the vote for white candidates. While a black (generally a man) may have been given a patronage position, very little else could be expected to go to the black community.[22]

Even though she had not been a winning candidate, Jordan's growing political visibility represented a power with which to be reckoned. It is not surprising, then, that after her defeat she was appointed to a position as the administrative assistant to Judge William Elliot of the Harris County Court—a political appointment that she held for a year. In 1966, after a year, she told the judge that she was leaving to run for the newly redrawn Eleventh Senatorial District.

For African Americans in politics, 1966 was the beginning of a new era reflecting a political revival because of the enactment of the 1965 Voting Rights Act. Jordan's prospects this time, like those of other blacks, had changed. For the first time since Reconstruction, blacks in the South would be able to participate in the democratic process without the constraints of poll taxes and other discriminatory tactics used to diminish their political power. Within the context of Jordan's political story, it is important to note that the not-so-invisible hand of President Lyndon Baines Johnson was evident in the passage of the act. Through his shrewd legislative maneuvers—building upon the foundation of the agitation of the civil rights movement—blacks, minorities, and the poor would be able to fully participate in the electoral process for the first time since the turn of the century. A bloody legacy faded into the background as the act and the court rulings on one-man, one-vote literally changed the complexion of the nation's state, local, and federally elected officials.

For Jordan, the Eleventh Senatorial District as redrawn included a voting population that was more than 50 percent minority. However, it was not just the district's composition that had changed this time. Jordan had also changed. Her first two campaigns were conducted according to the white Harris County Democratic formula—an office uptown and white handlers who contacted the media to make the candidate's case for endorsement. *Grassroots* was the operative word for the candidate this time, so she used her law office that was right in the heart of the black community, and she personally went to the press to gain endorsements.

She changed the rules of engagement in the campaign by telling the editorial boards of the two major newspapers, "If you know you can't bring yourself to endorse me, then consider not endorsing my opponent either."[23]

Jordan's opponent, Charlie Whitfield, accused her of injecting race into the campaign —an irony that defied analysis. Stepping outside the confines of the party patriarchs, Jordan ran on her own terms, using her own strategy, and won the Democratic primary with more than 60 percent of the vote. Because Texas was still a one-party state, winning the Democratic primary was tantamount to general election victory. In November, she became one of two blacks in the state legislature; the other was Curtis Graves, who won a seat in the lower house. He would later challenge her congressional bid.[24]

The state senate was made up of white men, many of whom wanted the prestige of the senate office and the opportunity to use it to bestow government largess on selected constituencies, rather than to engage in writing copious legislation. Jordan had to retrofit herself into this staid, unmalleable structure. The question was how would she do it? As the only black, she refused to rely on race for access or favor.

Her strategy, whether conscious or unconscious, was to become "one of the boys" in a nonthreatening way and at the same time to take the time to master the state legislative process. In an age when black power and protest politics characterized much of African American leadership, she was unique in her nonconfrontational and noncombative approach to dealing with the Texas politicians in the senate.

"I wanted them to see me first-hand and not just read about this great thing that had happened in Houston," she wrote. "I wanted them to know I was coming to be a senator, and I wasn't coming to lead any charge. I was not coming carrying the flag and singing 'We Shall Overcome.' I was coming to work and I wanted to get that message communicated personally."[25]

In the final analysis, Barbara Jordan was a Texan, a believer in the Constitution, and a sympathizer but not an active participant in the civil rights movement of the 1960s. Even though she was a member of the NAACP and had joined some of the most politically active women's clubs, such as the LINKS and the Delta Sigma Theta Sorority, she was different from the contemporary black leadership. For her, the legislative process was really the answer, and while she was very much a part of the black experience in America, she did not indulge herself in its protest movements.

For the time being, her milieu was the Texas Senate, and she intended to hunker down and conquer it. Being the only female—the other had been gerrymandered out of office— did not keep her from becoming a part of the senate's powerful inside network. She joined the senators on the annual quail hunts, playing her guitar while the others hunted. From sitting in on the afternoon drinking sessions with state senators Jake Johnson or Dorsey Hardeman—two powerful allies—to listening to off-color jokes and not showing distaste for them, Jordan cultivated and maintained relationships that enabled her to effectively get her legislation through the senate without rocking any boats.[26]

"She conducted herself in a most commendable manner from the start. [She was] not forward in any respect. She didn't press her race or color. She was very modest and circumspect, which gained her the respect of the senate," said one old-line Texas Democratic state senator.[27]

As Jordan became more of a public figure, she privately yearned for the days when friends were friends and it was always possible to determine who they were. Her close circle of friends and advisers had not changed much since high school. Her private life centered around her sisters and their husbands, her father and mother, a favorite cousin and her husband, and the family friends Evelyn and Mary Elisabeth Justice and their husbands. This circle opened a bit in Austin, just wide enough to let in Nancy Earl, an educational psychologist who ended up as a longtime companion and part of Jordan's network of trusted relationships. In 1976 the two would build a home together in Austin, Texas, where Jordan would spend the last twenty years of her life.[28]

If her private life was expanding only a bit, her public life was moving beyond Austin into the national arena. Aiding this national exposure was an invitation in February of 1967 from President Lyndon Baines Johnson. Johnson invited black leaders such as Roy Wilkins of the NAACP, Whitney Young of the National Urban League, Dorothy Height of the National Council of Negro Women, along with other heads of major organizations and state senator Barbara Jordan to the White House for a briefing on his proposed fair housing initiative. The mere fact that the president had sought out Jordan, who had not been identified in the past with any major civil rights efforts outside of Texas, gave rise in the media to speculation that Johnson had hand-picked a black leader outside of the traditional civil rights community. The positive articles spoke to Johnson's actions when he deferred to the state senator for a response to his query about the initiative. Her answer was not as significant as the fact that he had posed the question to her. Of course, in the Washington political parlance, the act was enough to elevate her to the status of a new black national leader.

But Jordan was seemingly unaffected by the national attention and would not be deterred from her efforts to pile up what was amounting to an impressive legislative record. She had already gained a reputation as an effective, cautious politician who exercised considerable power within the Democratically controlled state legislature. Her six years in the state senate were legislatively productive and historically noteworthy. She authored bills that aided and improved the quality of life of the poor, minorities, and women. In the main, she focused on ensuring fair employment practices, creating agencies such as the Texas Department of Community Affairs, giving firemen reimbursement benefits for college credits, developing programs for the education and training of the handicapped, and reforming workers' compensation and state administration.

She was the first black elected to preside over the state senate; the first to chair a major committee—Labor and Management Relations—and the first freshman senator ever named to the Texas Legislative Council.[29]

Probably most significant on a historical and a personal level was her designation as the first black woman to be named "Governor for a Day," an essentially ceremonial event honoring the president pro tempore of the senate. The governor and lieutenant governor arrange to be away from the state capitol for a day, and the line of succession calls for the president pro tempore, the presiding member of the senate, to take over the governor's office. It is a day generally filled with festivities, gifts from lobbyists, and the signing of ceremonial proclamations in front of constituents and friends.

It was in this way that on June 10, 1972, she became "Governor Jordan." Schoolchildren and constituents were bussed into the state capital in Austin from Houston to join her inner circle of friends and family, which included her ailing father. The Reverend Benjamin Jordan had suffered a heart attack earlier and was in guarded condition. However, with a steady resolve, he sat through the morning ceremonies as planned, and he heard the reading of the proclamation declaring his daughter "Governor for a Day." As the ceremony progressed, he took ill again and had to be rushed to the hospital, where he died early the next morning. Needless to say, for Jordan it was both a day of high praise and honor coupled with personal loss and heartfelt condolences. The "Governor for a Day" honor was one of the last high-profile acts before she left the state senate to run for national office.

Jordan was already in the running for the newly created Eighteenth Congressional District, which was created by the state senate's Redistricting Committee, of which she was vice chair. The district was created to include a voting age population that was 19 percent Hispanic, 42 percent black, and 39 percent white. Not surprisingly, from its inception, the creation of this district was controversial. The most damaging criticism came from state assemblyman Curtis Graves. He accused Jordan of agreeing to the decimation of her state senate district for a chance at creating and running for the new congressional district.

The trade-off in the creation of the minority Eighteenth Congressional District appeared to be the gerrymandering of Jordan's state senate seat to minimize the chances of a black candidate winning it again. Such a political maneuver was viewed with skepticism by factions within the black community led by Graves. He accused her of forfeiting her seat for the chance to serve in Congress and leaving Houston without any chance of an African American presence in the state senate.

It was a rare moment of criticism against Jordan, who was generally praised for her work in the legislature. It was not unlike the dilemma political scientists in the future would face as they attempted to decipher Jordan's political philosophy beyond the overwhelming impression her splendid rhetoric created. The puzzle fueled the creation of conflicting political portraits. One described a talented black machine politician and power broker; the other, a member of the African American community struggling for political change that would eliminate that very machine. Because machine politics had been used against their political progress in the past, having a popular African American politician embracing the machine was problematic for many black politicians.

Graves, the candidate who challenged Jordan in the primary for the U.S. House seat, raised the issue of machine politics in his bid against her. However, he faced a no-win situation. Jordan had participated in the process of eliminating her own seat and would probably benefit from it, yet she continued to be a popular candidate. In spite of this arcane political tactic, ordinary people would vote for her to go to Congress.

Still, Graves would not be dissuaded; he took his opposition to the courts and lost, and then he took it to the people and ran against her for the Democratic nomination for the new congressional seat. He sought an endorsement from the Harris County Democrats while lambasting Jordan for being disloyal to the party. Side-stepping the issue, the county Democrats endorsed both Jordan and Graves. In the end, of course, it was no contest. Jordan defeated Graves and another black candidate, getting 80 percent of the vote in the primary and going on to the general election, where she defeated Republican Paul Merrit with 81 percent of the vote.

The Congressional Years and Beyond

Jordan was elected to serve in the Ninety-third Congress in November 1972, the first African American woman from the South to be elected to the U.S. House of Representatives. With one person less in her closed circle of family—her father, the Reverend Benjamin Jordan—and friends, she headed for Capitol Hill.

Former president Johnson held to a promise to back Jordan as she moved from state politics to Congress, and she used that commitment to gain a favorable committee assignment.

While at a pre-swearing-in workshop at Harvard's John F. Kennedy School of Government, she contacted Johnson and asked for help in securing a seat on either the House Judiciary Committee or the Armed Services Committee. He, in turn, called Arkansas Democrat Wilbur Mills, the powerful chair of the House Ways and Means Committee, and asked him to put the freshman on the Judiciary Committee—a choice Johnson felt was more politically advantageous to her. It was yet another confirmation that Jordan was first and foremost a bona fide Texas Democrat and now a member of one of the most powerful political blocs in the House of Representatives. Mills's action signaled to others that she was also unusually well-connected for a freshman member. It was one of Johnson's final acts of power on her behalf. On January 22, 1973, before he could see the congresswoman in full force in the House of Representatives and just weeks after her swearing-in ceremony, he collapsed and died of a heart attack.[30]

Barbara Jordan entered the House of Representatives as a member of another emerging power bloc, the Congressional Black Caucus (CBC). The number of blacks in the House of Representatives increased from six in 1969 to sixteen in 1973. Although she identified more with the Texas caucus than the CBC, Jordan was nonetheless one of the most visible black members on Capitol Hill. That same year, 1973, three women joined Shirley Chisholm (D-N.Y.) as the only African American women in Congress—Jordan, Yvonne Brathwaite Burke (D-Calif.), and Cardiss Collins (D-Ill.). The three new women's style was a lot less confrontational than Chisholm's. This fact may have contributed to their assuming significant positions within the Congressional Black Caucus—two eventually became chairs of the CBC.

Although they benefited from Jordan's prominence and respected her legislative accomplishments, the CBC could never quite reconcile itself to her ties to the Texas party machine. Though it had tried to wean earlier Chicago CBC members from the Daley machine, there is no evidence that any attempts were made to meddle with Jordan's loyalties.

One act in particular characterizes Jordan's penchant for machine politics—her response to a request by the Democratic National Committee chair, Texan Robert Strauss, that she act as a character witness in the grand jury investigation of former Texas governor John Connally. Connally was no friend of civil rights; in Texas he had blocked major legislation aimed at helping poor and minority communities. Jordan had balked at supporting him as a favorite son candidate in a previous presidential primary and had openly wept when she overheard his comments regarding the death of Martin Luther King, Jr., which she reported as: "When you live by the sword, you die by the sword."[31]

Despite the overwhelming respect for her by black leaders, her decision to testify on behalf of Connally raised questions about Jordan's continued Texas allegiance. It so happened that in 1975 Connally needed a character witness in front of a predominantly black jury in Washington, D.C. The former governor was being tried for conducting fraudulent activities with milk manufacturers. He needed a character witness, she consented, and the CBC members flinched.

The Connally incident was the exception rather than the rule, however, and Jordan's six-year tenure in the House of Representatives resulted in the introduction of the legislation authorizing cities to receive direct Law Enforcement Assistance Administration (LEAA) grants, thereby eliminating the need to go through the state bureaucracy. She also refused to vote for confirmation of Gerald Ford as vice president because of his dismal civil rights record. She fought for the inclusion of Hispanics, Native Americans, Alaskan Natives, and Asian American language minorities in the 1965 Voting Rights Act extension. She also cosponsored legislation to extend the state ratification deadline for the proposed Equal Rights Amendment from 1979 to 1986.

Her greatest legacy, however, was her ability to voice the country's anguish over presidential excesses during the Watergate hearings. It was the overwhelming impact of that moment that led her to make history once again when she was invited as the first black to give the keynote speech at a major party's political convention.

The 1976 Democratic National Convention will be remembered for nominating Jimmy Carter for the presidential bid, but it also will be remembered as the convention that honored one of its major political stalwarts—Barbara Jordan. Standing before the cameras of the nation, once again Jordan turned in an unsurpassed performance.

"One hundred and forty-four years ago, members of the Democratic Party met for the first time in convention to select their presidential candidate. Since that time, Democrats have continued to convene once every four years to draft a party platform and nominate a presidential candidate. Our meeting this week continues that tradition," said Jordan, opening her keynote address with what had become her oratorical style. It was a style that began with a historical context of exclusion, contrasted with the unlikely presence of an African American in the contemporary context. She continued: "But there is something different about tonight. There is something special about tonight. What is different? What is special? I, Barbara Jordan, am a keynote speaker."[32]

The speech garnered rave reviews from the media and from Americans who saw her as a likely candidate for Carter's cabinet, if not for the vice presidential slot. But it was not to be. Carter, after using the popular congresswoman to campaign for him, refused to appoint her to any position that represented power and control, such as attorney general. This was the position that Jordan wanted, and the call that she waited to receive from the successful presidential candidate. It never came.[33]

Jordan served another term, and then in 1978, to the surprise of many, the Texan with the booming voice and the electrifying rhetorical style announced to an unsuspecting world that she was leaving politics to return to her home. Stricken with multiple sclerosis—a diagnosis that the very private Jordan described as a degenerative bone disease—she returned to private life as a professor at the University of Texas's Lyndon B. Johnson School of Public Affairs in Austin. In an interview with Dan Rather of CBS News in 1979, she said, "Getting there is more fun than being there" in reference to her decision to leave Congress.[34]

In her six years, she had reached the top in terms of national exposure and appreciation as a public official, but personally she had exhausted her desire to continue fighting a recalcitrant and lethargic House of Representatives. She wanted to move into public policy deliberations and to use the academy as a place to engage new minds and future leaders. It would become her love for the remainder of her life. Although she retired from elective office, Jordan continued to be involved in public service, even after a swimming accident in 1988 left many apprehensive and concerned about her health.[35]

Jordan rebounded from the accident and five years later, in 1992, she was back in the spotlight as the keynote speaker at the Democratic National Convention, which nominated Bill Clinton as its standard bearer for the presidency. But the American icon and symbol of pride for a generation of African Americans was criticized by key black leadership for engaging in the ongoing battle in the Democratic party for the political middle ground, and she was accused of taking the side of the centrists. The schism had been exacerbated by Bill Clinton's use of a little-known rap singer, Sister Souljah, to divide black leadership and deflect attention from Democratic progressives, such as the Reverend Jesse Jackson. Many blacks thought that Jordan used her gift of oratorical prowess to deliver a centrist party line, thus carving an even larger wedge between the Jackson and the Clinton factions. "Jordan was carrying the water of the strategists that want to bring us back to the right of center in the [Democratic] party," Jewell Jackson McCabe, founder and chairwoman of the National Coalition of 100 Black Women, told a *Los Angeles Times* reporter after the speech. "It was as though she—a black woman, one of my role models and heroes—was carrying the message of white men to black people. I was shocked, saddened and confused because I didn't understand what she meant or why she would say that."[36]

McCabe's advocacy group has a reported membership of seven thousand, and she represented the new politically conscious and more independent wave of black women in politics. The remarks she referred to were these from Jordan's address to the convention: "We are one, we Americans, and we reject any intruder who seeks to divide us by race or class. We seek to unite people, not divide them, and we reject both white racism and black racism. This party will not tolerate bigotry under any guise." In particular, McCabe and others objected to her use of the term "black racism." Most black leaders felt strongly that blacks could not be racist without having control of the power to implement their ideas. It was a volatile debate within the African American community, and some felt that Jordan's remarks showed signs of betrayal rather than just a difference of opinion. Furthermore, they felt that she engaged in the same rhetoric of division that Clinton had used to malign Jackson.[37]

The former congresswoman was indeed a Clinton Democrat, and she actively supported much of his legislative agenda, including the controversial North American Free Trade Agreement—an issue on which many black politicians differed. Even as Jordan chaired the administration's efforts to review immigration laws, she ran into resistance from her previous allies in the Democratic party. Still, she retained her national reputation as a conscience of the Constitution up until her death.

In her last years, she also remained enamored by the classroom, teaching new minds and becoming an oracle for the integrity of the political process. Even though she had received the Presidential Medal of Freedom in 1994, for Jordan it was the classroom that gave her the most pleasure. Summing up her love of teaching, she said in an interview before her death: "Well, I am living a very full life and enjoying it. I enjoy teaching my students. I teach a seminar that is titled, 'Political Values and Ethics.' And this is a seminar which is designed to teach young people the kind of future public servants should have. And I have an opportunity to impact the next generation of public officials in what I do, and that pleases me."[38]

What was evident from the many eulogies following her death in 1996 is that dignitaries, students, and ordinary people alike believed that Barbara Jordan had also pleased America as the quintessential public servant.

Chapter 4

Yvonne Brathwaite Burke

A Savvy Leader in a Male-Dominated Political Arena

My career was greatly affected by having a child while in Congress, and it was why I made a decision to leave.[1]

Résumé

Yvonne Brathwaite Burke

Personal

Born	October 5, 1932 Los Angeles, California
Family	Married to William A. Burke; two children
Religion	Baptist
Party	Democrat
Took office	Age 40, January 3, 1973

Education

A.D.	University of California, 1951
B.A.	University of California at Los Angeles, 1953
J.D.	University of Southern California School of Law, Los Angeles, 1956

Professional/Political Background

1956	Admitted to the California bar
1956–1965	Attorney
1965–1966	Hearing officer for Los Angeles Police Commission
1967–1972	Assemblywoman, California General Assembly
1973–1979	U.S. House of Representatives
1979–	Supervisor, Los Angeles County Board of Supervisors
1981–1983	Partner, Law firm Kutak, Rock and Huie
1984–1987	Partner, Law firm Burke, Robinson and Pearman
1987–	Partner, Law firm Jones, Day, Reavis and Pogue

Selected Awards/Organizational Affiliations

Loren Miller Award, National Association for the Advancement of Colored People; fellow, Institute of Politics, John F. Kennedy School of Government (Harvard); Chubb Fellow, Yale University; president, National Coalition of 100 Black Women; Los Angeles vice chair, University of California Board of Regents; member, Ford Foundation Board of Trustees; delegate and vice chair, Democratic National Convention 1972.

Congressional Data

Thirty-seventh Congressional District of California: Watts and other parts of Los Angeles

Committees: Interior and Insular Affairs; Public Works and Transportation; Appropriations

93d Congress:	1973–1974
1972 general election results:	60 percent of the vote
94th Congress:	1975–1976
1974 general election results:	80 percent of the vote
95th Congress:	1977–1978
1976 general election results:	80 percent of the vote

Yvonne Brathwaite Burke

*The First African American Woman
Elected to Congress from California*

Thirty-seventh District, California
Democrat
93d–95th Congresses, 1973–1978

The first African American woman elected to Congress from California—Yvonne Brathwaite Burke—was a trailblazer who made pioneering look effortless. Early in 1972, before her victory at the polls, Burke had already gained national exposure as the first woman to serve as vice chair of the Democratic National Convention. Not only did she receive recognition for the history-making position, but she also was applauded for her adept handling of what was predicted to be a polarizing and chaotic convention, with delegates representing candidates that ranged from Congresswoman Shirley Chisholm, making her historic presidential bid, to the supporters of the paralyzed target of an assassin, segregationist governor George Wallace.

Burke's history making did not stop once she was sworn into the House of Representatives in 1973. That same year, what may be a footnote in American history became a milestone in women's history. On November 23, she became the first woman in Congress to be granted maternity leave by the Speaker of the House. Given the history of prohibitions on pregnant women in public positions, Burke's decision to violate the norm was a significant step in 1973. While today her pregnancy may appear to be of little import, it was a liberating act in the early seventies, when women were coming into their own in politics and in the society at large. In comparison, the second woman in the House to deliver a child while in office—Congresswoman Enid Greene Waldholtz (R-Utah)—received scant media coverage of her maternity leave in September 1995. (Unfortunately, her headlines resulted from another source—alleged fraudulent campaign practices that prevented her from seeking a second term in office.) Despite Burke's other significant historic contributions and legislative accomplishments, she is most often identified as the first woman to deliver a child while in Congress.

In a way it is a misleading label because Yvonne Brathwaite Burke was not a mere symbol of a liberated woman; on the contrary, she was a tough legislator who spearheaded substantive legislation through the California General Assembly and the U.S. House of Representatives. In the political arena—a charming, sophisticated, and attractive woman—she catapulted to the top of a male-dominated world because of her above-average intellectual capabilities and her proven political abilities. At a time of ambivalence about women in public office, it was rare for a woman to be sought after as a political leader among men. However, Burke was consistently identified as a leader in historically male-dominated institutions such as the Congress, among black leaders, and within the Democratic party as a whole. For example, in 1976 she became the first woman to lead the Congressional Black Caucus (CBC)—an organization that had earlier shunned the leadership efforts of Shirley Chisholm.

Burke was a unique leader, a woman with a comfortable and respected niche in the traditional Democratic party, as well as in the nontraditional black empowerment movement of the 1970s. Perhaps because of her ability to mesh the world of black activism with an established party, she stood out, demanded, and received considerable respect across the board.

The Early Years

The image of the pretty woman with the chestnut brown skin, an oval face, elegant features, and an ever-present ladylike one strand of pearls was instantly imprinted on America as Burke became a political star following the 1972 convention. Not surprisingly, success was anything but overnight. Born Perle Yvonne Watson in Los Angeles on October 5, 1932, to James A. Watson and Lola Moore Watson, Burke had a loving home environment that contrasted with hostile segregated school experiences. The combination shaped personal resolve and fostered dreams beyond her neighborhood, where a vision of a different future was being formed.

Help with those dreams came from her father, a janitor at the MGM film studios, and her mother, a real estate agent. The Watsons made every effort to give their only child every advantage they could afford. She took dancing, piano, violin, and speech lessons and was encouraged to explore her full potential. She showed promise as a young student and was placed in the University of Southern California's "model school," where she was the only black pupil. There she also experienced the kind of racism that the 1940s engendered. But it really was not until she grew older, moving from elementary to middle school and on to high school that she began to recognize the value of racial protest. When she was just fourteen, her father had her join him on the union picket lines, giving her a firsthand look at how protest could be launched even when great risk accompanied it. "He always encouraged me to fight for whatever I believed possible," she once said. She described another incident to Brian Lanker for his book, *I Dream a World:*

> I was one of two girls in the women's honor society at my high school. We were going on a field trip to Popswillow Lake and we had all looked forward to it. When I went to school to meet the bus that Saturday morning, there was no one there except the other girl. We sat and we sat. Finally we went to her house and her mother called the lake. They said that blacks

were not allowed. I was in the principal's office at eight o'clock Monday morning. "Why would you have me sitting out there all morning?" I asked her. "Why would you do that?" She said, "I just didn't want to hurt your feelings." That probably hurt me most. I feel it as much today.[2]

Sometime between her high school years and college, Perle Yvonne Watson became Yvonne Watson, dropping her first name because she did not like it. After high school she went on to the University of California at Los Angeles, majoring in political science and working her way through school as a model. In addition to appearing in magazines such as *Ebony,* she also tried her hand at acting. Like many young people growing up in Los Angeles, she had visions of show business, but after experimenting with an acting career, she found it difficult to accept the parts offered. At one time she found work on an "Amos n' Andy" radio show to be so offensive that her desire to go into the industry abruptly ended. Eschewing the silver screen, Watson went on to graduate with honors from UCLA, then easily moved on to the University of Southern California Law School. But academic ease was one thing, social and racial ease was another.

She graduated from law school in 1956 in the top third of her class, but not before she had to confront racism once again. Women in law school were discriminated against, but even within their small group, there was prejudice. Being black and female was just as limiting as being Jewish and female. Neither group was allowed in the women's professional sorority. In protest against such discrimination, she joined two Jewish students and started a rival professional sorority that lasted beyond her years in the school, continuing to fill the need of those who were excluded.

Burke found very little difference in the outside world. Because she was a woman and black, neither work in government nor in a private law firm was open to her. Consequently, in 1956, after passing the California State Bar examination, she went into private practice handling routine probate cases and other basic legal work—a decision born out of a lack of opportunity more than desire.

The following year, she married Louis Brathwaite, a mathematician. The marriage ended in divorce less than a decade later, as she found herself moving into politics—a public arena.

The Political Odyssey

By the time of her divorce in the mid-1960s, she was on her way to a life in politics. Los Angeles led the country in what was becoming a turbulent era—the Watts riots broke out in 1965, destroying lives and property. The aftereffects of the riots changed the lives of many, including Yvonne Brathwaite. In response, she organized a legal defense team for the rioters and later served as an attorney for the McCone Commission, which was created to investigate the cause of the disturbance. In addition, she worked with the NAACP Legal Defense Fund team and produced an in-depth analysis of housing conditions in the greater Los Angeles area, a report that shed light on some of the underlying causes of the riots. Yvonne Brathwaite was becoming enmeshed in the politics of California and liking it.

She was bitten by the political bug while volunteering for President Lyndon B. Johnson's 1964 campaign. In 1966 she entered her first race, running for the California state legislature. She defeated a field of six men in the Democratic primary for the seat created in the California General Assembly representing the Sixty-third District. Winning the seat against her Republican opposition in the general election would be more difficult. This time it was a victory that came after a malicious campaign, in which she was labeled as a militant and a communist by one of her ultraconservative John Birch Society opponents. It was true that she had a grassroots African American following that included some militants, but she was more of a progressive than a militant herself.

Her politics would become more apparent as her legislative agenda unfolded. She pushed for legislation that reflected her unique concerns and constituency. Her record, which some might call "womanist" today, centered around removal of the stumbling blocks placed before women, minorities, and the economically disadvantaged. Her term in the California legislature produced legislation in the areas of equal job opportunities for women, child care for the disadvantaged, federal aid to education, and free day-care centers on college campuses.

The Congressional Years and Beyond

After six years of service, however, she became impatient with the slow movement of the legislative wheels in the state assembly. Her ambitions were in the direction of Washington and the Congress. Not that the pace would be any quicker there, but she believed the issues would be larger and the visibility greater. Her chance came after the 1970 census, when the Thirty-seventh Congressional District was created by court-ordered reapportionment of California. She entered a five-way race for the majority black district and won with 54 percent of the vote. Her major opponent in the Democratic primary was Billy Mills, a lawyer and a city councilman, whose campaign aide was William A. Burke. On June 14, 1972, two days after her primary victory, Brathwaite and Burke were married.

William Arthur Burke had been born May 13, 1939, in Zanesville, Ohio. This marriage was his second. He held a bachelor's degree from Miami University and a 1977 doctorate in education from the University of Massachusetts. A veteran officer in the U.S. Air Force, Burke entered into civilian life and engaged in a number of business enterprises. He was a past president of the Los Angeles Marathon, the tennis commissioner for the Twenty-third Olympiad, president of the Fish and Game Commission of California, and a management consultant in health care.[3] The two became an early prototype of the two-career, professional-political couple.

The year 1972 proved to be an eventful one for Yvonne Brathwaite Burke. Besides her marriage and the victory in the primary, she was asked to be the keynote speaker at the Gary Convention—an assemblage of more than eight thousand African Americans who had crafted a black political agenda to be presented later in the summer at the Democratic National Convention.

The two conventions were linked in that the black leadership in Gary consisted of influential Democrats engaged in party reforms to be implemented in the convention. Burke would be one of the beneficiaries of those reforms. She made such an impression in Gary as an honest broker that she garnered enough allies to promote her as the vice chair of the 1972 Democratic National Convention. She was the choice of an overwhelming majority of the black delegates, with the minority opposition led by an unexpected source—congresswoman and presidential candidate Shirley Chisholm. After many CBC members won the battle to have the first black woman elected to the position of vice chair, Chisholm refused to back Burke and chose instead to support Patsy Mink (D-Hawaii).[4] It was an act that marred otherwise unified black support for Burke and highlighted the fractious relationship between Chisholm and some members of the CBC.

The Democratic National Convention in 1972 was bracing for the most diverse group of delegates to date. Naming Burke meant that the convention leadership put in place someone who had the credibility to gain the respect of the new groups represented by the delegates—the increased number of African Americans, minorities, women, and youths who were the beneficiaries of the new Democratic reforms. Key among those reforms were a new formula for allocating votes; a more representative makeup on the Rules, Platform, and Credentials Committees; elimination of floor demonstrations; and equal representation of men and women on committees and among convention officers. In addition, the convention officials also had to field the platform battles and delegates pledged to the wide spectrum of party ideologies. The 1972 presidential primaries included the extremes of Governor George Wallace of Alabama on the right and Congresswoman Shirley Chisholm and Senator George McGovern on the left, with other moderate candidates in the middle.

Burke was responsible for overseeing the platform debate that would bring the various agendas to the convention floor. As it turned out, her style, which was firm, even-handed, and even-tempered, kept an often raucous convention from dissolving into polarized special interest groups.

Despite the behind-the-scene dynamics, the convention turned out to be a national debut for the erudite Burke. She gained a national constituency that included African Americans and women. She was a high-profile political figure for whom the sky was the limit. This popularity was proven when she sailed through the general election in November with 60 percent of the vote. The convention was a success and her performance was applauded throughout the country. She, in turn, praised the party for "opening up to women, minorities and youth." Although it did not help the presidential campaign—Senator

George McGovern of South Dakota lost—the party was actually showing signs of reform, the kind that produced results on the local level in elections such as Burke's.

A national celebrity, Burke left the convention and went back on the campaign trail, where she was able to garner support from most of the major feminist and black political organizations. Heading into the general election, she was far more visible than her opponent, Republican Gregg Tria. In the heavily Democratic, minority district, she won a landslide victory.

The enigmatic Chisholm was now being joined by not one but two black women in the House of Representatives—Burke and Congresswoman Barbara Jordan (D-Tex.). The dynamic threesome would become the most identifiable black women ever to serve on the Hill. Early in the term, a special election in 1973 would bring a fourth black woman, Cardiss Collins (D-Ill.), to Congress.

When Burke was sworn in to Congress in January 1973, she was the only woman in the California delegation and the first black woman ever to be elected from the state. She came there as an advocate for the rights of women across economic and racial lines. Just as she had done in the state legislature, she backed bills to raise the standard of living for low- and middle-income workers by supporting legislation to increase the minimum hourly wage; extend unemployment compensation coverage to other workers, including farm workers, domestics, and the employees of state and local governments. She also supported the issuance of food stamps to striking workers, backed emergency mortgage subsidies for employed workers who faced the loss of their homes, and voted for child nutrition programs.

One quantitative effect of Burke's work in Congress was the $255 million in contracts that minorities and women received from the Alaska pipeline legislation. In 1974 she introduced an amendment to the Trans-Alaska Pipeline Authorization Act requiring that affirmative action be taken to ensure that construction contracts be awarded to minority-owned businesses. A version of this amendment would eventually materialize as the Burke Amendment, which required that any project receiving federal funding implement an affirmative action plan.

Throughout all of this, she was also juggling the scheduling demands of a new bicoastal marriage. The Burkes lived in an exclusive suburb of Washington, known as Potomac, and commuted to a home in California. It was a dizzying schedule for the two professionals. Despite this, the forty-year-old congresswoman decided along with her husband that she could also handle a child.

Even though Burke was ready for the new addition to the family, she was not prepared for the response she received from the public. She did not know that there had never been another woman to become pregnant while in Congress, so she was unprepared for the reaction. The reality was that in the 1970s, forty-year-old women were not having babies in large numbers, and certainly not congresswomen. Conventional wisdom and taboos dictated that women avoid middle-aged pregnancies. As with everything else, Burke was forthright in her skepticism about conventional wisdom. "I had a heavy program and I wanted a baby," she said. "The simple matter is that I didn't let any fears or ungrounded compuctions become a consideration."[5]

Thus, in November 1973 Burke established another milestone in the movement of women toward equality, she delivered a healthy daughter—Autumn—whom she proudly proclaimed would someday become president of the United States. The event was also a banner day for women in politics and public life, because Congresswoman Burke proceeded to turn in top-notch performances on the floor of the House and take on additional leadership roles even as she reared a new child. Obviously, the voters were not troubled by the feminist pioneer. They returned her to office with an 80 percent landslide victory over Republican Tom Neddy in the 1974 election. That year, she made history once again, when she was elected as the first woman to chair the Congressional Black Caucus. The CBC was beginning to show signs of numerical strength. By the time she was elected chair, Burke was one of seventeen blacks serving in Congress, and the CBC had begun to establish yearly agendas for legislative action.

About her first term as chair, Burke says: "I started the CBC Foundation because the caucus was in tremendous debt. We were trying to get the CBC going into a new direction. It had been in debt and did not have enough to function."[6]

Burke went on to develop a financial base for the caucus. The foundation would later become the major fund-raising vehicle for CBC projects; through its annual legislative weekend and dinner, major contributions would pour in from around the country for decades after her term in office.

A year into her chair, she joined with other members of the caucus and tried to persuade Attorney General Edward Levi to abstain from filing a brief with the Supreme Court supporting a Boston plan that would oppose school busing. She joined with the National Urban League in criticizing President Carter's record on civil rights and social programs, warning Carter that he could lose black support. Her contribution to the CBC leadership also included planning and seeing through strategies. Congressman William L. Clay (D-Mo.) writes, "A second legislative agenda was formulated concentrating the priorities in ten issue-oriented areas: full employment, health care, urban revitalization, rural development, civil and political rights, education, welfare reform/social insurance, economic development/aid to minority businesses, the economy, and foreign policy."[7]

Her intent during the two-year term was to tackle these issues, but she became sidetracked by another controversial and potentially explosive issue—the harassment of black elected officials by the Department of Justice. Much of her time was taken up fighting the Justice Department and other investigative arms of the government that had begun to investigate black members of Congress disproportionately. She found herself going before the attorney general asking for explanations for the overzealous attempts to smear African American members of the House of Representatives by initiating investigations and leaking information to the press.

One incident involved Congressman Clay (D-Mo.), a founder of the CBC and an outspoken critic of the government's treatment of blacks. He had been the target of Justice Department investigations from 1974 to 1977. After three years the department announced they were dropping all charges against him with no indictment. The investigation was then resumed by the Internal Revenue Service. As chair of the caucus, Burke tried to mediate between the Department of Justice and the CBC. Her efforts, while noteworthy, did not deter the Department of Justice. The investigations continued against others for another fifteen years. Half were or eventually would become targets for prosecution or investigations. This pervasive government effort, however, produced two major convictions among black members of Congress: Congressman Charles Diggs (D-Mich.) was indicted for fraud, and in 1995 Congressman Mel Reynolds (D-Ill.) was convicted on sex offenses. The others spent inordinate amounts of money in legal fees before being cleared but not before losing bits and pieces of their reputations.

In her attempt to highlight these tactics, CBC chair Burke wrote to the *Wall Street Journal*. "Apparently you have joined what is looking more and more like a conspiracy between certain federal agencies and some elements of the media to undermine the integrity, and ultimately the effectiveness, of black leaders," she said.[8]

Burke remained in the House of Representatives until 1978, when she decided for personal reasons not to run for reelection. "I left to raise my daughter," she would later say. But at the time, hopes were dashed by her decision to depart. The congresswoman for whom unlimited political horizons loomed professionally defended her decision on the grounds that the legislative process was too slow and deliberative to be an agent of change. Political analysts, however, had other interpretations of her abrupt departure. Some attributed it to the fact that her husband was in the throes of a federal bankruptcy, resulting from his business dealings, and that Burke did not want a public airing of those issues, especially during a campaign.

Whatever the true reason, historians have lamented the fact that Burke, with all her potential, left Congress with plenty of work left undone—work that she could have turned into credible and much needed programs for the country and for minorities and women in particular. Her seat was filled by Julian Dixon, the African American state legislator who earlier filled the California General Assembly seat she vacated six years earlier.

Burke left Washington in 1978 but did not leave politics. That year she went back to California and launched a campaign for state attorney general, but lost to Republican George Deukmejian. In 1979 she was appointed by the governor to the Los Angeles Board of Supervisors, where she is today. Burke served on numerous boards of directors, including the Ford Foundation and MGM, where her father had once worked as a janitor.

Yvonne Brathwaite Burke had once said: "When I walk into a room, I assume I have to prove myself. I know that I'm accustomed to that. But I also know I can prove myself."[9] It was that spirit that made her stand out from the crowd and gave her the courage to go against the odds. She may not have served in Congress as long as her supporters would have liked, but she served long enough to make a difference.

Yvonne Brathwaite Burke's 1972 Democratic National Convention Vice Chair Acceptance Speech

Yvonne Brathwaite Burke was elected as the vice chair of the 1972 National Democratic Convention on July 10, 1972, at Campaign Headquarters in Miami, Florida. She was the first African American and the first woman to hold such a key position in a national presidential convention. The following is her historic acceptance speech, delivered at the convention.

Thank you very much, Mr. Chairman, and thank you to the women's caucus and to the black caucus for their support of my nomination.

Mr. Chairman, and fellow Democrats, I am indeed honored and proud to participate in this 1972 National Democratic Convention, which is undoubtedly history-making in its development and its composition.

For the first time the poor, blacks and browns and other minorities, women, the young and old, are participating and are represented. They are truly represented in selecting the person that will be the next President of the United States.

The Vice Chairperson and Vice Chairman is a new office for this Convention. It is symbolic of the new politics that we have been implementing. The significance of this new office is that it is defined to assure that women participate equally at the top level in the operation of this Convention. We are demonstrating the Democratic reform and we are demonstrating that they are viable. I am confident that this viable process can work to bring Democrats together. I am confident that we Democrats of this country realize we must come together and it makes no difference which candidate we came here pledged to support, that we will work together and elect the nominee of this Convention and make sure that we will have a new person occupying the White House next year.

The entire world is looking at this Convention to see if there is really a democratic process in our political system. We are setting an example in this Convention of how every sector of American life, no matter whether rich or poor, can participate and can work together in harmony, and we are certain that, coming together, we will select a person who will head this ticket that will set forth new principles that can bring peace to this nation and make sure that every citizen will enjoy full opportunity.

That is our challenge for this 1972 National Convention.

Thank you very much.

Source:
Official Proceedings of the 1972 Democratic National Convention (Washington, D.C.: Democratic National Committee, 1972), 232.

Chapter 5

Cardiss Robertson Collins

Twenty-three Years in the House of Representatives—the Longest Service of Any African American Woman

I would be remiss if I didn't say that one thing that I'm very proud of having done was to have introduced the first mammogram bill ever in the House of Representatives, and when that finally became a reality and became payable under Medicare, it was a very proud moment for me.

Résumé

Cardiss Robertson Collins

Personal

Born   September 24, 1931
        St. Louis, Missouri

Family Widowed (Congressman George Collins died in office, 1972);
        one child

Religion Baptist

Party   Democrat

Took office Age 41, June 7, 1973

Education

Attended Northwestern University, 1949–1950

Professional/Political Background

1973–1996 U.S. House of Representatives

Selected Awards/Organizational Affiliations

Selected Honorary Degrees: Winston-Salem State University, Spelman College, Forest Institute of Professional Psychology.

Affiliations: National Association for the Advancement of Colored People; Chicago Urban League; LINKS; Coalition of 100 Black Women; Black Women's Agenda; National Council of Negro Women; Alpha Kappa Alpha and Alpha Gamma Phi Sororities; secretary, Congressional Caucus for Women's Issues; Democratic whip-at-large, U.S. House of Representatives.

Congressional Data

Twelfth Congressional District of Illinois: Chicago and Oak Park

Committees: Commerce; Government Operations (renamed Government Reform and Oversight in the 104th Congress)

93d Congress: 1973–1974
1973 special election results: 93 percent of the vote (the special election filled out the term of her late husband, George Collins)

94th Congress: 1975–1976
1974 general election results: 88 percent of the vote

95th Congress: 1977–1978
1976 general election results: 85 percent of the vote

96th Congress: 1979–1980
1978 general election results: 86 percent of the vote

97th Congress: 1981–1982
1980 general election results: 85 percent of the vote

98th Congress: 1983–1984
1982 general election results: 87 percent of the vote

99th Congress: 1985–1986
1984 general election results: 78 percent of the vote

100th Congress: 1987–1988
1986 general election results: 80 percent of the vote

101st Congress: 1989–1990
1988 general election results: 100 percent of the vote

102d Congress: 1991–1992
1990 general election results: 80 percent of the vote

103d Congress: 1993–1994
1992 general election results: 81 percent of the vote

104th Congress: 1995–1996
1994 general election results: 79 percent of the vote

Cardiss Robertson Collins

The First African American Woman
Elected to Congress from Illinois

Seventh District, Illinois
Democrat
93d–104th Congresses, 1973–1996

At the age of sixty-five, having served twenty-three years in the U.S. House of Representatives, Cardiss Robertson Collins joined the exodus of 1996, as more than a dozen senators and almost twice as many members of the House chose not to seek reelection. The unassuming Chicago politician had remained in Congress longer and acquired more power than any African American woman in history. Yet, with the exception of politically active men and women and her Chicago constituents, many Americans were not aware of her accomplishments.

The single exception was her brief moment of fame after a 1994 hearing she convened on gangster rap music. The rap hearings placed her at the forefront of the battle for values and against sexually explicit and misogynist music heard on radios and televisions around the country. It was February 11, 1994, and the congressional staff expected a standing-room-only crowd in the committee room, but the weather in Washington, D.C., changed expectations. Snow- and ice-covered roadways kept many government workers home. But the young students from area high schools would not have missed it for the world. They wanted to see and hear the testimony of their music idols, such as Yo Yo (Yolanda Whittaker) defend their generation's music—gangster rap. For parents, it would have been better had the woman before them—chairing the House of Representatives Subcommittee on Commerce, Consumer Protection, and Competitiveness—been the students' role model. She was the first African American woman elected to Congress from Illinois, and had served in the U.S. House of Representatives longer than any black woman in history. Even the fact that she chaired the subcommittee was historic—no black woman had ever done that. However, this was not a generation vested in history, and so Congresswoman Cardiss Collins (D-Ill.) opened the session with a bit of perspective of her own.

> Welcome to today's hearing, which will be the first in a series of hearings on the production, sale and distribution in interstate commerce of music which contains sexually explicit, violent and misogynist lyrics. I am not here to legislate morality, but I do believe that this series of hearings will raise the moral consciousness of the country. Parents and others have

been questioning music lyrics for ages. In fact, when I was 7 or 8 years old, I remember my grandmother calling me an infidel because I was singing the lyrics of a Bessie Smith song called "In the Dark." I didn't have any idea what those lyrics meant, but I happened to have liked the music, so I was singing it. During the 1950s I remember a song called "Work with Me, Annie," by Hank Ballard and the Midnighters, which was changed to "Dance with Me, Annie," because the title was considered too suggestive.[1]

Historical context notwithstanding, it was the contemporary controversy that brought this seeming overreaction to a music art form of inner-city youth to the point that congressional hearings were being conducted. Chairperson Collins, her matronly bearing more prominent than usual, gave voice to the problem.

As the news media camped out in front of the witness tables, the unusually high-profile hearing placed Collins in the political spotlight focused on gangster rap—a music that had been the lightning rod for a number of political, financial, legal, and artistic debates in the 1990s. Several months before, a U.S. district court had ruled the music of a group called 2 Live Crew to be obscene, whereupon the promoters appealed the ruling to the Supreme Court and received a reversal. More than twenty municipalities across the country had enacted restrictive laws governing the sale of music with sexually explicit messages to minors. Even presidential politics entered the fray—politicians saw rap as a handy tool for defining adversaries or attracting supporters. Bill Clinton began the trend with the 1992 presidential primaries, using the previously little-known rap singer Sister Souljah as a vehicle for separating himself and his candidacy from the progressive black agenda of the Democratic party, led by former presidential candidate Jesse Jackson.

It was a politically defining moment for the candidate, and it divided black leadership ranks—for example, providing a litmus test for Clinton supporters. By the time Clinton was up for reelection long after the Collins hearings had ended, references to rap music as a political scapegoat had come full circle. The then Senate majority leader and 1996 presidential candidate Bob Dole launched his Republican campaign with an attack on the same music and the entertainment industry, singling out gangster rap as one of the chief contributors to the country's moral decay.

This focus on rap artists, who were primarily black, had another affect on the established black leadership, who bristled at the attention being given to the artist-as-spokesperson. Their voices inside such established civil rights organizations as the NAACP, the National Urban League, and the Southern Christian Leadership Conference, as well as the Congress, were publicly nullified by the media's reliance on the articulation of the conditions of black people by the artistic expressions of rap music. In other words, their leadership as authentic voices of and for the poor, black, and disenfranchised was in jeopardy.

The fact was that the music was just a verbal expression of a harsher reality plaguing the neighborhoods, such as the one Collins represented in Chicago. The critics questioned why the hearings were being held on the music and not the conditions that created the music. In fact, the promoters testified that there was more power and politics put into taming the messenger than in improving the conditions behind the message; calling into question the motivation behind Collins's hearing.

She had little choice politically on whether to hold the hearings. As the chair of the subcommittee with a history of support for women and minorities as well as accountability to the media, she had responded to an outraged stalwart in the movement for political empowerment for black women, the chair of the National Political Congress of Black Women, Dr. C. Delores Tucker. She was a former secretary of state for Pennsylvania, a formidable traditional civil rights leader, and a political powerhouse who stood behind every black woman in Congress at that time.

Her organization, founded by former congresswoman Shirley Chisholm, took on this battle as an act of conscience, but also as a way of reestablishing its leadership position in the black community. Affirmative action, set-aside programs, and economic development initiatives helped those who were inside the mainstream and capable of benefiting from the success of the programs. They did not necessarily represent the people whose lives were depicted, however crudely, by rap artists. It was already too late. The traditional leadership, in some respects, had been too successful and because of that success was separated from the realities of the poor—a cultural divide manifested in some respects in the gangster rap music.

By the time of the hearings, Tucker had already enlisted the help of popular singers Dionne Warwick and Melba Moore in her nationwide campaign against gangster rap lyrics and had combined forces with William Bennett, the conservative former secretary of education and drug czar under the Reagan and Bush administrations. Bennett had proclaimed himself an arbiter of a return to moral and virtuous behavior. They were an odd couple, Bennett and Tucker, but both were powerful forces within their spheres of political influence—Tucker with black politicians, businesses, and entertainers, Bennett with white conservative politicians and businesses.

Aligned with the gangster rappers and profiteering from their musical expression was the powerful entertainment industry, for whom the music was a hot financial property. Time-Warner, a target of the Tucker and Bennett partnership had purchased 50 percent interest in Interscope, a producer of some of the most offensive rappers, for $120 million several years earlier. The music was not contained within the confines of the inner city either. It was pervasive. Even more disconcerting to the cultural conservatives was the fact that the music was also as close at hand as the suburban enclaves of middle-class white and black Americans, where 50 percent of the sales were made. Because it enjoyed constitutional protection, the music was beyond legislative reach. The best that could be hoped for was that the music industry would regulate itself—not a likely scenario, since taming the music would be tantamount to killing the proverbial "goose that laid the golden egg."

A solution was being sought as public pressure began to mount and black women jumped into the vanguard on this issue. Tucker, Collins, and Senator Carol Moseley-Braun (D-Ill.) were against the gangster rappers and saw no redeeming qualities in their anti-social and anti–black woman lyrics.

There was no question but that the significance of the hearings represented a changing of the paradigm of black leadership. But not everyone aligned themselves with this group. One person who willingly challenged the black leadership status quo on this issue was Collins's colleague, Congresswoman Maxine Waters. The Democratic congresswoman from California stood with the gangster rappers. Hers was another point of view, and she came forth to make it a part of the record as well as to remind the chair that this music had an economic component, which if harnessed could be used to improve conditions of poor people.

"You heard today that Los Angeles is rather a special place and I guess that is said about us all the time in many ways," said the congresswoman representing L.A.'s South Central District, where conditions created the underlying reality of the music. "But you heard today that so-called gangster rap originated in our area, and you heard some reference to gangs and to the despair and the problems of my city. Those references, of course, are absolutely correct."[2]

Waters went on to defend the young people who found an outlet for their anger in an art form that was originally ignored and rejected by major producers, spawning an entrepreneurial opportunity for many young black promoters. Ironically, Waters viewed the history of the industry almost as an American success story. Seeing the young rappers selling makeshift tapes on street corners, the young black entrepreneurs organized production and promotion companies and created a niche in the emerging market before major record companies discovered the wealth inherent in the product. What Waters did not tell the committee was that even after the industry decided to produce the rap music, musical outlets such as MTV, the popular music video venue on cable television, which today transmits rap music around the world, would still not showcase black artists. The rappers found an outlet instead in another African American–owned enterprise, Black Entertainment Television (BET). The early segregated marketing had created economic opportunities and enhanced black involvement in the management and entrepreneurial side of the entertainment industry.

In reality the rappers had proven some of the black leadership wrong because they were now real players in the American dream of economic success, without any overt artificial protections such as affirmative action or minority set-asides. They believed in their music; it was novel, new and different. Initially financing it themselves, they created a market. Ignored by the industry, they actually created their own. By 1994 the people before the committee had become more independent than any civil rights organization—all of whom had fallen on hard times, either through lack of vision, mission, leadership, contributions, or sound management. In contrast to Collins, Waters treated the rappers as powerful, financially capable constituents and exacted accountability. She encouraged promoters, artists, and the industry to put some of the profits back into the community and provide support for the education and development of young people in South Central Los Angeles through a program she originated.

This was Waters's position. And it was not alien to Collins. She had a lot in common with the business side of gangster rap music. In the past, she took the leadership in getting more minorities into the communications industry by pushing the Federal Communications Commission (FCC) to use the licensing process as a leverage for getting television and radio stations to increase the presence of blacks, minorities, and women in front of and behind the camera. Fitting right into her legislative mission and as a part of her trademark was the story of economic development and the expansion of opportunity in the entertainment industry.

Gangster rap grew from music depicting less violent conditions. Early lyrics—while suggestive and full of sexual innuendo and the same staccato sound of rhyming words over sometimes original musical scores—had a different, more upbeat message. One music critic testifying before the committee said in essence that when the times got hard so did the rap.

Nelson George, a journalist and author told the committee: "You can almost look at the indices of gangster rap being created, particularly 1989, 1988 when Dr. Dre, Ice Cube, et. cetera came out. . . . The amount of violence in the black community in cities like D.C., for example, New York City, L.A. all escalated with the introduction of crack cocaine. . . . Gangster rap is very much a reflection of this new environment that was created by crack cocaine."[3]

George's testimony was a reminder that the offensive music represented a more offensive reality—too many youths dying, drug infested neighborhoods, homeless children, and moral decay starting at a young age. In short, the music was political, showing a world outside of Congress different from the one Cardiss Collins left in 1973, when she was first sworn into office. Twenty years after the civil rights era and after twenty years of legislation such as the affirmative action and set-aside bills Collins had authored, there was still an ever widening gap between the have's and the have not's. These hearings revisited the basic issues facing Collins and other black legislators. The powerful committee chair watched as the hearings, which were begun as an admonition to the record industry turned into a challenge to legislators who represented blighted urban areas—areas similar to her own.

An expanse of some of Chicago's poorest neighborhoods on the West Side and some of its most profitable enterprises in the downtown Loop, the Seventh Congressional District was created as a minority district in the early 1970s. As in the rap hearings on a local scale, Collins was both a protectionist for Chicago's business interests and an advocate for its poor and disenfranchised, an amalgam that required a balancing of economic interests and political focus. However, most of her legislative initiatives benefited middle-class women and minority workers and entrepreneurs. In her early years, she also stretched her legislative activism to include global and progressive causes for human rights and international justice. Her legislative persona evolved from that of a political ingenue without a balanced focus during her first term (1973–1974) to a sanguine "can do" legislator after more than two decades in office.

Subdued by the sudden loss of her husband, Cardiss Collins was different from the other three African American women who served with her during the early 1970s. Shirley Chisholm (D-N.Y.), Barbara Jordan (D-Tex.), and Yvonne Brathwaite Burke (D-Calif.) gained national prominence as outspoken, independent, and strong voices, shaping public opinion and advocating change during their years in the House of Representatives. Charting a different course, the pensive Collins maintained a low-key presence, steeping herself in the routine work of committee assignments, which resulted in her mastery of the powerful committee process of conducting productive and relevant hearings, getting substantive legislation drafted, and strategizing to get bills passed on the House floor. As the three other trailblazers left the House, all voluntarily, with national accolades for their pronouncements and positions on issues, Collins remained behind building a base on the seniority system that fueled the power, privilege, and perks of the House of Representatives. She became one of the most powerful members of Congress, black or white, male or female.

It was a surprisingly productive tenure for a woman who had nothing in her background that pointed to a burning desire to become a politician. Actually, she had been content to be the political wife. In this respect she mirrored most of the white women in Congress before the 1970s, who made their way to Capitol Hill as the widows of congressmen rather than through personal ambition. When George Collins, one of the original members of the Congressional Black Caucus (CBC), was killed in a plane crash shortly after reelection to his second term, it was Mayor Richard Daley, Sr., who encouraged Cardiss Collins to run to complete her husband's term. It was a significant endorsement coming from the man who was described as the originator and "boss" of the powerful Chicago political patronage machine. His endorsement virtually assured her election.

Planning to serve only eighteen months, Collins reluctantly accepted—only to end up serving more than twenty-three years. It was a time of political growth for the woman who had taken a "wind beneath your wings" approach to her marriage to the ambitious alderman turned congressman.

The Early Years

Born Cardiss Robertson, in St. Louis, Missouri, on September 24, 1931, she was the only daughter of Finley and Rosia Mae Cardiss Robertson. Her mother, a nurse, and her father, a laborer, moved the family to Detroit when she was ten years old. She was sent to Bishop and Lincoln Elementary Schools and later to Detroit's High School of Commerce; after graduation, she moved to Chicago to find work. Her high school diploma in hand, the future congresswoman got a job as a Chicago factory hand-tying mattress springs, and from there she went to work as a stenographer for a carnival equipment company. In her late twenties, while attending night school at Northwestern University, she met George Collins. The two married in 1958. The night-school program conferred on her an accounting certificate, assisting her in upward mobility in her job with the Illinois Department of Revenue.

In the meantime, her husband, George Collins, was working his way through the Chicago patronage system. George Washington Collins was a Chicago native born on March 5, 1925. After serving in the U.S. Army, he attended and graduated from Central YMCA College in 1954. He continued his studies at Northwestern University, earning a degree in business in 1957 while working as a clerk at the Chicago Municipal Court. From 1958 to 1961, he was deputy sheriff of Cook County and served as secretary to the Twenty-fourth Ward's alderman, Benjamin Lewis. After Lewis's death in 1963, Collins succeeded him as ward alderman for seven years.

In 1969, Congressman Daniel J. Ronan died in office, and Collins ran in a special election to fill the vacant seat of the Sixth Congressional District. The successful campaign placed George Collins in Congress in November 1970. During his first term, the Daley machine supported the Illinois state legislature's efforts to restructure his district, making it a minority district with a 67 percent black constituency and relabeling it the Seventh Congressional District. The result was a safe seat for Congressman Collins, a party loyalist and a lieutenant in the Daley machine.

Collins was an effective legislator in his short time on Capitol Hill. Serving on the Public Works and Transportation and Government Operations committees, he supported increased funding for elementary and secondary education, introduced legislation to compensate for urban residents removed from their neighborhoods by road construction, and introduced a bill requiring the Treasury Department to provide free tax preparation services for low- and moderate-income taxpayers. He was also one of the congressional reformers who wanted to change the operations of the Federal Housing Administration after hearings revealed low-income homeowners had been defrauded. When his plane crashed on December 8, 1972, a month after his reelection, Congressman Collins was en route to his district to deliver toys for the annual children's Christmas party.

The Congressional Years

The plane crash changed the course of Cardiss Collins's life. She became the single parent of a thirteen-year-old son and heir apparent to her husband's seat in Congress. With no political experience to speak of, she reluctantly ran in the special election in June 1973, winning her husband's seat with 93 percent of the vote. The move to Congress was quite a stretch for the woman who described herself as holding "a female supportive capacity to her husband—planting seeds during Lady Bird Johnson's Beautification Program and pouring tea at the Bismarck Hotel when her husband met with dignitaries. . . . 'I was glad to see George do it and worked with him to further his goals, but I never had political aspirations myself.' "[4]

It was true that she had not sought to become a politician, but what Collins lacked in ambition, she made up for in diligence, perseverance, and consistent effort. Characterizing Collins politically is best done by looking at her legislative record and assessing the trends in her initiatives over the years. She is best known in the communications field as the person who pushed through the Energy and Commerce Committee the FCC legislation that gave minorities and women access to ownership and jobs in the television and radio industries. By holding hearings on affirmative action and challenging the FCC to use the licensing process to exact parity in hiring and ownership, Collins changed the face of the industry over the course of her time in the House. Her legislative efforts resulted in more minorities and women entering the various on-air and behind-the-camera professions, as well as owning radio and television stations.

In the area of consumer protection, she fought for financing and research concerning women's health issues and for improved regulations for airline safety. Her advocacy for Chicago's business interest was evident when she parted with the Clinton administration and her colleague Senator Moseley-Braun by refusing to support the North American Free Trade Agreement (NAFTA). Collins saw it as hurting businesses in her district and eliminating much-needed jobs for her constituency. Despite her leadership in all these areas, Collins never was well known among blacks and women outside of Chicago and Washington. In twenty-three years, she never achieved the name recognition and national reputation of Chisholm, Jordan, or Burke. Even though she was in the vanguard of the Free South Africa movement and was one of the first to forcefully advocate an arms embargo against South Africa in 1977, she is not identified normally with progressive Pan African leaders either. The first time she emerged as a vocal black leader was in 1979 as the second woman to chair the Congressional Black Caucus. Hers was the strident voice representing a disenchanted CBC that felt betrayed by the Carter administration. Collins took over the leadership of the CBC during the Ninety-fourth Congress (1979–1980). At that time there was great ambivalence within the caucus about continuing its support for President Jimmy Carter.

What started out as a powerful alignment of black Democrats with southern whites had disintegrated by the time Collins began her term as chair. The political combat even threatened to fracture the CBC. President Carter started out with the support of most members of the CBC and the civil rights establishment. Relying heavily upon the Georgia civil rights icons—Andrew Young, Coretta Scott King, and Martin Luther King, Sr. (Daddy King)—Carter was able to parlay his relationships into political leverage with other black leaders around the country.

Carter, a former governor of Georgia, more than any other politician struck a chord with black elected officials. They saw in him an opportunity to break away from the conservative Republican stranglehold on the White House since President Lyndon Johnson's departure in 1969. Throughout his campaign the alliances worked. Once in office, however, what appeared to be a liberal agenda became a policy of fiscal conservatism. Black legislators found that the Carter administration's goals actually caused the loss of black jobs as inflation cut deeply into the already dwindling buying power of the working poor and as hoped-for social programs failed to materialize. Even Carter's commitment to the King family became enmeshed in a quandary of unfulfilled promises. Collins, as chair of the CBC, found herself labeling Carter a "racist" for his staff's attempts to derail the battle of Congressman Conyers to get a Martin Luther King, Jr., holiday bill enacted.

Collins told the members of the CBC that they would have to fight the president's fiscal conservatism to trim social programs for the poor. Concerned that attempts would be made to roll back gains in civil rights, she led the caucus to defeat an antibusing amendment to the Constitution, monitored the 1980 census to protect minorities from an undercount, and pushed for economic sanctions against the apartheid government in South Africa. While her intent was to bring the caucus together as a unified and unifying voice, the Carter issue was one that threatened its very existence. The division in the CBC was so great that calls for unity at the Democratic National Convention in 1980, where Carter was seeking renomination, fell on deaf ears.

Collins's own call for solidarity went unheeded. Carter was elected as the Democratic standard bearer again and CBC members divided into Carter loyalists, supporters of Senator Edward Kennedy, and independents. Some would not support Carter under any circumstances. The real showdown between Carter and the caucus came at the annual Congressional Black Caucus dinner in 1980, where ten thousand or more African Americans gathered. As a candidate for reelection, it offered an ideal opportunity for Carter to speak to a large black constituency. President Carter wanted to use the high-profile event to capture black decision makers and consensus builders as a part of his overall campaign strategy for corralling the black vote. There was one hitch, however, he was not invited to speak. Instead the keynote address would come from former United Nations ambassador Andrew Young.

Earlier that year, Carter had pressured Young into resigning his ambassadorship because he had met with members of the Palestine Liberation Organization (PLO). Because of the Middle East conflict between the Israelis and the Palestinians, the CBC accused American Jews of pressuring Carter to fire Young, and they blamed the president for caving into the pressure. The CBC was incensed that the impact of the Jewish lobby also meant that Young was being treated differently from other government appointees, who had also admitted to holding such meetings without any consequences.

When word reached Carter that Congressman William Clay (D-Mo.) had threatened to literally pull the microphone out of the socket if the president invited himself to speak, the White House strategy changed. Instead a reception was held in the White House ostensibly in honor of CBC chair, Cardiss Collins. The president lavished her with praise and flowers and invited all of the CBC dinner participants to attend. Derailing the CBC chair, though, would take more than flowers and White House receptions; Collins was just as critical after the event as she had been before it. "The issue did not end with the President's decision not to attend," writes Congressman Clay, who was the chair of the dinner. "That night Cardiss Collins delivered an address at the dinner calling for extreme militancy in pursuit of the goals of the black agenda."[5]

Just as Collins was gaining national attention as a voice for black leadership, she lost the pulse of her own community. The same year she assumed the CBC chair, Chicago politics took a turn in another direction. In spite of the fact that she was in the House performing Herculean tasks, getting legislation passed for women, minorities, and the poor, political conditions in her hometown were undergoing a dramatic change. She would face one of the toughest realities of her congressional career—Mayor Daley had died in 1976, and his machine had given way to a new independent black political movement of which she was not a member. It had taken hold of her city and her district.

The new independent black movement grew out of the politics of disenchantment with the remnants of the Daley machine—most notably, Jane Byrne, who inherited the seat of the late mayor. Byrne, elected in 1979, was not a candidate of the black community. She disregarded their interests and never connected with the leadership. Collins, who was out of touch with the new independents, supported Byrne for renomination against the black candidate, former congressman Harold Washington.

It was a slap in the face for blacks who were attempting to gain political independence. Black activists considered her out of touch with the people's will and a part of the dismantled machine. Washington won both the primary and the general election, becoming the first black mayor of the city and carrying with him a strong organization, which included many of the West Side black activists in Congresswoman Collins's district. For the first time in her congressional career, Collins was faced with a formidable opponent during the 1984 Democratic primary. Alderman Danny Davis, a Washington candidate, received 38 percent of the vote in the primary to Collins's 49 percent, and although he did not win, it was enough of a wake-up call for Collins to get in touch with her constituency a little more and to make herself better known in the process.

Of course, in the general election she continued to carry the lion's share of the vote as she had done throughout her tenure. Davis made another attempt in 1986 but received fewer votes than before. Collins, in the meantime, heightened her profile and embarked upon a legislative program that had a broad reach into the emerging behemoth known as the telecommunications industry. As for her reelection bids, she began a pattern that she continued until her last campaign in 1994—a year-round continuous campaign posture.

In an effort to concentrate more on her committee assignments, and as a way to quell the criticism that she was spending more time on issues that did not immediately affect her Chicago constituency, Collins turned down the offer to chair the African Subcommittee on Foreign Affairs, after pejoratively being labeled "Mother Africa" by her critics. She took instead a position on the Manpower and Housing Subcommittee of Government Operations. And there she began a decade of what would be one of her most prolific legislative periods while in Congress.

When asked about some of her accomplishments during that time, Collins identifies three that she considers important.

"One thing that I'm very proud of having done was to have introduced the first mammogram bill ever in the House of Representatives, and when that finally became a reality and became payable under Medicare, it was a very proud moment for me."

Secondly, she referred to her set-aside legislation for minorities and women in television and radio acquisitions and her push for affirmative action in the communications industry. "I am proud that as a member of the Subcommittee on Telecommunications that I was able to be of benefit to a lot of African Americans who had not had the opportunity to become an integral part of the print and especially the television media. It was just something that had to be done and something that I wanted to do. And we were able to make some inroads there."

The third measure was her early support of gun-control legislation. Collins was one of the first to introduce legislation to control certain firearms.

These measures were introduced during the Ninety-seventh and the Hundredth Congresses (1981–1988)—Collins's most productive. However, there were other legislative efforts in these years that were also significant. For example, her hearings on affirmative action in the airline industry in 1988 uncovered the fact that the vast majority of black airline employees were low-wage and unskilled workers; black pilots were experiencing multiple rejections for employment from large commercial airlines. Airlines had failed to institutionalize and incorporate affirmative action into corporate policy; and the Office of Federal Contract Compliance had failed to monitor adequately the airline industry for affirmative action compliance. As a consequence, the committee recommended that the FAA assume a role in affirmative action oversight of the airline industry, that the Equal Employment Opportunity Commission initiate a systemic investigation of at least four major air carriers, and that the air transport association elevate affirmative action issues on the agendas of its member airlines.[6] It was a scathing report on the airline industry, one that followed Congresswoman Collins's successful efforts in the previous year to establish a 10 percent set-aside for women and minorities to participate in airport concessions.

It was also during the Hundredth Congress that Collins introduced the legislation to which she refers today with pride—the provision that allowed Medicaid payments for screening of breast and uterine cancer. In addition, during that same year, she used her position on the Telecommunications Subcommittee to get the Federal Communications Commission (FCC) to become pro-active in its recruitment of women and minorities to enter the broadcasting industry. She continued until she succeeded in offering legislation that gave preferences for minority and female applicants seeking broadcast licenses from the FCC.

The Hundredth Congress may have been her most productive, but the 101st (1989–1990) found Collins suffering from an illness that kept her away for a good part of the term. However, rebounding in the 102d Congress (1991–1992) with renewed commitment and new allies, she found herself in the company of three new African American congresswomen. It was a welcomed event, because from 1985, after the departure of Katie Beatrice Hall (D-Ind.), Collins had spent three terms as the only African American woman in Congress.

She was so overjoyed by the prospect of having three more black women in Congress that she wanted to celebrate. It was a classic photographic opportunity, the four African American congresswomen of the 102d Congress, dressed in sequins and celebrating their newfound political unity. Each had come from inner-city districts and had a lot to coalesce around—improving conditions for brown and black inner-city poor people, battling against a conservative Republican White House headed by President George Bush, and expanding remedies to gain parity for traditionally disenfranchised Americans. These new women heralded from cities with names that told of the triumphs and trials of urban America—South Central Los Angeles, Washington, D.C., Detroit, and Chicago.

Collins welcomed Eleanor Holmes Norton (D-D.C.), Barbara-Rose Collins (D-Mich.), and Maxine Waters (D-Calif.). At a cost of $4,000, paid to a posh Washington restaurant, it was an unusual orchestration of a major public event. Unusual, too, was the opulence of the celebration. It spoke to the passions that the congresswoman exhibited for the political and economic advancement of women and minorities. With much fanfare, Collins greeted the new black women and said farewell to the lonely six years that preceded their election.

In the following Congress, the 103d (1993–1994), an additional five African American women joined her in the House, and one won a Senate seat. To Collins, there were enough women to form an African American Women's Caucus. From her home state of Illinois, Collins welcomed Senator Carol Moseley-Braun, the first black woman in the Senate. Joining her in the House from newly drawn districts in the South were Eva Clayton (D-N.C.), Cynthia McKinney (D-Ga.), Eddie Bernice Johnson (D-Tex.), Corrine Brown (D-Fla.), and Carrie Meek (D-Fla.). They, Collins, and the three women from the 102d Congress formed the largest contingent of African American women to ever serve in the House of Representatives up to that point.

The bonding of the African American women in Congress was so great that newspaper and magazine articles began to label them the "Sisterhood." Although Collins had aligned with the 102d entrants in her opposition to the nomination of Judge Clarence Thomas to the U.S. Supreme Court and on other legislative issues, nothing compared to the united front of the black sisterhood of the 103d Congress.

Never were they more united than when what had become an annual debate over the Hyde Amendment to the appropriations bill began. The women in the House of Representatives came together in an effort to block the amendment—which prevented poor women from having abortions paid for by federal funds. The spirited debate quickly turned ugly when Collins's colleague from the neighboring Sixth Congressional District of Illinois, Republican Henry Hyde, said, in defending his amendment, "We tell poor people, 'you can't have a job, you can't have a good education, you can't have a decent place to live. ... we'll give you a free abortion because there are too many of you people, and we want to kind of refine the breed.'"[7]

Collins responded, "I am offended by that kind of debate."

Hyde retorted, "I'm going to direct my friend to a few ministers who will tell her just what goes on in her community."[8]

The women in the House of Representatives all came to Collins's aid, demanding that Congressman Hyde retract his statement and expunge his words from the record. Hyde, who was known for his acerbic remarks, later apologized but never fully grasped why the ire of the black women was so intense. He would later describe the scene to one reporter as "looking up and being surrounded by angry black women."[9]

Collins said that normally she would have let the comment go, but she had had enough and demanded that Hyde apologize. Meanwhile the anger of the African American women in the House had by now spread to the Senate. There, Collins was backed up by an angry senator, Carol Moseley-Braun (D-Ill.), who in protest refused to vote on the feminist-backed Freedom of Choice Act, which codified *Roe v. Wade* and essentially allowed middle-class women a right to abortion because they could afford it, while the Hyde Amendment effectively eliminated that right for poor women.

Buttressed by her seniority, Collins continued through the 103d and 104th Congresses, initiating and supporting high-profile and not-so-high-profile legislation. She led the fight for gender equity in collegiate athletics and pushed for the television industry to provide parity for athletic games played by historically black colleges and universities.

To the 104th Congress (1995–1996, Collins's twenty-second and twenty-third years), an additional black woman was elected to the House from Texas, Democrat Sheila Jackson-Lee, expanding the number of African American women in Congress to eleven and the total number to have served in all to fifteen. Collins had served with all of them.

The 104th Congress also brought a militant conservative Republican majority into both the House and the Senate, and Collins lost her chairmanship and her majority status on committees. She remained, however, as the ranking minority member on the Government Operations Committee and continued to hold up a faltering Democratic presence in the House.

Throughout this transition from Democratic to Republican control, she maintained a strong position in an institution where seniority defined the scope of power. She also stood as a single frame of reference for the extent to which African Americans have exercised influence within the U.S. House of Representatives. Longevity is not Collins's only hallmark however; she was a quiet force in the quest for parity and more economic opportunities for women and minorities. She weathered the storms of the conservative years of Republican presidents Richard Nixon, Gerald Ford, Ronald Reagan, and George Bush and the dashed hopes of Democratic presidents Jimmy Carter and to some extent Bill Clinton. A remarkable reservoir of history resided with Collins because of the span of time she served and the integral role she played in shaping legislation for almost a quarter of a century.

The gangster rap hearings were a case in point. Congresswoman Collins did make headway with her hearings. As was typical, the low-key response kept a nation from knowing her role in the outcome. A year after her hearings, due to political pressure, Time-Warner divested itself of the multimillion-dollar Interscope producers of gangster rap music.

The quiet force in the House of Representatives who had been transformed from a Chicago machine politician to an independent, focused, and accomplished legislator had made her mark. After almost a quarter of a century in the House of Representatives, Cardiss Collins, now a grandmother, joined the record number of Democrats and Republicans in the congressional exodus in 1996.

Chapter 6 **Katie Beatrice Green Hall**

Sponsor of the Martin Luther King, Jr., Holiday Legislation

The legislation before us will act as a national commitment to Dr. King's vision and determination for an ideal America, which he spoke of the night before his death, where equality will always prevail.[1]

Résumé

Katie Beatrice Green Hall

Personal

Born April 3, 1938
 Mound Bayou, Mississippi

Family Married to John Hall; three children

Religion Baptist

Party Democrat

Took office Age 44, November 29, 1982

Education

B.S. Mississippi Valley State University, Itta Bena, Mississippi, 1960

M.S. Indiana University, Bloomington, Indiana, 1968

Professional/Political Background

1960–1982 Teacher, Gary, Indiana, school system

1974–1976 State representative, Indiana House of Representatives

1976–1982 Senator, Indiana Senate

1982–1984 U.S. House of Representatives

1985– Gary, Indiana, city clerk

Selected Awards/Organizational Affiliations

Outstanding Legislator Award in Politics, city of Gary, 1975; Outstanding Woman in Politics, Indiana Black Political Association, 1975; delegate, Democratic Mini Convention, Memphis, Tennessee, 1978; chair, Indiana State Democratic Convention, 1980.

Congressional Data

First Congressional District of Indiana: city of Gary

Committees: Public Works and Transportation; Post Office and Civil Service

97th Congress: 1981–1982

1982 special election results: 57 percent of the vote (the special election filled out the last two months of the term of the late Adam Benjamin)

98th Congress: 1983–1984

1982 general election results: 67 percent of the vote

Katie Beatrice Green Hall

The First African American Woman
Elected to Congress from Indiana

First District, Indiana
Democrat
Part of the 97th–98th Congresses, 1982–1984

Catching up with former congresswoman Katie Beatrice Green Hall in the 1990s meant being squeezed in between her private responsibilities and her duties as city clerk for Gary, Indiana, and government teacher for senior citizens. The schoolteacher-turned-politician is still as active as that day in 1982 when she stepped out of the Indiana state senate into the U.S. Congress as the representative for the First District of Indiana.

Hall served in the House of Representatives from November 1982 to December 1984—a short tenure distinguished by her successful shepherding through Congress of the legislation declaring the birthday of Martin Luther King, Jr., a federal holiday. In so doing, Hall brought closure to a fifteen-year campaign that produced some of Congress's most acrimonious and emotionally charged debates.

The Early Years

Born in Mound Bayou, Mississippi, April 3, 1938, to Jeff Green and Bessie Mae Hooper Green, Katie Beatrice Green attended Mississippi's segregated public schools. Upon high school graduation, she went to Mississippi Valley State College in Itta Bena. In 1957, before graduating in 1960 with a bachelor of science, she married John Hall. The Halls moved to Indiana and there reared their three children—Junifer, Jacqueline, and Michelle. Katie Hall began teaching in the Gary, Indiana, public schools in 1961, a career she continued until she left for Washington in 1982. The ambitious Hall went on to graduate school and received a master of science from Indiana University in 1969.

It was during her teaching years that she became involved with the political career of the up-and-coming Richard Hatcher, who would become mayor of Gary and her mentor. In 1974, she was elected to the Indiana House of Representatives, and in 1977 she was elected to the Indiana Senate. Between her years in the state senate and the 1982 election to Congress, she served as chair of the Lake County Democratic Committee.

The Political Odyssey

Hall's national political career began when she was selected in a hotly contested process to fill the seat left by the death of Congressman Adam Benjamin, Jr. The First Congressional District congressman's sudden death from a heart attack in his Washington, D.C., apartment in September 1982 occurred just weeks before the Democratic primary, in which Benjamin had no opponents. The Democrats in the district were left without a candidate in the upcoming election. The Republicans, who had all but conceded the race to Benjamin, had no formidable candidate to field either. They had put forward an unemployed schoolteacher, Thomas Krieger, as a political sacrificial lamb.

The First Congressional District consisted of three counties: Lake, La Porte, and Porter. Lake County included the city of Gary—Indiana's third largest urban area—which was 70 percent African American and Democratic. Gary made Indiana's First Congressional District unique and a radical departure from the rest of the state. The demographics for the district, skewed by the Gary population, gave it the following characteristics: 71 percent white, 24 percent black, 8 percent Hispanic, and predominantly Democratic. The demographics for the state as a whole were much different. African Americans made up 8 percent of the population to 91 percent for whites and less than 2 percent for Hispanics. In addition, Indiana was known as a largely Republican and conservative state.[2]

Although the Democratic strongholds were no bastions of liberalism, the changing demographics of Gary led the Democrats there to concede the city to Hatcher's leadership. Yet, expanding his influence beyond the city into the surrounding suburbs of Lake, La Porte, and Porter Counties could not be done by fiat and was highly unlikely. The First Congressional District was the line in the sand, and Hall's selection brought the unspoken dividing line of power into the open. Even though she did not have to invoke race in the 1982 campaign, it would become a major issue in her bid for reelection in 1984.

Mayor Hatcher, as First District Democratic chair, had the legal authority to choose the Democratic nominee to replace the late congressman. The three white county Democratic chairs wanted to place Benjamin's wife, Patricia, in the seat to serve out the two months of his unexpired term, but Hatcher named Hall instead, signaling a basic schism in the district's Democratic committee. Robert Pastrick, the Democratic chairman of Lake County, joined the chairs of Porter and La Porte counties in a lawsuit to block the mayor from naming Hall. But the court sided with Hatcher, ruling that he did have the proper authority to make the selection without consultation with the county chairs.[3]

For Hatcher, Hall was a natural choice. An ardent supporter in three of his campaigns (1967, 1971, and 1975), she was also an integral part of the emerging vanguard of Gary's black progressive politics. Hatcher's control over the selection of the Democratic candidate was evidence of the strength of the progressives, but it was also seen as another grab for power within the region.

Hall had two months to mobilize, raise funds, and launch a campaign. Two elections would determine her fate. She would have to be voted on for the full term of the Ninety-eighth Congress, and a special election-day vote would determine whether she could serve the remainder of Benjamin's term in the Ninety-seventh Congress. Not only was the time short, but Hall would raise only a fraction of the campaign funds that would have been available to the veteran lawmaker, Benjamin. Fortunately for her, her state senatorial record enabled her to mobilize funds from labor and women's groups both outside and inside of Indiana. She was aided by the fact that her Republican opponent, Thomas Krieger, was relatively unknown and not a serious contender. Krieger raised $10,500, just a quarter of the money raised by Hall.

It was a low-profile campaign—Krieger injured himself and for the most part did not attend any debates. His failures worked to Hall's advantage. Because her support was not very strong among white Democrats, she spent time trying to win their votes. Many were still intent on putting Benjamin's widow in the seat. It was not that Patricia Benjamin was qualified for the seat but rather that supporting her gave the white Democrats an opportunity to redirect their efforts to a formidable white candidate to run later.

A far more qualified candidate than either Krieger or Benjamin's widow, Hall had served in the upper house of the Indiana legislature since 1977. Prior to that she was in the Indiana House of Representatives from 1975 to 1976. While in the state legislature, the former social studies teacher concentrated on education as well as labor and women's issues. She was successful in pushing through legislation clarifying Indiana's divorce laws by defining marital property, and she authored a bill speeding payments to those eligible under the state victims of crime law. She also devoted much effort in the legislature to advocacy for the Equal Rights Amendment, which the state ratified in 1977.[4]

It was this record that proved Hall to be the most qualified candidate, and, though not in overwhelming numbers, the voters agreed. In the 1982 congressional race, Hall received 57 percent of the vote, winning the right to serve out Benjamin's unexpired term. A 63 percent victory over her Republican opposition also earned her a seat in the Ninety-eighth Congress and a place in the history books—she was the first black elected to Congress from Indiana.

On the eve of the departure of the first black woman in the House of Representatives—Shirley Chisholm (D-N.Y.)—Katie Hall entered the Ninety-seventh Congress in 1982 to complete Benjamin's term. Congresswoman Chisholm had decided not to seek reelection, leaving Congresswoman Cardiss Collins (D-Ill.) as the lone African American woman to greet Hall when she began to serve her first full term.

The Congressional Years and Beyond

During that one term, Hall was able to accomplish more than the average freshman. In looking at her record, we see a dual characteristic to her voting pattern.

First and foremost, she focused on legislation that contributed to the economic well-being of Indiana, which in the 1980s was experiencing a recession because of the eroding steel industry. Employment bills and legislation that had an impact on the social conditions created by poverty and unemployment were among her interests.

To that end, she endorsed the Fair Trade in Steel Act, which was intended to revitalize the steel industry. She supported the Humphrey-Hawkins bill for full employment and measures to prevent child abuse and family violence. She considered unemployment the most serious problem facing the First Congressional District—in 1982 it had an unemployment rate of 25 percent—and its side effects, she felt, diminished the quality of life for those caught in the economic turmoil. Her view was that mortgage foreclosures, divorce, mental illness, and child and spouse abuse were part of the domestic fallout of economic recessions. Where possible, she believed legislative remedies should be sought.[5]

Hall was also a social activist on a national and international scale. She supported the proposed Equal Rights Amendment to the Constitution and called on South Africa to abandon its policy of placing blacks in so-called "black spots" after removing them from their ancestral lands. She also sponsored and served as floor manager for the King holiday legislation.

Up to the time Hall entered Congress, the fight for the King holiday bill had been long and arduous. Since 1968, the year of Dr. King's assassination, fifty bills had been introduced in the Congress to commemorate the martyred leader's life and works—many of them introduced by Congressman John Conyers (D-Mich.). Conyers's tireless efforts began three months after Dr. King's death, when he introduced the first bill to set aside January 15, as a national holiday. That bill never made it out of committee.

It was just the beginning of Conyers's relentless efforts, which the Michigan lawmaker turned into a virtual crusade by inaugurating a national grassroots movement in support of the King holiday legislation. A unified Congressional Black Caucus (CBC) joined Conyers as he mobilized a cadre of supporters, including the King family, Dr. Ralph Abernathy of the Southern Christian Leadership Conference, entertainers, and state and local officials who organized petition drives and protest marches and enacted local laws designating the January holiday.

At one point, Abernathy's petition drive produced three million signatures, which he personally delivered to President Richard Nixon. But Nixon and his three immediate successors—Presidents Gerald Ford, Jimmy Carter, and Ronald Reagan—refused to support the legislation. While a negative response could have been expected from the three conservative Republicans, more was expected of Carter. In his presidential campaign of 1976, the former Georgia governor relied heavily on the support of King's widow, Coretta Scott King, the Reverend Martin Luther King, Sr. (Daddy King), and the civil rights leadership to gain access to black voters. He also gave indications to the King family and the CBC members that he supported the legislation. Once in office, he allegedly sabotaged the CBC's efforts to get the Conyers bill through by lobbying southern congressmen to propose a Sunday holiday bill to supplant their efforts. The "Sunday holiday," of course, would be no holiday at all. Although there were other issues and broken promises that caused the rift between Carter and the CBC, the King holiday legislation was surely on the mind of Congressman Conyers when, just as Carter was about to launch his bid for reelection, he organized a "Dump Carter" campaign.[6]

Carter, Congress, and the other presidents were actually out of sync with the mood of their constituents. By 1983, when Hall introduced the bill, ten states had already declared January 15 an official day of commemoration of the life and works of Dr. King. Other forces within the Congress were working as well.

Congressman William Clay (D-Mo.) states in his book, *Just Permanent Interests*, that one of the events that led to more receptivity to the 1983 legislation was the impact of the congressional investigation of Dr. King's assassination: "House Speaker Thomas P. ('Tip') O'Neill, Jr., appointed Congressmen [Louis] Stokes and [Walter] Fauntroy to the committee that conducted official investigations into the assassinations of John F. Kennedy and Dr. Martin Luther King, Jr. . . . When their committee concluded the inquiries and issued final reports, pressure to pass the Dr. King holiday bill increased dramatically."[7]

By the 1980s, the pace had picked up. The investigation and a narrowly defeated Conyers-sponsored bill in 1980 made supporters cautiously optimistic. Invigorating the movement further was the 1981 March on Washington calling on Congress to act on the legislation. It was hard to measure the impact of thousands of people from across the nation marching down Pennsylvania Avenue to the theme song "Happy Birthday," but it clearly gave a renewed impetus to the movement's leadership. The song's composer and a demonstration organizer was the popular performer, Stevie Wonder. Wonder—arm-in-arm with Coretta Scott King, members of the CBC, civil rights leaders, and other entertainment celebrities—led a star-studded demonstration that gained national headlines.

The media exposure did much to increase the numbers in the grassroots lobby and intensify pressure on Congress. So much so that by the time Hall began, the momentum had built to the point that there was sufficient support to consider pushing the bill through the House in the Ninety-eighth Congress. Her success was the result of the confluence of a number of events. One was the unified support of the CBC. Unlike other legislative initiatives, the quest to pass the King bill overshadowed personal political agendas of members of the caucus. All agreed that it was necessary.

Secondly, the CBC had become proficient in building coalitions around common interests. The caucus had reached a point where its considerable clout gave its leaders access to behind-the-scenes bargaining power with respect to committee and subcommittee assignments—enough to place Hall, a freshman, on the appropriate committee to introduce the bill. Clay writes:

> In 1983, Congressman William Ford, chairman of the House Post Office and Civil Service Committee, and like Conyers, a Democrat from

Michigan, supported Katie Hall, a freshman House member from Indiana, for chairman of the subcommittee that had primary jurisdiction over the Conyers's holiday bill. Hall introduced her own bill designating the third Monday in January as the day to commemorate Dr. King. Her committee held hearings and on July 3, 1983, passed the bill out of subcommittee. Chairman Ford, a key supporter of the bill, called for a full committee mark-up and reported the bill to the House floor for a vote in August.[8]

And now in the midst of the August debate, it was clear that some of the fifteen-year-old arguments of the legislation's opponents had been revived and were being delivered with renewed vigor. Despite the ground swell of support, some hard-liners remained adamantly opposed to the legislation. This became evident when Congressman Larry P. McDonald (R-Ga.) launched into a tirade, beginning with:

> I rise in strong opposition to . . . a bill designating the third Monday in January of each year a legal public holiday to commemorate the birthday of Martin Luther King, Jr.
>
> At best Martin Luther King, Jr.'s prior associations and activities are questionable. This fact is reflected in the action taken by Attorney General Robert F. Kennedy, certainly one of the most liberal men to hold that high post, when he authorized wiretaps and other forms of surveillance of Martin Luther King, Jr., after the FBI developed evidence that King was associated with and being manipulated by communists and secret communist agents.
>
> Unfortunately, neither the Congress nor the American people have any idea what information was gathered by the FBI. Under court order of 1977, the FBI's surveillance records and tapes on Reverend King were sealed in the National Archives for fifty years or until the year 2027. . . . Before acting prematurely, this House should either request that the records be made available or delay consideration until the information is released.[9]

Hall handled such acrimony with great aplomb, allowing congressmen like McDonald to have their say, and proceeding to go on to the next speaker. It earned her bipartisan praise for her skill in floor management. Moving the legislation to the point where the opposition did not overwhelm the support, was not an easy job, but it was made less difficult because of the presence of a new generation of legislators, many of whom, like Hall, had benefited from the many gains from the civil rights movement.

Congressman Robert Garcia (D-N.Y.) spoke for a number of his colleagues in the Ninety-eighth Congress when he said:

> The question about whether Dr. Martin Luther King deserves a national holiday is one that, as far as I am concerned, means a resounding yes. To many of us, especially myself, I was elected to the New York State legislature in 1965, as a result of the Voting Rights Act which passed in 1964. Had it not been for the work of Martin Luther King walking the corridors

of Congress to get that Voting Rights Act through, many of us in this Congress, especially those with brown faces and black faces, would not be sitting here today.[10]

In the end, despite a price tag estimated annually at $225 million in lost production and productivity in the federal workforce, fiscal conservatives such as the future Speaker of the House Newt Gingrich (R-Ga.), and liberals such as Representative Ronald Dellums (D-Calif.), joined together in bipartisan support to pass the landmark legislation.

On the floor of the Senate, the bill was confronted by the expected negative rhetoric and legislative maneuvers of Senator Jesse Helms (R-N.C.), whose filibustering was halted by a vote to limit debate. Helms then introduced several amendments that were soundly defeated. One called for the president to pardon Marcus Garvey, the black nationalist. Another would bar a national holiday for King unless one was declared for Thomas Jefferson. In the end, the Senate passed the House version of the bill intact by a vote of 78 to 22.[11]

On November 2, 1983, flanked by members of the King family, the Congressional Black Caucus, Stevie Wonder, and major civil rights leaders, a reluctant President Ronald Reagan signed the Dr. Martin Luther King, Jr., holiday legislation into law. There were strong undercurrents of profound meaning in the snapshot of a conservative Republican president who vehemently opposed the legislation now with pen in hand signing the bill into law. It spoke not only to the power of the King legacy and Conyers's grassroots crusade, but also to the skill and temperate manner with which Hall had managed the House floor debate, keeping it from turning into a protracted and bitter partisan debate as it had been in the past.

Fifteen years in the making, the King holiday legislation had miraculously been shepherded through the House and the Senate and signed into law in just four months. The historic act of having for the first time a federal holiday named after an African American was quite a feat for a freshman congresswoman.

Meanwhile, the First Congressional District had become more racially polarized while Hall was in Washington. When she returned to run for reelection in 1984, she found herself embroiled in a bitter Democratic primary from which she would not recover. She eventually lost her 1984 bid to Benjamin's former aide, Peter Visclosky. In addition to Visclosky, Hall was challenged in the Democratic primary by Lake County prosecutor, Jack Crawford. Both her opponents attacked her on the basis of her close political ties to Mayor Richard Hatcher.

"Mrs. Hall does the bidding only of Mr. Hatcher; she fails to represent the entire district and has been absent when key House votes were taken," said Visclosky as campaign claims and counterclaims were hurled around. "She serves one constituent out of 500,000, the Mayor of Gary."[12]

For her part, Hall saw the attacks as racially motivated:

"If I wasn't black and female, there wouldn't be a contest," Hall declared in a debate at Purdue University. "I have an excellent record, and under other circumstances I wouldn't even have an opponent."[13]

Crawford's attacks also dealt with Hall's record in the Congress. After having to publicly apologize for sending out campaign literature with a racially divisive message, which implied that a split in the white vote could mean that Hall would win the primary, he began attacking the incumbent on her House activities. "She went on to Africa and Europe last summer to observe poverty and hunger at the same time we had 50,000 people on public assistance and people lined up blocks long in Government cheese and milk lines."[14]

In the face of such illogic, Hall put up a valiant fight. Chicago mayor Harold Washington attended a labor rally endorsing her candidacy, and the labor unions made a public presentation of a $4,500 check for her campaign coffers. Even after losing, Hall would not accept defeat. The primary vote was close. The results were as follows: 32.6 percent or 42,345 votes for Hall, 34 percent or 44,712 votes for Visclosky, and 31.4 percent or 40,775 votes for Crawford. Because the race was too close for her to accept, she called for a recount on the premise that racism played a role in her opponent's 2,367 vote lead. It was to no avail; the recount did not change any of the votes, making Hall one of the few incumbents who did not return to the Ninety-ninth Congress.[15]

The political defeat was particularly difficult for her on another level. The 1984 Democratic primaries were also considered a bellwether for Jesse Jackson's presidential campaign. It was assumed that other liberal Democrats and blacks in particular would benefit from having Jackson at the head of the ballot. The thinking was that voter turnout in the black community would be strengthened by Jackson's first run for the White House and that on his coattails other African American and progressive candidates would gain victory at the polls. Yet this did not happen for Congresswoman Hall.

Dissuaded but not discouraged, she attempted to regain her congressional seat twice after the 1984 defeat—once in 1986 and again in 1990. Both times she was defeated in the primaries by incumbent Peter Visclosky.

Katie Beatrice Hall left Washington, albeit reluctantly, and returned to Indiana intent on continuing to shape and mold the state's politics. She served as vice chair of the Gary Housing Board of Commissioners after returning to Lake County, and in 1985 was elected as the city clerk of Gary, serving there for over a decade. Hall can be counted as one of the African American women who transformed Congress with her vibrant presence and a tenacity that, at a propitious moment, put closure to a fifteen-year odyssey to honor the slain leader of the civil rights movement—Dr. Martin Luther King, Jr.

Part Two

The Urban Women
of the 102d Congress

Chapter 7 **Delegate Eleanor Holmes Norton**

Fighting the Battle to Gain Statehood for Washington, D.C.

It is a blemish of hypocrisy on this country that 600,000 Americans, most of them African Americans, who live in this city [Washington, D.C.] are without the ordinary rights that each and every one of you have unless you happen to have been born in the capital of the United States.[1]

Résumé

Eleanor Holmes Norton

Personal

Born	June 13, 1937 Washington, D.C.
Family	Separated; two children
Religion	Episcopalian
Party	Democrat
Took office	Age 53, January 3, 1991

Education

B.A.	Antioch College, 1960
M.A.	Yale University, 1963
J.D.	Yale Law School, 1964

Professional/Political Background

1965	Admitted to the Pennsylvania bar; admitted to practice in the District of Columbia and before the U.S. Supreme Court
1964–1965	Law clerk, Judge A. Leon Higgenbotham, Federal District Court, 3d Circuit
1965–1970	Assistant director, American Civil Liberties Union
1970–1976	Chair, New York City Commission on Human Rights; executive assistant to the mayor of New York
1977–1981	Chair, Equal Employment Opportunity Commission
1981–1982	Research fellow, Urban Institute, Washington, D.C.
1982–1990	Professor, Georgetown University Law School
1991–	U.S. House of Representatives

Selected Awards/Organizational Affiliations

Selected Honorary Degrees: Fisk; University of Southern Connecticut; Ohio Wesleyan University; St. Lawrence University; University of Wisconsin; University of Massachusetts; Smith College; Spelman College; Howard University; Brown University; Bard College; Princeton University; Yeshiva University.

Selected Awards: One Hundred Most Powerful Women in Washington, *Washingtonian Magazine*, September 1989; Ralph E. Shikes Bicentennial Fellow, Harvard Law School, Fall 1987; Visiting Phi Beta Kappa Scholar, 1985;

Chancellor's Distinguished Lecturer, University of California Law School; Yale Law School Association Citation of Merit Medal to the Outstanding Alumnus of the Law School, 1980.

Affiliations: Yale Corporation Board (1982–1988); U.S. Committee to Monitor the Helsinki Accords; Board, Martin Luther King, Jr., Center for Social Change; Board, Environmental Law Institute.

Congressional Data

District of Columbia nonvoting Delegate: all of Washington, D.C.

Committees: Post Office and Civil Service; Public Works and Transportation (renamed Transportation and Infrastructure); District of Columbia; Government Reform and Oversight; Joint Committee on the Organization of Congress (The reorganization of the committee structure by the Republicans of the 104th Congress placed the District Committee under the Government Reform and Oversight Committee, relegating it to subcommittee status.)

102d Congress: 1991–1992
1990 general election results: 62 percent of the vote

103d Congress: 1993–1994
1992 general election results: 85 percent of the vote

104th Congress: 1995–1996
1994 general election results: 85 percent of the vote

Eleanor Holmes Norton

The First African American Woman Elected to Congress from the District of Columbia

District of Columbia
Democrat
102d Congress–present, 1991–

Long before black women were elected to Congress in any appreciable numbers, there was a woman giving leadership, a woman serving in strategic places, a woman who could argue the case. She gave of her time. Not only did she serve in the Carter Administration, but this is a woman who provided leadership and contact among women's organizations all over this country when few of us were represented in the emerging power. You see her today as she argues the case in Congress. You see her today as she takes on the right wing. She does it well because she came prepared. She's from the District [of Columbia] and she knows how to represent Washington, D.C. Ladies and Gentlemen, welcome Eleanor Holmes Norton, the representative for the District.

—Maxine Waters introducing Eleanor Holmes Norton
during the National Political Congress of Black Women,
Congressional Black Caucus Legislative Weekend, 1993

There was something tragic, intriguing, and triumphant about Eleanor Holmes Norton's decision to run for Congress. It was tragic because a twenty-five-year marriage would have to withstand public scrutiny and eventually it would fail. It was intriguing, because as a well-known and well-respected civil rights lawyer, Norton could easily have taken her more than one hundred honorary degrees and awards and continued an uncomplicated, revered life in academia rather than endure a public tarnishing of a well-deserved reputation. And it was triumphant because, despite a temporary setback that would have eliminated a lesser candidate, Norton rose above and soared beyond adversity, making believers out of naysayers and affirming the wisdom of the ordinary voter over the established political pollsters and pundits.

With her decision to run for Congress in 1990, Eleanor Holmes Norton added statehood for Washington, D.C., to the long list of issues that she had championed in her professional career—a career that included defending the First Amendment rights of free speech for segregationists, petitioning the Democratic party on behalf of an independent political party, and revitalizing a dormant federal agency charged with eliminating employer discrimination. Now her political task was to explain to a basically disinterested Congress why they should give the capital of the free world full voting representation in the nation's legislative body.

The battle to get congressional representation and statehood for the District of Columbia was parochial rather than national, making the job of the D.C. delegate one of marketing, educating, and legislating. District residents paid federal taxes, but had only one nonvoting delegate in the House and no representation in the Senate. Moreover, every bill passed by the D.C. City Council had to go before the Congress before it was enacted into law.

Although Norton fought for "citizenship rights" for others, she and three generations of her Washington relatives had never enjoyed full representation. That was because Washington, D.C., was a unique hybrid of a city and state without the full rights of either, and it was home for Norton. She was born Eleanor Holmes on June 13, 1937, to a couple who could trace their ancestry back to three generations of Washingtonians—a distinction that was often made to separate those who had roots in the city from those who were recent transplants, while at the same time conferring a unique and prestigious status on the former.

The Early Years

Thus, she and her two sisters represented a fourth generation of Washingtonians. They were born to Vela (Lynch) and Coleman Holmes. Vela, a schoolteacher, and Coleman, a government worker, reared the three girls in the protected and sheltered environment of Washington's segregated black middle class of the 1940s and 1950s. Norton, the oldest, felt that "more was expected" of her. It was a feeling that contributed to her becoming the trendsetter, the example, and the one who paved the way for her two sisters. The close-knit family nurtured and encouraged the bright and intelligent Eleanor as she went through Dunbar High School—at the time, the school for Washington's black elite in the segregated nation's capital.

In later years, when she defined turning points in her early social consciousness, Holmes evoked a protest she witnessed by the famed and revered suffragette and human rights advocate, Mary Church Terrell (1863–1954). Terrell was a key figure in Washington's reform movement—a movement that was supported by a rich cultural base of the city's black intelligentsia. However, there was no amount of intelligence or culture that could mitigate or eliminate the petty incidents of segregation that demeaned people of color through the minor daily practices of merchants and entertainment owners. Most Washingtonians could recite the litany of such occurrences, for instance store clerks not allowing black women to try on hats before buying them or movie theater ushers routinely showing them the way to the balcony rather than seating them on the first floor.

Norton recalls a scene where Terrell was demonstrating against segregation. It could have been one of many launched by the human rights icon. In the late 1940s and 1950s, at a time when she was in her eighties, Mary Church Terrell continued her crusade to ban discrimination in Washington, D.C.'s public and commercial establishments. One such demonstration was against one of the city's leading department stores, the Hecht Company, where the management would allow blacks to spend their money in the store but not allow them to use the bathrooms—a minor indignity, but to Terrell, a denial of a fundamental right.

Young Eleanor was impressed by the icon Terrell, and witnessing such demonstrations, undoubtedly helped shape her personal philosophy about what it meant to be undaunted, black, and female in America: "You could say race was an obstacle to me, you could say sex was an obstacle to me, but I refused to own them in that way. I was black and female, but I never conceived that those were supposed to keep me from doing what I wanted to do."[2]

It was an attitude that took her a long way. It saw her through graduation from Dunbar High School in Washington, D.C., and to Ohio, where she attended Antioch College and graduated with a B.A. in 1960. She became one of the few black women at that time to attend Yale Law School, entering in 1960, just when the doors were opening a little wider for blacks and women. As a graduate student, Holmes was full of energy and curiosity about the world that she was about to enter, and she saw sound preparation as essential to her success.

Energetic and intellectually curious, she not only studied law at Yale, but in 1963 she earned a master's degree in American Studies. In 1964 she received her law degree. While at Yale, Norton met another woman, Marian Wright-Edelman, who would land in the bosom of the civil rights movement with her. Edelman was attending Yale Law School after graduating from Spelman College. Both became pioneers as female lawyers supporting the civil rights movement and later dedicating their professional lives to human rights causes. Wright-Edelman became the director of the Children's Defense Fund, an advocacy group for the welfare and rights of children. And of course, Norton would become identified with equal rights and equal opportunity enforcement. From her work as a staff member for the 1963 March on Washington to her early involvement with the Student Nonviolent Coordinating Committee (SNCC), she remained active for more than three decades in major civil and human rights movements.

For example, in the early years she worked behind the scenes in the historic Mississippi Freedom Democratic party (MFDP) challenge to the Democratic National Convention. The MFDP was an organization identified with the late Fannie Lou Hamer. Founded in 1964, it was an independent political party formed to challenge the legitimacy of the segregated Mississippi Democratic party. The MFDP's efforts were undergirded by a youthful and committed SNCC organization. Norton, as an early SNCC member, provided support for MFDP's challenge to the 1964 Democratic National Convention (DNC). The MFDP petitioned the convention, requesting that it seat the MFDP's sixty-eight-member integrated delegation. It was a singularly significant and progressive political event. So historic was the challenge that many analysts trace the reforms that followed in 1972, such as proportional representation in delegations, to the impact of the MFDP.

The twenty-seven-year-old Eleanor Holmes—along with Wright-Edelman and other advisers—prepared a legal brief pleading the case for full representation for the MFDP delegation. It attempted to gain access to the floor and credentials process and participation in the convention. The strength of the party's position was fortified by what writer Paula Giddings referred to as their well-prepared legal case, which was "good enough to make President Johnson edgy." She writes further, "not only was the technical challenge intact, but testimony from Fannie Lou Hamer, broadcast over the television networks, made their cause even more compelling."[3]

Hamer's emotional and graphic recitation of incidents of prison beatings she had endured, just because she sought to register to vote, was riveting. The combination of her presentation and the legal brief helped to force the convention officials to the table to discuss negotiated alternatives to the group's protest. While the MFDP went home without gaining access to the convention (they would not compromise for limited access), all was not lost. The convention rules were eventually changed, making it impossible ever again to have a segregated delegation.

The next year, 1965, was pivotal in Norton's life. While clerking in Philadelphia with the respected jurist, Justice A. Leon Higgenbotham of the federal court, she passed the Pennsylvania bar examination. In the same year she accepted a position with the American Civil Liberties Union (ACLU) in New York. It would lead to her national exposure and would serve as the foundation for her reputation as a principled and even-handed civil rights attorney. The last event of 1965, and by far the most significant, was her marriage to Edward Norton.

Edward Worthington Norton was born in New York in 1938. His trail from New York led to Yale University, where in 1959 he received a bachelor of arts degree before serving in the U.S. Navy (1959–1963). In 1966 he received a law degree from Columbia University. He would later go on to hold a series of high-profile government positions in federal and state agencies, including deputy general counsel for the U.S. Department of Housing and Urban Development and deputy director of the Legal Services Program for the northeast region of the Office of Economic Opportunity. Although he combined his professional career with a number of social outreach programs, such as work with the 100 Black Men and the Harlem Lawyers Association, Norton never achieved the fame of his wife, who by 1968 was already making a national name for herself.

At the ACLU, Norton was the assistant director in charge of litigating First Amendment–rights cases. In the process of defending the most fundamental American right of freedom of speech, she came head-to-head with two unlikely clients—a white supremacist and a segregationist politician. These two cases launched her career as a respected civil rights lawyer. She argued and won her first case before the U.S. Supreme

Court when she defended the rights of a white supremacist group to hold a rally in Maryland. In the second case, one with more political symbolism, she successfully defended freedom of speech for the 1968 presidential candidate and governor of Alabama, George Wallace. He had sued to hold a rally at New York's Shea Stadium.

The defense of Wallace was newsworthy partly because of the juxtaposition of the attorney and client. Pictures of the governor of Alabama blocking the doorway to the state university as National Guard troops escorted black students to class had become a symbol of southern white resistance to integration. Segregation was anathema to all that Norton held dear, of course, but she felt compelled to protect the governor's rights, especially if the same rights were going to be upheld for those in the civil rights movement. "It was not difficult for me as an ACLU lawyer to represent people with whom I had profound disagreements such as George Wallace," Norton would say. "There's no way to argue, nor should there be, that black people ought to have freedom of speech and racists shouldn't. If the principle is going to live at all, it's got to live for anybody who wants to exercise it."[4]

Norton's successful defense brought her to the attention of her opponent in the case, the city of New York. Mayor John Lindsay asked her to come on board in 1970 as head of the New York City Commission on Human Rights. No longer an outsider, Norton accepted her first political appointment. As commissioner, she swore she would "attempt to see that no man is judged by the irrational criteria of race, religion, or national origin. . . . And I assure you I use the word 'man' in the generic sense, for I mean to see that the principle of nondiscrimination becomes a reality for women as well."[5]

She remained in this position for seven years. It turned out to be a good proving ground for what was ahead. She was given a broad exposure to the area of civil rights enforcement and, equally important, she gained in-depth administrative experience as the head of a regulatory agency. Controversial in some quarters, because of her ability to separate emotion from performance while still maintaining a passion for the rights of others, she became a lighting rod for militant blacks and a scapegoat for conservative whites. Black male leaders felt that she concentrated more on the rights of women than they might like, and whites criticized her for continuing her activism while in office.

Through it all, Norton evolved what was becoming a philosophical basis for her professional persona. She once described herself as "existential," being outside of herself in terms of what she felt she had to do in the present or the future. "Most people who know me would speak of my passion. But I pride myself as well on the ability to think coldly through a problem. In the middle of a revolution, you don't want somebody who is just going to go out there and raise a flag and say 'follow me.' You want somebody who has figured out how to get through this battle."[6]

For Norton the battle was not just for the rights of blacks. It was also for the rights of women and other minorities. In the early and formative years of the 1970s, a crucial divide faced many black leaders, and she was no exception. The activism of the women's movement was about to eclipse the traditional civil rights movement, and black women in leadership roles were placed at the crossroads and viewed with suspicion if they tried to serve both. Highly visible, with a weekly television program in the popular New York market, and a frequent speaker on major civil and human rights issues, Norton was a likely political target for those who felt that they were losing political power and access. The black community critiqued her performance, sometimes harshly. But she was not deterred.

In 1973, while still with the commission, she became one of the founders of the National Black Feminist Organization (NBFO), which attempted to organize black women who had been summarily left out of the white women's movement. The NBFO, according to its charter, was created to "articulate the need for political, social, and economic equality specifically for black women." Referring to the reticence of black women to label themselves as feminist, Norton later added, "it took us some time to realize that we had nothing to fear from feminism." The organization went on to gain more than two thousand members in cities throughout the country.[7]

More important than the growth of the organization was the fact that Norton had tackled head-on the colliding agendas of the civil rights and the women's movements by staking her claim in the emerging black women's feminist movement. She would later continue her advocacy for black women as one of the founders of the National Political Congress of Black Women, Inc.

Her activism, though controversial back at the commission, did not keep her from being reappointed in 1974 by Lindsay's successor Mayor Abraham Beame—an appointment she accepted, staying on until 1977, when she was tapped by President Jimmy Carter to become the first woman to head the Equal Employment Opportunity Commission (EEOC).

As chair of the EEOC, Norton was one of the Carter administration's success stories. For though Carter had placed more blacks in cabinet, agency, and subcabinet positions than any other president before him, African American political leaders and particularly the Congressional Black Caucus, found fault with what they considered his "duplicitous" manner in dealing with the established black leadership. Norton, however, was not caught up in the controversy surrounding Carter. As a matter of fact, she received high praise for bringing the moribund agency back to life. She is credited with reducing the EEOC backlog of cases, creating a high profile for its work and mandate, and strengthening and reshaping its administration. It was during her years as chair of the EEOC that Norton received most of her awards and honorary degrees, and in 1975 she coauthored a book, *Sex Discrimination and the Law: Cause and Remedies*. She became a noted advocate for equal opportunity and was constantly called upon to give focus to affirmative action and its practices and future.

With Republicans back in office and the civil rights movement in a lull, Norton left office at the end of the Carter administration in 1981. She went to work at the liberal think tank, the Washington, D.C.–based Urban Institute, where she was a senior fellow until 1982, at which time she joined the faculty of Georgetown University Law School. It was during her time as a tenured professor at Georgetown that she threw her hat into the ring for the 1990 campaign for the nonvoting delegate seat representing Washington, D.C.

The Political Odyssey

Although Washington, D.C., was home, Norton had stayed away from its local politics. Her focus had been more national in scope, while her hometown was left in the hands of former SNCC members who had settled in Washington and established a political base, many of them colleagues from her civil rights days. For example, Mayor Marion S. Barry and D.C. city councilmen Frank Smith and John Wilson all had roots in SNCC and had come into power through effective grassroots organizing and voter education and registration. At first Norton watched as others fought for the political enfranchisement of her hometown.

The road to enfranchisement for the District had been rocky and fraught with racial animus and power plays. By 1990, the year of Norton's entry into local politics, the city had experienced two decades of home rule, one failed 1978 attempt at getting a statehood amendment ratified by the states, and a series of financial and budgetary setbacks.

The seat for which Norton decided to run was first filled in 1971, by the Reverend Walter Fauntroy, a local minister and follower of Martin Luther King, Jr. Fauntroy remained in office for nineteen years, until his resignation in 1990. Having been the only delegate to ever hold the seat, he shaped the voters' expectations about the limits of the delegate's office. All in all, he used it as a bully pulpit for lobbying Congress for statehood, basically following the legislative intent of the law. Norton would promise and eventually deliver a broader vision of what the nonvoting delegate could accomplish.

Fauntroy had been energetic and visionary in the early years, but by the time of his resignation there was no sign of those early traits. For example, during his early days, Delegate Fauntroy conducted voter registration drives in the South Carolina district of Congressman John Macmillan (D-S.C.). Macmillan was the powerful chair of the District of Columbia Committee in the House of Representatives for more than twenty-five years. During that quarter of a century, he kept the District government filled with patronage positions and prevented the city from gaining home rule and voting representation in Congress.

Fauntroy's tactics were eventually successful; Macmillan lost his seat. Waiting in the wings to take the chairmanship of the District Committee was Congressman Charles Diggs, the black Democratic representative from Detroit. Diggs's first move was to introduce home-rule legislation for the District, giving it an elected mayor, school board, and city council but retaining the congressional oversight of the budget and giving the House the authority to overturn any laws, while at the same time giving the president control over the city's judicial system. Fauntroy was a key player in all of these early efforts. Over time, however, he became burdened by old methods of tackling new problems, many of which were not effective. A change was in the wind for all of Washington's top elected officials, and the proof was evident in Fauntroy's run for mayor in 1990 after his resignation from the House. He lost resoundingly, garnering only 10 percent of the vote.

It was indeed a watershed year for D.C. politics. Since home rule, the District had elected only two mayors—Walter Washington and then Marion S. Barry, who served three terms. A native of Itta Bena, Mississippi, by way of Memphis, Tennessee, the charismatic Barry defeated Washington, a native of the District, in 1978. While he received credit for being a reformer his first term, by the time Norton announced her candidacy in 1990, Barry's reputation was in sad decline.

The District of Columbia was bursting at the seams politically and racially following Barry's arrest on charges of smoking crack cocaine. The arrest brought to the surface tensions that existed in almost every aspect of the city's life, but nowhere more than in the media.

Washington, D.C., has a thriving alternative black media—one of the few in the nation.[8] And while it was no match on a large scale with the powerful *Washington Post,* the black press (including radio, television, and print) reached a large segment of the majority African American population and, to its credit, enjoyed the community's trust. Many of the columnists and editors sat on local mainstream news commentary and talk shows on television and radio, shaping opinion and offering contrasting views to mainstream reporting.

Racial division in the city crystallized during the election for mayor and D.C. delegate, leading the black-owned and -controlled press to coalesce into an ad hoc group called the African American Media Coalition (AAMC). The coalition became an informal forum for political candidates' presentation and discussion of issues. It also monitored local mainstream coverage of the Barry story and in two instances held community forums on the harassment of black elected officials and the future direction of the city. The presence of the C-SPAN cameras gave the community forum a national audience.

In another instance, the tension between the mainstream media and the AAMC was so great that an unprecedented three-hour meeting between the coalition and the general manager and production team of the local NBC affiliate resulted in the station canceling a two-hour special on the indictment of Barry. The point of conflict arose over the right of Barry to be treated as innocent until proven guilty. In the meeting, the AAMC argued that the proposed program, by allowing the U.S. attorney a half-hour to discuss the case the day the indictment was to be handed down, was a violation of the mayor's rights. In addition, the producers had no one who would agree to speak on Barry's behalf. The result would have been the loss of the presumption of innocence and a slanted televised special to be aired the day of the scheduled indictment of Barry.

The general manager, although not in agreement with the AAMC, nevertheless pulled the show because he considered their arguments to outweigh those of his producers.

Norton learned quickly about these two media markets and their separate powers. At a fund-raiser at the home of a political activist and former SNCC member, Florence Tate, Norton marveled at the support she received from Cathy Hughes, a radio talk show host and successful entrepreneur. Hughes had a loyal grassroots following she called the "WOL radio station family," and her political endorsement meant a great deal to aspirants for office in Washington, D.C. The various audiences of the black press were the hidden arsenal that made Norton's candidacy successful, even after the revelations about her evasion of taxes and abandonment by the mainstream press. In a city so scandal-ridden already, the report that Norton and her husband owed $80,000 in back taxes was devastating news. That they had not even filed for several years only made matters worse.

Before she announced her candidacy in 1990, Norton was the well-known half of a handsome, popular, and high-profile professional husband and wife team. By the time she was sworn in to her first term in January 1991, her official biography listed her marital status as "separated," and by the time the official 103d congressional biography of Eleanor Holmes Norton appeared, her status was "divorced." The woman who had once decried the single female–headed household as one of the major problems in the black community, was now a single parent—albeit an extraordinary one—of two children.

It all began with a mysterious defamatory fax that was sent to newsrooms around the city. The source of the fax was never revealed because the return fax address had been deleted and the point of origin was never clear. The fax almost spelled the death knell for Norton's campaign. Before it, she was the front runner; after it, she was viewed as a long shot. The fax showed tax records that revealed Norton and her husband owed back taxes in excess of $80,000.

The barrage of negative stories and news commentaries that followed not only attacked Norton for not filing taxes, but also criticized the veracity of her explanation. She continued to profess that she knew nothing about the unpaid taxes because it was the role of her husband to take care of financial matters. For an arch feminist, Norton's response was hard to imagine, and as a candidate for a congressional seat, such lack of accountability, not surprisingly, produced suspicion.

Up to this point, many had considered Norton the ideal role model for local politics—a native Washingtonian and national personality running for office to lead the charge for statehood. Still other voters were skeptical about her sincerity, since she had never been involved with any local issues. But if the tax issue made her candidacy suspect to the white mainstream press and white voters, it gave her a more human connection with the everyday voters, who were predominately black. It also gave them a chance to get to know who the candidate really was. So that in an odd way, the personal angle was the best thing to come out of the scandal.

At about 5 feet 6 inches, Norton is a tall and a strikingly attractive woman with a wide smile, a reddish brown afro hairstyle that she has maintained for decades, and a light brown complexion with a hint of freckles. A plain dresser, she wears very little makeup and very little jewelry. Given to understated suits without collars and high-necked blouses, her dress style typifies her cordial but professional business attitude.

This unpretentious persona, in some respects, won her a place in the hearts of the voters, because with all of her achievements, she remained the affable, bright woman next door who made her neighbors proud. This was evident when, just weeks before the Democratic primary, in almost tribunal fashion, she stood on a platform before the voters with her two children and her husband, declaring her innocence. A sea of voters listened intently and applauded to show their approval of her response to the charges. For the first time voters saw Norton in all her many roles, a woman, a mother, and a wife. Eleanor Holmes Norton—the woman—told the crowd, that she would not let the media and all of this criticism destroy her marriage of more than twenty-five years. And as a mother she stood in front of the crowd with her two children at her side, a son, John, and a daughter, Katherine. It was the first time that many voters knew that Norton was the mother of a child with Down's syndrome. And as the wife she came before them, first acknowledging that her husband had held the responsibility for filing the taxes, acknowledging that he had not done what he was supposed to do, and then forgiving him and swearing they would immediately pay the back taxes, which they did. The noble response was little help in covering up the fact that a bond of trust had been severed in a longstanding marriage.

The relentless media analysis and commentary followed Norton for the rest of the campaign. A lifetime of achievement was being destroyed with each mention of the tax issue. Possible prosecution was also mentioned as a part of the remedy for the tax liability and lack of filing. Norton, attacked by the mainstream media, began courting the black press—a press that had editorially supported her throughout the campaign and continued to do so, even after the disclosure. The racial division began to emerge as the *Washington Post* endorsed her white opponent, Betty Anne Kane, a former member of the city council. The *Post* endorsement was generally a signal as to which candidate would get the vote of the predominantly white Ward 3.[9]

The paper went on to endorse Sharon Pratt Dixon (Kelly),[10] who up to this time had only received serious coverage in the black press. Heretofore, the mayoral Democratic primary race had been the most significant, but now with the Norton story, the nonvoting delegate race was the one to watch. The polls showed that the race for the nonvoting delegate seat was really one between Kane and Norton, even though there were more than half a dozen other people running in the primary.

Racial symbolism was unavoidable. Most of the black press endorsed Norton, while the *Washington Post* endorsed Kane. Each saw a different candidate and each viewed the Norton scandal differently. The *Post* treated her tax situation as an unforgivable sin, and the black press in general took Norton at her word. One publication remarked that "no man" would ever be able to get away with the explanation that Norton gave; he would not only not be believed but he would be laughed at.

In the end, the voters spoke, and the media was left reporting on the election and analyzing the results. When the polls closed, Norton was the victor. She defeated Kane with 36 percent of the vote to Kane's 33 percent, with the remainder of the candidates splitting the rest. In the predominately Democratic city, the general election was assured to the victor in the Democratic primary. Not surprisingly, it was a bittersweet victory for Eleanor Holmes Norton. In 1993 she and her husband were divorced, ending a marriage of almost three decades.

The Congressional Years

In a particularly poignant way, Congress offered an opportunity for a professional and personal renaissance for Norton. The zeal and commitment that she brought to the job was extraordinary. In the community, she was a regular at meetings, conferences, radio shows, schools, and churches. Her constituent services surpassed those of her predecessor, as well as those of the newly elected mayor—Sharon Pratt Kelly. But it was not just constituent services that earned her instant praise. She turned the office into a viable political post by expanding its possibilities and its role. "I wrote a legal memorandum, which for the first time gave the District a vote on the House floor. I vote in the Committee of the Whole, but on final passage, I don't vote," Norton proudly proclaimed. It was one of a handful of concessions that she wrested from Congress during her first and second terms (1991–1994).

With that legal memorandum, Norton gained for the District of Columbia and the four territories the right to vote in the Committee of the Whole, a technical term referring to the full House of Representatives.[11] Prior to this time, the delegates could only vote in committee.

The victory was significant but temporary. It was stripped away in her third term. The road to enfranchising Washington, D.C., historically has always been fraught with racial animus, manipulation, and abuse of power. While politicians deliberate on giving the District the franchise, more than half a million taxpayers, most of them African Americans, are without rights of full citizenship, even though they fight wars, pay taxes, and shoulder all of the duties and responsibilities of other Americans.

Norton, however, made significant strides toward home rule during her first two terms in Congress. Other than getting the vote, she, along with newly elected mayor Kelly, received an additional $100 million in emergency funds from the Congress to defray the financial burden of the cash-strapped city. Late in the 102d Congress, Norton held debates and a vote on District statehood. It was the first time in two hundred years that such a debate had been held. Although the bill was defeated by a vote of 277 to 153, it was an accomplishment that buoyed Norton's hopes for the future. She swore to return to the issue and attacked the status of the District as the exception to the American principles of democratic representation and self-government.

Norton moved on to the 103d Congress with a sound victory in the polls, no significant opposition, and a glowing endorsement from the *Washington Post.* If Norton's star was rising, Mayor Kelly's was not. Voters began to compare the two as public servants with two extreme responses to their public service obligation. They contrasted Norton's quick response to their concerns with the slow and nearly nonexistent service they were receiving from the Kelly administration. Not only was Norton's warm and open personality being compared to Kelly's aloof and acerbic persona, Kelly's actions were driving the two Washingtonians apart politically.

The delegate found her biggest struggles in Congress to be the defense of some of the actions of the Kelly administration. Because of the District's unique quasi-independent status, a close working relationship between the mayor's office and the delegate was essential for gaining support of Congress. In most instances, the mayor had not even given her the courtesy of briefings on measures that Norton would be forced to defend on Capitol Hill, in effect blindsiding her on critical issues.

For example, when Kelly announced that she was considering introducing casino gambling to the District, Norton was caught off guard when queried about the matter. Norton felt gambling would hurt the city's chances for statehood, and she could not believe that Kelly had thought through the project and its consequences before making the announcement.

Of course, in public Norton was diplomatic, but in private aides say she was really furious because her first knowledge of the casino issue came through the press and not from the mayor's office. Kelly did the same thing with the issue of a commuter tax for Washington suburbanites—a volatile issue and one that could adversely affect Norton's dealings with the neighboring Virginia and Maryland congressional delegations. The major issue that had a lasting and detrimental effect on relationships between the two and that would eventually push back the cause of statehood was Kelly's alleged mishandling of the city's finances.

When the 103d Congress convened, the honeymoon for the new mayor was over. Constant trips out of town, nonresponsive administrators, cold and off-putting personal traits, and seeming incompetence became the trademarks of her administration. Norton, much more politically aware, had reached out to the new president, Bill Clinton, to gain further leverage for statehood, while Kelly had not. As early as the 1992 Democratic National Convention, Norton had pushed to get statehood on the party platform and had elicited a promise from Clinton that, if elected, he would not sign any legislation tampering with the District's home-rule charter.

In another concession, Norton was able to get the president to commit to allowing her to submit names to him for appointments to district court judgeships and the U.S. attorney's office. That move resulted in Clinton's making the appointment of the first black U.S. attorney for the predominately African American city. Eric Holder, a former member of the Justice Department, was one of three names Norton submitted to the president for consideration for the highly sensitive post.

Norton's ability to reduce the District's political limitations would soon come to a halt with the entrance of a hostile 104th Congress (1995–1996) led by Republicans. On the first day the new Congress convened, the Speaker, Newt Gingrich (R-Ga.), held the House in session past midnight. That session proved to be a disaster for Norton's statehood mission. Gingrich, whom Norton had erroneously referred to as a friend of the District, spearheaded the raucous Republican majority in first stripping away her right to vote on the floor of the House and then relegating the District of Columbia Committee to subcommittee status, placing it under the Government Reform and Oversight Committee. The latter shift in committee status meant that the District's issues would assume less prominence and priority in the workings of the Congress.

Without a vote, Norton returned to her early SNCC tactics and launched a protest candlelight vigil outside the House of Representatives while the members were in session. The strategy proved useless, and by March her approach had changed.

Faced with the threat of complete congressional takeover of the city, Norton joined the Republican-led District subcommittee in passing legislation that would put the District finances under a presidentially appointed Financial Control Board. The board, led by Andrew Brimmer, a former member of the Federal Reserve Board of Governors, was responsible for oversight of the District's budget and all fiscal issues.

By this time Norton resigned herself to a Republican-controlled Congress intent on putting additional constraints on the District's autonomy, and she tried to negotiate for the least intrusive options. The establishment of the Financial Control Board was one battle that she attempted to handle strategically. She cosponsored the bill on the condition that it would not violate the city's home-rule charter. The Congress already had fiscal control over the District, and following a damaging General Accounting Office (GAO) report on the disarray of the city's finances and fault-finding with the accounting practices of the former Kelly administration, it moved to establish the board as a source of outside accountability.

The 1994 elections not only changed the makeup of Congress but also changed the political leadership of Washington, D.C. The former mayor, Marion Barry, was elected in 1994 as irate voters removed the incumbent, Mayor Kelly. She received less than 20 percent of the vote, and voters returned a rehabilitated Barry to office. Barry, a favorite of the people, was not a favorite of the members of Congress—Republican or Democratic. What Norton conjectured was that the Republican defiance to the will of the people to be governed by their elected representatives could not be eliminated but perhaps mitigated. She also felt that the Financial Control Board recommended by the GAO had its merits and said that a bill to establish this Financial Control Board would literally save the city. She stood alongside the other city officials as President Clinton signed the legislation into law.

Norton had embarked upon still another challenge by maintaining some semblance of control over the diminishing self-government and statehood movement. It was a battle that she would single-handedly wage in the halls of Congress as the District's only representative. Establishment of the Financial Control Board was followed by congressional inquiries into gaining control of the District's education and the police department. At one point, during the 1995–1996 deadlock on the federal budget, Congress considered a voucher program for the District, which would provide scholarship funds for poor children. It would be the Republicans' way of introducing a pilot program in Washington, D.C., to push their political agenda for school vouchers.

Norton found herself moving from one legislative proposal to another as a virtual brush fire of bills were proposed. In early 1996 the proposals were so meddlesome and harmful to the fiscal soundness of the city that the city's land-grant college, the University of the District of Columbia, through its Office of Alumni Affairs, led by Irene Bush, staged a rally denouncing cuts in the budget. The rally quickly turned into a major protest, with students blocking one of the main thoroughfares and the mayor issuing orders to the police to leave the area so that the protest could proceed. For Barry and his SNCC veteran in the Congress, Eleanor Holmes Norton, the days of protest sparked new life into what had been a city stymied by apathy. Congress and the Financial Control Board began to talk about perhaps providing the city with additional funds to tackle its beleaguered financial condition. Working behind the scenes and sometimes in front of them, Norton was back in her element, poised for confrontation and renewed in her resolve to fight for full statehood for the District.

To put it differently, it did not take long before Delegate Eleanor Holmes Norton went back to her protest days. Before the end of the first session of the 104th Congress, she was out in front of the Capitol demonstrating and holding a rally to save home rule from the Republicans' continued intrusion into the self-governing rights of the city. An outsider on the inside, Eleanor Holmes Norton, at fifty-eight, had found the spirit of the octogenarian Mary Church Terrell and moved from the comforts of the congressional corridors to the confrontation in the streets, seeking social reform and justice—this time for the basic franchise for Washingtonians.

The District of Columbia and Its Search for Statehood

In 1790 Congress authorized the selection of a new site for the nation's capital, one hundred square miles between Maryland and Virginia on the Potomac River. The city was planned by Major Pierre Charles L'Enfant, a French patriot, who left before completing the assignment. The completed city plans were carried out by Major Andrew Ellicott and black mathematician and astronomer Benjamin Banneker. On December 1, 1800, the seat of government was officially transferred to Washington, D.C., from Philadelphia after a brief hiatus in Princeton, New Jersey. The new capital was a city with a booming commerce in the selling of human beings—enslaved Africans. It was also a town with a large free black population.

The Congress kept political control over the city until Reconstruction. In 1871 Republicans gave the city control over its local government. The vote was given to black men and white, with or without property. The elected governor/mayor at the time was Alexander "Boss" Shepherd, who drove the city into bankruptcy. His fiscal abuse brought together two groups who wanted to take the franchise away from the citizens of the District—white women suffragettes and the business community. While the businessmen just wanted to gain control of the city, a task that they could better perform by giving bribes to members of Congress, the women were determined that if white women could not vote, neither could black men. Both groups went to Congress and struck a compromise. Congress would withdraw the voting franchise from the city and take back control.

Saying that suffrage puts them at the mercy of a "property-less majority fortified by ignorant, irresponsible Negroes," the Congress agreed with the dissenters and enacted the 1878 Organic Act, which replaced the elected officials with three commissioners appointed by the president.

The three-commissioner form of government remained until the 1960s. Home rule for the District of Columbia, while not a hue and cry, became a murmur within the 1960s civil rights movement. At that time much of the attention had to do with the city's majority black population. In 1961, the Twenty-third Amendment to the Constitution was passed, giving Washingtonians the right to vote for president and vice president through three electoral votes. It was not a full franchise, since the number of electoral votes had to be "not more than the least populous state," as stated in the amendment.

But it was a beginning, and the 1964 elections were the first in which District residents could register to vote for president of the United States. It was the first in a series of steps leading toward a limited enfranchisement. In 1968 District residents first elected a school board; 1971 saw the first nonvoting delegate in Congress; and in 1974, District residents could vote for a mayor and a part-time city council. In addition, elections were held for nonpaid, nonvoting members of Advisory Neighborhood Councils, and two shadow senators, and one shadow representative. The "shadow" positions were to serve as unpaid lobbyists for statehood. Even with this "home rule" configuration, the District residents still did not maintain control of their finances or judicial system.

The president was in control of the judicial system, appointing all district judges and the U.S. attorney, while the district's purse strings were controlled by Congress. Congress maintained veto power over the District's budget and any laws promulgated could not be enacted without their approval. In addition, in lieu of taxes for federal lands, the Congress would pay the District a subsidy for the federal enclave, and that amount would be determined by Congress on a yearly basis—making budgeting virtually impossible.

With the reelection in 1994 of Mayor Marion Barry after his release from prison on charges of possession and use of crack cocaine, and with the worsening of the city's financial crisis following the Kelly administration, the Republican Congress immediately attempted to take the reins of control from the city's elected officials. By 1996, home rule and statehood had become moot points, and Delegate Eleanor Holmes Norton was left fighting just to keep the Congress from dismantling the few rights that the citizens held.

Chapter 8 **Maxine Waters**

*The Voice of South Central
Los Angeles*

My name is Maxine Waters. I'm a black woman. I'm a sister. And I think I'm very clear about who I am and what I care about. This discussion is so important today because there is a concentrated, well-organized effort to keep our voices closed and shut down on the discussion of race.[1]

Résumé

Maxine Waters

Personal

Born   August 15, 1938
        St. Louis, Missouri

Family   Married to Sidney Williams, U.S. ambassador to the Bahamas; two children

Religion   Christian

Party   Democrat

Took office   Age 52, January 3, 1991

Education

B.A.   California State University, Los Angeles, 1970

Professional/Political Background

1970–1976   Teacher's assistant, Head Start

1976–1990   Assemblywoman, California Assembly

1991–   U.S. House of Representatives

Selected Awards/Organizational Affiliations

Selected Honorary Degrees: Spelman College; North Carolina A&T State University; Howard University; Central State University; Bishop College; Morgan State University

Affiliations: Board, Trans-Africa Foundation; National Women's Political Caucus; chair and founding member, National Commission for Economic Conversion and Disarmament; Board, Center for National Policy; Clara Elizabeth Jackson Carter Foundation (Spelman College); Minority AIDS Project; cofounder, Los Angeles Black Women's Forum.

Congressional Data

Thirty-fifth Congressional District of California: South Central Los Angeles

Committees: Veterans' Affairs; Small Business; Banking, Finance and Urban Affairs (name changed to Banking and Financial Services during the Republican-controlled 104th Congress)

102d Congress: 1991–1992
1990 general election results: 80 percent of the vote

103d Congress: 1993–1994
1992 general election results: 83 percent of the vote

104th Congress: 1995–1996
1994 general election results: 78 percent of the vote

Maxine Waters

The Second African American Woman
Elected to Congress from California

Thirty-fifth District, California
Democrat
102d Congress–present, 1991–

On the west African island called Goree, where human cargo was shipped across the Atlantic to America, Africans who refused to go quietly or without a struggle were placed in cubicles labeled "recalcitrants." They refused to participate in their own enslavement. When it comes to yielding to extreme conservative positions and legislation that goes against her South Central Los Angeles constituency, Maxine Waters is a recalcitrant. She refuses to allow America to slip back into its pre–civil rights mode of disenfranchising African Americans. At no time was that label more apropos than in 1994, when the Republican rebellion began its self-imposed mission to destroy significant social programs.

The congressional elections of 1994 produced what America called the "Year of the Angry White Man." While most pollsters attributed this anger to preferential hiring programs due to affirmative action, the real issue was not more women and minorities in the workplace but a changing economy that could not promise jobs to anyone. The advent of the technological age meant that many white men, who were still the dominant group in the workforce, would never again work and earn at the same level. Rather than explore remedies for the economic reality, politicians chose instead to seize upon the opportunity to fan fears with racial scapegoating.

It was an election year framed by a national conservative Republican platform that touted a Contract with America—a list of ten issues that were to be turned into legislation and passed within the first hundred days of the 104th Congress (1995–1996).

The ten provisions of the Contract—fiscal responsibility, taking back the streets, personal responsibility, American dream restoration, job creation and wage enhancement, national security restoration, senior-citizen fairness, family reinforcement, citizen legislature, and commonsense legal reform—formed the basis for the undoing not only of government programs that provided entitlements for the poor but also, voters would later discover, for decreasing entitlements to the middle class.

The Contract had become a bible for conservative Republicans who were buoyed by right-wing radio talk show hosts, a key element in the mobilization of conservative voters. As the political right championed the reform-sounding provisions of the Contract, liberal Democrats condemned them—calling it instead, a Contract *on* America. As far as the Democrats were concerned, the provisions were a cover-up for efforts to decrease funding for entitlement programs for the poor, to censor and eventually eliminate funds for the arts, and to institute stringent law-and-order measures against crime.

Riding high on the Republican victories, in July 1995 the National Republican Congressional Committee (NRC) launched its Project 28, aimed at unseating liberal Democrats by using the same angry white male voters who were credited for creating the 104th Congress. They had not counted on one thing—a still angry black woman—Congresswoman Maxine Waters, who represented California's Thirty-fifth Congressional District. It is a district with landmarks as famous as the great Western Forum, where the L.A. Lakers played to thousands, and as infamous as the intersection of Normandy and Florence, where Reginald Denny, a white truck driver was dragged from his truck and beaten during the 1992 riots in South Central Los Angeles.

"This 'Wanted Poster' is a scurrilous and irresponsible escalation of Republican hostility toward black, Jewish, and women legislators and toward government itself," Waters told the Capitol Hill press corps. "It is sexist, racist, and anti-Semitic," she went on to say in response to the Project 28 attack. As a strategy, the NRC issued a fund-raising flyer along with a letter to its financial backers, which depicted headshots of President Clinton and twenty-eight House Democrats in the format of a wanted poster. Of the members of Congress, there were ten African Americans, nine women (four of them black, including Waters), Jewish and Hispanic members, and an openly gay congressman, Barney Frank (D-Mass.).

The poster was captioned with these lines: "Liberal Democrat Wanted Poster: Wanted for voting against at least 7 out of 10 provisions of the Contract with America and for aiding and abetting President Bill Clinton's big government, pro-tax, anti-family, anti-military agenda in the House of Representatives."

The clash came at a very critical period in the changing political and philosophical mood in the country. A threat such as this by Republicans to remove Waters from office would have seemed impossible, or at least improbable, a year earlier, when she had just defeated her Republican opponent, Nate Truman, with 78 percent of the vote in a minority district. To fulfill their threat, however, the Republicans had a weapon: the "politics of change" had shifted in their direction. What changed were the rules by which the new Republican majority played. This wanted poster was indicative of the vitriolics that turned a normally civil House of Representatives into a combat zone of ideological differences.

For instance, in June 1995, during the first session of the 104th Congress, the U.S. Supreme Court ruled that minority districts had to pass strict scrutiny to insure that they were not created with race as the overriding factor. Although Waters's Thirty-fifth Congressional District (previously the Twenty-ninth District) was more than three decades old, it was still vulnerable under the new ruling—making a potential defeat feasible.

The Republican majority knew that the threat held potential now more than ever before, but Waters was not intimidated. In fact, she was emboldened by the new Republican majority in the House.

Along with her Democratic colleagues, she returned to the 104th Congress to find that after forty years in control of the House of Representatives, the Democrats were now the minority party. Committee chairs were now in the hands of Republicans, and the new Speaker of the House, Newt Gingrich (R-Ga.), had become an overnight voice of fiscal responsibility, change, and congressional reform in the first half of the 104th Congress.

Where other Democrats tried to meld into the conservatism of the times by moving toward the political center, Waters was intractable. She fought the Republican majority and what some called their mean-spirited approach to the social programs that she considered important and fundamental to her political agenda. Since many of her colleagues were less vociferous about traditional liberal issues, it appeared, at times, that Waters was alone in her fight for the poor and disenfranchised.

As for the poster, Waters saw it as just another diversionary tactic of an overzealous Republican party that set a tone for right-wing hostility spreading throughout the country. Calling the poster racist and antigovernment propaganda, Waters criticized the NRC's action as a polarizing effort that could easily have turned the poster into a hit list of congressional liberals.

Labeling the poster as a potential "hit list" was not hyperbole. Times had changed. Waters, who once angered members of Congress by calling the Los Angeles disturbance of 1992 a "rebellion" instead of a riot, was in the midst of a rebellion of another sort—that of white men in America. Her reaction to the poster was a case in point. She called for the FBI and congressional security to advise her and other members on the possible security risk created by the distribution of the poster. It was an unprecedented response by one member of Congress to the actions of an opposing party.

Waters should have expected that she would appear on the Wanted poster, because she had been relentless in her hand-to-hand combat with Gingrich. While most Democrats of the 104th were licking their wounds and lamenting the loss of forty years of control, not so the congresswoman. She was attacking the new Republican Speaker each time he claimed a victory.

When he went to great lengths to announce a victory for the Republicans for keeping the campaign promise to vote on all of the provisions of the Contract within the first hundred days, Waters responded with an attack on the Speaker's ethics. In a statement with the title "The Real Story of Newt Gingrich's First Hundred Days," Waters attacked his character by accusing him of delivering the Republicans into the hands of wealthy special interest groups.

She recited a litany of ethics complaints against him ranging from a million dollar book deal from media mogul Rupert Murdoch to the hiring of his wife, Marianne, by the Israel Export Development Company after Gingrich had given political support to a proposal by American investors while talking with the Israeli government. Waters's recitation of these ethical breaches followed on the heels of the House Ethics Committee's announcement that Gingrich's actions would become the subject of an investigation. Before the end of the session, a special counsel would be called in to conduct an independent investigation.

The very nature of the Contract, of which Gingrich was the architect, meant that the 104th Congress had a fight between Republicans and Democrats not unlike the South Central Los Angeles Crips and Bloods gang battles in the inner city—except that this one was in the Congress. When Waters entered the House of Representatives in 1991, her battle was to maintain and expand the liberal agenda of the Democrats who controlled the House, but by this, her third term, it took all of her political chutzpah to fight the new "angry white men" who were intent on diminishing or eliminating many of the programs that she considered significant for her constituents. It was almost as though a new gang had entered the House of Representatives, and Maxine Waters found herself needing to use the tactics of gang warfare to do battle with the Republican rebellion. Once again she had to be tough and impolite, a stance that masked a deep empathy for the people she represented.

The Early Years

Waters's affinity for the poor came from roots that were not far from those of the people she served. She knew what it took to get from public housing in St. Louis, Missouri, where she was born in 1938, to the U.S. House of Representatives, where she began serving in 1991. One of thirteen children, she grew up on welfare in St. Louis and attributes some of those experiences to shaping her aggressive political persona. "When you have twelve sisters and brothers and you are competing for everything from space in the bathroom to the most favorable bed, I suppose it helps to shape the personality an awful lot."[2]

Waters came to political consciousness early, just trying to figure out how as a black person she fit in the system of the Constitution and most of all the Bill of Rights. She often repeats the story of how as a high school student, she was intrigued by the Bill of Rights, but recognized that it did not include her—she just did not know how wide the gap was between those who were covered by it and others who had a history of not being included. Although she never attached her meager living conditions to those rights or the lack of them, she did witness the injustices of a life with social workers and bill collectors who daily violated the basic rights of human dignity of poor people.

Yet, in spite of it all, Waters did manage to identify a role model of sorts. The image she carries in her mind even today, is that of the social worker who came to the housing projects with a briefcase and wearing a suit—looking professional. Waters was determined that she would grow up and become that social worker—not just any social worker—but the best there was. In a way, her path to the Congress and even within the House has borne out that early desire.

Married before she was twenty, Waters and her first husband, Edward, left St. Louis and moved west. Living in Los Angeles in 1961 at the age of twenty-three—married with two children—she held a series of jobs: garment-factory worker, waitress in a segregated restaurant, and telephone company employee. The early marriage ended in divorce in 1972, turning Waters into a single parent.

Although a time of crisis, it was during this period that Waters speaks of the bond she established with black women who fed her children while she worked, fed her when she returned home, and provided a nurturing, warm, and caring environment for her during trying times. It is also one reason why Waters collects black memorabilia, some of which include the controversial Aunt Jemima image. Most black women consider Aunt Jemima— the character on the pancake box—as a negative stereotype, but for Waters it is a tie to those women who were there for her when she had to forgo lunch and a bus ride home in order to save money for her children. Her resistance to the black pressure to denounce the Aunt Jemima image is one example of her refusal to be defined by black society or white.

Through all the hardship, Waters never let go of her ambition to earn a college degree and become a social worker. In 1970 she earned a B.A. in sociology from California State University. Persistence and hard work had paid off nine years after her arrival. Now in her early thirties, she was a college graduate, with a ticket to a larger world of opportunities and possibilities. She began working as an assistant in a California Head Start program and became a part of the movement by community organizers that politicized inner-city activists during the 1970s.

The Political Odyssey

Noninstitutionalized California politics in the 1970s were radical, pro-black, and strong. Waters was a part of that movement. After having worked in a number of political campaigns, she decided to run for office herself. In a heated contest, she won a seat in the California Assembly in 1976, embarking on a new career in politics and a new personal journey as well.

In 1977, a year after her election, she married Sidney Williams. Williams, a luxury car salesman, was a former National Football League player who had played for the Washington Redskins and the Cleveland Browns. In the presence of the tall, handsome Williams, the normally combative Waters would often let down her defenses and exude a rare warmth and serenity seldom evident in her day-to-day political dealings.

The personal renewal would soon give way to the beginning of a high-profile political life of controversy. It began by Waters introducing herself to her new colleagues in the state assembly by confronting them on the use of the term "assemblyman." She fought to have the nomenclature changed from "assemblyman" to "assembly member." It was a small victory, but eventually it was overturned. However, the effort and the publicity ensured her a coveted place in the burgeoning political feminist movement and started her down the legislative path that became her hallmark—the issues of women, blacks, and the poor. Her fourteen-year tenure in the state assembly was characterized by legislation that focused on creating set-aside programs for minorities and women, initiating legislation that created the first public school in a public housing project, and fighting to get California to cease investing in South Africa. The latter she considers her most important accomplishment. She led the fight to get the state to divest its pension funds from South African investments, which it finally did in 1986.

She was able to maintain a favorable voting base in spite of her outspoken and, in some circles, controversial stance. For all of her social consciousness, she was no "do-good social worker" gone astray but rather a seasoned and skilled politician, a survivor with a penchant for mastering the nuances of the political game.

A nonconformist who feels that she had to learn to navigate her way through the state legislature without any mentors, she says: "When I came to this legislature, I did things my own way because I really didn't have any guidepost. Even if I had been a willing pupil, there were no teachers for women."[3]

A recent account of Waters's days in the state assembly modifies her comments about a lack of mentors by pointing to her strong political alliance with a former Speaker of the California Assembly—Willie Brown. Brown owed his early election as Speaker to Waters's support and strategic attack on his opponent. Waters's support gave her considerable leverage in the assembly during the fifteen years of Brown's tenure, netting her historic firsts as majority whip, chair of the Democratic Caucus, and chair of the Rules Committee and Budget Conference Committee.[4]

Awaiting her next political step after the state legislature, for example, she targeted the seat of the venerable congressional pioneer and veteran, Augustus Hawkins (D-Calif.). By 1990, when Hawkins decided not to seek reelection, he had already served twenty-eight years in Congress and had previously served twenty-eight years in the California Assembly. Hawkins had been an enduring presence in the U.S. House of Representatives since 1963. An original member of the Congressional Black Caucus who was affectionately referred to as the "silent warrior," he authored more than one hundred bills, which included minimum wage compensation for all women, the Fair Housing Act, and the establishment of the Equal Employment Opportunity Commission. From his historic perch as chair of the Education and Labor Committee, he also coauthored the Humphrey-Hawkins Full Employment Act, one of the most significant employment bills passed by Congress during his tenure.

His legislative history notwithstanding, Hawkins's retirement was imminent. Working with state legislators on redistricting, Waters began restructuring Hawkins's district to fit her politics. What had been Hawkins's old Twenty-ninth Congressional District became after redistricting Waters's new Thirty-fifth, minus what she called a "rednecky" community that she saw as hindering her chances for a successful election. The result was a minority district with less than 20 percent white voters.

Once Hawkins announced his retirement, Waters was poised to launch her campaign. By that time she had already gained national visibility as one of the early and most vocal supporters of the 1984 and 1988 Jesse Jackson presidential campaigns. But, it was not national politics or national exposure that elected her in 1990. It was grassroots support that gave her a victory over her opponent with 80 percent of the vote.

The Congressional Years

She entered Congress in 1991, along with two other Democratic African American women who were sworn into the 102d Congress—D.C. delegate Eleanor Holmes Norton and Detroit's Barbara-Rose Collins. The three joined the veteran, Cardiss Collins (D-Ill.), who had been serving as the only black congresswoman for six years. Collins was so happy to have more black women in the House of Representatives that she threw a party to celebrate their arrival.

Cutting a different swath than her unassuming predecessor, the high-profile Waters chose to serve on the Veterans' Affairs, Small Business, and Banking Committees of the House of Representatives. She started her term on the Veterans' Affairs Committee by challenging the committee's Democratic chair to hire more blacks for the staff—upsetting the status quo in the House, as she had done so successfully in the California Assembly.

This time she had a major problem on her hands. She was not trying to be provocative just for the sake of it; her main objective was to find ways to focus national attention, money, and programs on South Central Los Angeles—a population that was alien to most of her colleagues. Her biggest challenge was to create alliances in order to enact legislation that addressed the unique needs of her constituents, such as ensuring through regulations that banking services would be placed in inner-city areas, ensuring that neighborhoods were drug-free and that opportunities for jobs and job training were available. In a House of Representatives that grappled with budget deficits, foreign relations, and defense spending, the question became: how can a member of Congress interest colleagues in finding legislative solutions to the problems that plagued an otherwise disenfranchised group?

Her answer was to go against the grain, be provocative, irreverent, and tough. It worked and it produced an image of the petite, impeccably dressed congresswoman as an outspoken, audacious, and controversial advocate for the poor and those outside of the mainstream. Although her constituency included others, Waters's focus was primarily on this group, her detractors say, to a fault. As an unapologetic, uninhibited voice for the disenfranchised, she was when she entered Congress and still is without peer, even among the institution's legendary radicals.

Neither euphemistic nor coy about her advocacy, Waters describes herself as the congresswoman who "does not have time to be polite." And she never tires of proving it.

Most notable was her decision during the 102d Congress to invite herself to the White House meeting called by President George Bush in April 1992. It was during the aftermath of the riots in South Central Los Angeles, and Maxine Waters heard on the morning news that the president had called the Speaker of the House, Tom Foley (D-Wash.), and other members of the Congress to the White House to discuss the disturbance. The riots had erupted after an innocent verdict was handed down by an all-white jury in the police beating of black motorist Rodney King.

If the morning news was about the meeting called by the president, the evening news was about the unceremonial presence of the uninvited Waters.

> White males talk about waiting their turn, but African American women don't wait their turn. We help to decide the agenda. . . . I was in the unfortunate situation of being in the middle of a rebellion in Los Angeles. And I had to give some definition to that. I had to give definition, not only in the national media, but in this institution [the Congress]. And when the leadership, for example, decided they would meet, basically white males, to talk about the problem, there were no African Americans from this House included in that meeting at the White House. And so, I defied tradition. I went to the White House uninvited and forced my way in and forced them to have to look at me and to talk with me and to hear what it is I know about my community.[5]

Whether sexist, racist, or partisan, Bush's slight was an affront not only to Waters, but to the rest of black leadership. She was just the only one bold enough to bring it out in the open.

When the Los Angeles riots broke out—the first full-scale riot in nearly twenty-five years—Maxine Waters had been in Congress a little over a year. Lasting thirty-six hours before President George Bush and Governor Pete Wilson deployed twenty-five thousand National Guard troops to end it, the disturbance spread largely due to Los Angeles police chief Darryl Gates's neglect. Gates was attending a political fund-raiser when the looting and fighting broke out. With tensions running high during the trial, it was expected that the police department would have had a contingency plan in place should there be an outbreak of violence following the verdict. He did not, and that inaction cost him his job.

As for America, it was jolted back into the realization that pockets of poverty, discrimination, and lack of opportunity still existed in a country that chose to disregard those conditions. That was Waters's message and her point of view. Obviously it was not a popular one shared by other members of Congress, nor much of the public, who saw the riot as just an opportunity for criminal activity that would not be penalized. Waters further angered an already disillusioned public with her intimation that the violence could spread beyond the confines of South Central, although it did not. She saw the Rodney King verdict as the immediate cause of the "rebellion," but the remote cause had its roots in institutions similar to the Congress, where intractable and entrenched white male power brokers held sway over the lives of poor people. Said Waters:

> This institution has been the domain of white males, for the most part. And because we've always had so few African Americans and so very few African American women, most of what ails us in our communities and most of our concerns were just never debated in this House. And so, I was determined that I would create a platform and forum and that I would ignore the traditions of the House.

She did just that by keeping her version of the events alive and out front through a full-page open letter reprinted in *USA Today,* appearances on national news shows and any outlet she could find to continue telling her story. So much so that after 1992, most of America needed no introduction to the congresswoman "with an attitude" and a reputation for "in your face" politics.

The savvy Waters took no prisoners in her fight for her constituency. Besides representing one of the toughest areas in the country—South Central—her district also included the middle-class Inglewood, Hawthorne, and Gardena districts. With a median income of around $25,000 and a racial mix of 42 percent black, 43 percent Hispanic, and the rest white and Asian, the district was one of the first minority districts, created thirty years prior to Waters's election. It is, however, also one of the nation's most troubled districts.

Depicted in blockbuster movies such as John Singleton's *Boyz N the Hood* and featured regularly on television sets around the world in the controversial gangster rap videos—the district is a place where a violent life leads to an art that imitates it. The violent life, of course, and to some extent, the art and publicity formed the basis for Waters's ability to move through Congress with force, demanding and giving urgency to a response to the urban issues of crime, housing, jobs, training, and respect for the poor.

Inflexible on issues of crime and justice, Waters is one of the few members of Congress who consistently stands up against capital punishment and for the rehabilitation of black youth. In fact, some might conclude that Waters is the only contemporary black leader that the generation of hard-core youth could count on in the halls of Congress to authentically represent their interests. She not only talked about the needs of young people who lived in an increasingly hostile environment, she used her position to act on it and her congressional platform to give legitimacy to their issues.

"We need to help build a bridge to get them back into the mainstream, or to get them in for the first time," Waters said when giving a rationale for funding job-training programs. "Some of them have been dropouts from school in our inner cities since they were 15 and 16, now they're 23, 24 years old. They've never worked a day in their lives."

She was equally adamant on crime:

> Our challenge and our chore is to try and argue the points on the floor and in committee that these are not the answers. America is going to have to look for deeper answers to how to redirect the problems of our cities and even our rural communities where drugs are now creating problems. So, people like me, you know, consider me whatever, a liberal progressive whatever. I'm never going to support a crime bill that kills children. I'm

> never going to support a crime bill that does not recognize the very seri-
> ous problems of our cities and at the same time that we talk about crime,
> we have to talk about an investment—an investment in communities
> and people that will help, not simply divert people from crime, but help
> people feel better about themselves and the fact that they can have an
> opportunity to realize their potential in this country.

Just as Waters would plead the case for young people on the House floor, she would also do it in public and in the press. When a *USA Today* photographer manipulated a front-page photo of a South Central gang member who was cooperating with a gun surrender program to make it appear that he was keeping rather than giving up his weapon, Waters attacked the newspaper and later received space for a full-page layout of an open letter dedicated to the people of her district: "The news media wants to whip us into a frenzy. Did you see the picture that *USA Today* had on its front page? Brothers with guns in their hands with a caption, 'L.A. Uneasy.' It was a bogus, set-up photograph. The brothers thought they were turning in their guns for jobs and thought the photo would help them."[6]

It was an effective act, forceful and typical Maxine Waters; *USA Today* apologized for the photo and disciplined the editor. When she ran for her second term, midway through the campaign she was so confident that she closed her campaign headquarters. Spending only a portion of the funds raised on her direct campaign, she contributed some of her money to other California politicians, such as successful U.S. Senate candidate Barbara Boxer.

She also focused some of her attention that election year on national politics. The year 1992 was not only the "Year of the Woman" but was also the year of the presidential race. George Bush, the incumbent Republican president; Ross Perot, a third-party candidate; and Bill Clinton, the Democratic nominee, had captured the political imagination of Americans. Although Clinton had not soundly convinced many progressive black leaders to support him—particularly after openly antagonizing some by his attack on Jesse Jackson, using an obscure black rap singer, Sister Souljah—his candidacy offered the potential of producing the first Democratic president in twelve years. It left the pragmatic Democratic politician with very little choice other than to support him. Waters was a pragmatic Democrat but not a blindly partisan one.

After endorsing the Clinton ticket at the Democratic National Convention that year, Waters told reporters, "I will never again vote for an all-white male anything." If the Democrats could not produce a ticket with a black or a female by the year 2000, she said she had no intention of supporting any future presidential tickets. With that she proceeded to throw her considerable political capital in the Thirty-fifth District behind Clinton's candidacy, delivering her district to him in landslide proportions. In return, she earned what she told her constituents was a "foot in the door." Her critics say, however, that it also bestowed upon her husband, Sidney Williams, an ambassadorship to the Bahamas.

Whether true or not, President Clinton's appointment of her husband did not buy unquestioned political loyalty to his policies and programs. While Waters would never be so impolitic as to call Bill Clinton "indecisive and insufficiently principled," as U.S. senator Bill Bradley (D-N.J.) is alleged to have done, she did say that he was capable of "double-crossing" African Americans. It was a position that set the tone for her second term in office and his first term in the White House.

Bill Clinton won and so did Maxine Waters. She was reelected to the 103d Congress, joining the largest group of black women ever to enter the House of Representatives. It was a dynamic Congress for Democrats, but it would also be their last as the majority party. With a Democratic president and control of both houses of Congress, they were awash with power, hubris, and invincibility. The president sought out support from black Democrats for his legislative initiatives, but the results were not what he expected. Many broke ranks from the party's president and created their own legislative priorities. Waters was one of them. Three presidential initiatives in the 103d Congress stood out as going against her interests—the Haitian policy, the omnibus anti-crime bill, and the North American Free Trade Agreement (NAFTA).

On the Haitian policy, Waters criticized Clinton for retaining President Bush's position on detaining Haitian refugees. President Bush had been criticized by Clinton during the campaign because he had detained Haitians and not allowed them to enter the United States, classifying them as economic rather than political refugees—a position opposed by black leadership. In May of 1994, Waters joined with Trans-Africa—the lobbyist that successfully awakened the world to the conditions of South African apartheid—which had now taken on the cause of the ousted Haitian president Jean Bertrand Aristide and the plight of thousands of Haitians who were languishing at the Guantanamo Bay Naval Base in Cuba. Trans-Africa's executive director, Randall Robinson, embarked on a hunger strike in protest of the Clinton policy, and Waters, along with Congressman Alcee Hastings (D-Fla.) and Congresswoman Nydia Velazquez (D-N.Y.), chained herself to the White House gate in protest of the administration's policies. She was arrested for demonstrating without a permit. It was not a wasted effort.

Her protest, along with the escalating pressure and publicity of Trans-Africa, forced President Clinton to step up U.S. involvement by bringing about a negotiated solution for the return of Aristide to Haiti. Engaging the help of the former head of the Joint Chiefs of Staff, General Colin Powell, and former president Jimmy Carter, Clinton was able to win a peaceful surrender of the military government that had ousted Aristide, returning him to power and instituting a democratic election.

It also came as no surprise that Congresswoman Waters was against the administration's omnibus anti-crime bill, which expanded the number of crimes that could lead to the death penalty and that allowed teenagers fourteen and older to be treated as adults when convicted of committing violent crimes. Unlike U.S. senator Carol Moseley-Braun—the only black in the Senate—who gave passionate pleas in support of the youthful offender amendment in the Senate version of the crime bill, Waters refused to accept the bill in its form:

> We're in a wild time in America. And the very narrow and almost dishonest response to crime by the white establishment is simply to lock them up, throw the key away, or to kill them. It is unconscionable for

adults, supposedly mature and intelligent people in a democratic society to talk about killing its children. Certainly, we are all pained by crime. We hurt very deeply about what is going on in many of our communities. And if we had a magic wand, we would just make it go away. No matter what the right wing has to say about us that we coddle criminals, that we're not for law and order, they're simply lies. We neither like nor take any pleasure in the fact that children are dying. But we also understand that much of what is going on in our communities is due to extreme poverty, a lack of a country directing resources in ways that will help to alleviate this policy, a lack of concern.

Waters was addressing in 1993 what would become patently evident in the next election in 1994, and that was that the political climate was slowly changing in America and liberalism was being challenged as fiscal and social conservatism was on the rise. She was also saying that she was not a wavering liberal, but it could be concluded that she considered President Bill Clinton to be one based on the policies that he promulgated. Where others saw Clinton as too liberal and needing a nudge to the center, from Waters's perspective he was not firmly liberal enough. More than ever, she found it necessary not to back away from what were becoming unpopular liberal positions. Her pronouncements were strong:

> You simply, whether you have a white community or a black community, cannot have people who are homeless, who are on general relief, who have no income, whose education systems are failing them, where drugs are being allowed into the country in increasingly larger and larger amounts, none of it manufactured in those communities but finding its way into those communities, children with no money in their pockets, lured by the fact that if they sell crack cocaine, they can earn money. Without trying to make excuses for crime, because, really, I would like to believe there are no excuses, except living in the real world, we understand and we know enough about human behavior to understand that people who are hungry enough, will find some food, even if they take somebody else's. People who are angry enough strike out because they don't like themselves.

Waters's protestations notwithstanding, the president's crime bill passed the House and the Senate, and he signed it into law.

When it came to economic development, jobs, training, and justice, it was easy to predict where Waters would vote. She refused to back Clinton in support of NAFTA, because it showed no promise of economic opportunity for people of color. The bill, which would open the borders of America to Mexico and Canada, benefited manufacturers who could now cross the border and open plants using low-wage workers and eliminate the need to adhere to government regulations.

> Well, frankly, there's not much promise of jobs attached to NAFTA. There has been some trading. This President is faced with a deficit ridden economy, he doesn't have a lot to give. Unless there was some very sturdy bridge for minority workers who already have been devastated for 20

years by the flight of jobs from these shores, it would be very difficult for somebody black to endorse NAFTA.

Not every member of the Congressional Black Caucus identified NAFTA with risk-taking. Many changed their minds and voted in favor of NAFTA, just as other members did, reversing themselves after receiving assurances from President Clinton that some of their pet projects would receive favorable attention. Waters would not yield.

The congresswoman was not always opposed to Clinton, and when she was not, he could not have had a stronger partnership. Gun control was an area where she shared the views of the president and where she gave her strongest supportive performances. Whether in committee or on the floor of the House, she would not back down from a fight nor shy away from a controversy on guns and crime.

With national statistics showing that homicide rates among fifteen- to nineteen-year-olds had grown by more than 60 percent in 1993, Waters battled her colleagues who were supportive of and supported by the National Rifle Association (NRA)—a lobbying group that waged costly fights against gun control. The powerful NRA lobby was a sacred cow in the fight against assault weapons and gun control by the Congress. The Democratically controlled House had a few recalcitrants who supported gun control and who could not be persuaded by the hefty campaign contributions that the NRA placed in the coffers of would-be nay voters, but it would be the 104th Republican-controlled Congress that would actually give the NRA the key to the Capitol.

The 103d Congress had been successful in passing the Brady bill, which banned the possession of hand guns. The bill, named after presidential press secretary James Brady, who was injured during an assassination attempt on President Ronald Reagan, had become a symbol of the pro-gun-control movement. The Brady bill had a fighting chance and passed, but the big issue before the 103d Congress was the assault weapons ban provision in the crime bill. The NRA pressured its supporters in the House to kick the provision out of the bill, but in the end they were unsuccessful in the 103d and successful in the 104th.

Waters was an aggressive and vocal opponent of legal assault weapons, since many of them found their way into the hands of inner-city youth, where they were used to settle disputes. These paramilitary weapons had already killed far too many of her constituents. Serving on the Joint Hearings on Gun Violence in the House Select Committee on Children, Youth and Families and the Senate Labor and Human Resources Subcommittee on Children, Family, Drugs, and Alcoholism, Waters questioned more than two hundred people. The assault weapons prohibition was signed into law, racking up another victory for Clinton's legislative agenda, also proving that having Waters in the trenches as an ally was much better than having her on the outside against you.

Clinton counted on her again when the House probed the failure of the Madison Savings and Loan and the suicide of presidential counsel Vince Foster. Republicans questioned the two events under the title of "The Whitewater Investigations," which was the name that came from a real estate deal in which both the president and the first lady had invested. A special prosecutor and congressional hearings, most partisan, spread over a major portion of Clinton's first term in office. Waters was a part of one of the hearings as a member of the House Banking and Financial Services Committee in 1993.

When the hearings became too acrimonious around the testimony of the first lady's special assistant, Margaret (Maggie) Williams—the first black woman to hold such a position—Waters leaned over the table and shouted to the congressman posing the questions, Peter King (R-N.Y.), to "shut up." The next day on the floor of the House, the debate flared up again, this time with an animated Waters telling King that "the day is over when men can intimidate and badger women." King's Republican colleagues came to his aid, but Waters kept on talking against the chair's request that she end her remarks. What followed was another moment of recalcitrance when the sergeant-at-arms was called in threatening to bodily remove Waters from the floor of the House.

She was also firmly against those within black leadership who misinterpreted and misrepresented her constituency. She knew her constituency, and she knew the public that maligned it and could be counted on to go against those in Congress who attacked them. When Congresswoman Cardiss Collins and Senator Carol Moseley-Braun were encouraged by Dr. C. Delores Tucker, president of the National Political Congress of Black Women, to hold hearings on gangster rap music, Waters testified both times in support of the rappers, her constituents. She defended them, promoting a different view than that of Tucker and other leaders. Her position was that the young people who created the music carved out a musical niche from the raw life they lived and that what needed to be changed were the conditions and not the music. The music, which had spread around the world, changed cultures and created a global musical revolution. What Waters did was to get the musicians to support projects for increasing opportunities for those left behind who still had to navigate a life filled with the ebb and flow of drugs, weapons, and death.

In the back of her mind and in the forefront of her politics, Waters was always moving toward training and job opportunities for South Central Los Angeles. One lasting hallmark will always be the tactic that netted the area a $10 million job-training grant following the riots. During the 103d Congress, Waters had not forgotten about the turmoil of the Los Angeles rebellion, and even though President Bush never really provided any support to people or property, but offered solutions to business instead, Waters was determined to do what was necessary to get funds into her district.

She found her chance in 1993, when midwestern members of the House were trying to push through an emergency relief bill for flood-ravaged areas in their districts. Waters attached an amendment onto the flood relief bill requesting $10 million for South Central. The money would be used to provide stipends for young people participating in the job-training programs. To expedite funding from Congress for flood relief, the Clinton administration made a back-door funding arrangement for Waters's project so that the House would be free to vote out the flood-relief legislations without a protracted debate on the amendment. It was the kind of incident for which she was derided by her critics for her tactics, but admired for her tenacity. Waters explained:

> We created the Stipends program for 17 to 30 year olds that would pro-
> vide $100 stipends for those who would re-enroll in school for vocational
> education, for GED, for job training, so that they could have money for
> haircuts and lunch money and the bare necessities while they were trying
> to get themselves into the mainstream. It caused quite a battle here [in
> Congress]. And we ended up, at one point, attaching the stipends program
> idea to the appropriation for the flood victims. Of course, you know,
> many people went absolutely nuts. But it did draw a lot of attention. And
> finally, this administration said, don't worry, we can do it. We can do it.
> And carved out a means by which to do that through the Labor Depart-
> ment, and so we have to keep doing those kinds of things.

These tactics were no substitute for sound legislative proposals, and by the end of
her second term in Congress, Waters had an impressive enough record in this regard to
run for reelection. She had successfully shepherded through Congress and had signed into
law the Gang Prevention and Youth Recreation Act and the Job and Life Skills Improvement Act, which provided $50 million to be appropriated for stipend-based job-training
programs nationwide. For her district, she secured a four-year $7 million Youth Fair
Chance Grant through the Department of Labor. She sponsored a community development banking bill that established a training and technical assistance program and had
successfully pushed through the Congress an expanded debt-relief authorization for
developing African countries.

As a member of the Veterans' Affairs Committee, she introduced the Women's Bureau
bill to create a Center for Women Veterans within the Department of Veteran Affairs (VA),
and she introduced, but was unsuccessful in enacting, the Veterans' Health Improvement
Act of 1993, which if passed would have mandated that the VA provide aggressive treatment to women veterans who were at risk of cardiac disease. The president also signed
into law Waters's bill for a $10 million grant to develop the Vermont Knolls section of
South Central Los Angeles, as well as the aforementioned amendment to establish a new
program of community involvement in bank branch closures. It was a strong and impressive "can do" record and it served her well as she sought reelection in 1994 and won.

Similar in many ways to the indomitable Shirley Chisholm—the first African American woman elected to the Congress—Waters makes no excuses for her attitude or her behavior because she makes a distinction between her Congressional accountability and that of
her colleagues: "People expect a lot. . . . They bring the problems that many white legislators don't have to deal with. But that's okay that they bring them to us, because African
Americans and poor people in general have been turned away from all the systems.
Nobody pays any attention. They're not treated fairly. And people don't answer their
questions." Maxine Waters not only listens to and answers their questions, the recalcitrant
from the Pacific Coast fights their battles in the Congress on the banks of the Potomac.

Chapter 9 **Barbara-Rose Collins**

*From Community Activism
to U.S. Congress*

When I was the state representative, I had my eye on Congress
because politics and government are all about power. The buck stops
here. It was the Congressional Black Caucus that helped to end
Apartheid in South Africa. Anytime I move from one office to another
I try to get to a higher level of power. The ultimate power was in
Congress.

Résumé

Barbara-Rose Collins

Personal

Born   April 13, 1939
Detroit, Michigan

Family   Widowed; two children

Religion   Shrine of the Black Madonna: Pan-African Orthodox

Party   Democrat

Took office   Age 51, January 3, 1991

Education

Attended Wayne State University

Professional/Political Background

1971–1973   Member, Detroit School Board

1975–1982   Representative, Michigan House of Representatives

1982–1990   Member, Detroit City Council

1991–   U.S. House of Representatives

Organizational Affiliations

Gamma Phi Delta Sorority; American Business Women's Association; National Political Congress of Black Women; past board member, Detroit Symphony Orchestra.

Congressional Data

Fifteenth Congressional District of Michigan: Detroit

Committees: Government Operations (renamed Government Reform and Oversight under 104th Congress); Post Office and Civil Service; Public Works and Transportation (renamed Transportation and Infrastructure)

102d Congress: 1991–1992
1990 general election results: 82 percent of the vote

103d Congress: 1993–1994
1992 general election results: 82 percent of the vote

104th Congress: 1995–1996
1994 general election results: 84 percent of the vote

Barbara-Rose Collins

The First African American Woman
Elected to Congress from Michigan

Fifteenth District, Michigan
Democrat
102d–104th Congresses, 1991–1996

"I had a strong antipathy toward black men, except the men I dated and my husband. But with other men, I felt that I could always find jobs and do what I wanted, but my brothers on the street never could," says Congresswoman Barbara-Rose Collins (D-Mich.) about her early political and racial consciousness—the decades before she pronounced that she would come to Congress and "save the black male." "I was very angry with them. I had a lot of inner anger toward black men."[1]

Collins's political rise to the U.S. House of Representatives is inseparable from the transformation of her political and racial consciousness. For the Detroit native, it was a journey that began with her membership in the socially active, nationalist Shrine of the Black Madonna, a church that had a major impact on Collins's life and politics.

For the past quarter of a century, Barbara-Rose Collins, a former purchasing agent for Wayne State University's Physics Department, has been either a state, local, or national elected official representing Detroit. Her political career includes three years on the Detroit School Board, six years in the Michigan state legislature, and nine years on the Detroit City Council, culminating in her historic election to the U.S. House of Representatives in 1990 as the first African American woman elected to Congress from Michigan.

A large-boned, statuesque woman with a radiant smile and luminous almond-shaped eyes—often framed in Kente-cloth patterned eyeglasses—Collins has a history of challenging the status quo. She has consistently moved in the direction of getting government to be more responsive to the needs of the inner city, the poor, and the working class. In the U.S. Congress, hers is a constant voice calling attention to the country's urban ills and the plight of the black male. Although she has been criticized for not instituting an aggressive enough legislative agenda to address the issues she raises, her supporters point to her vocal advocacy alone as essential to keeping the needs of the urban cities alive in the national dialogue. It was a position that became more acute during her third term, in the 104th Congress (1995–1996), when budgets were cut and austerity was the hue and cry of the conservative Republican majority.

However, urban ills and the plight of black males are causes that Collins had to grow to recognize as significant. It happened only after her exposure to the politically active and socially progressive African-centered Pan-African Orthodox Church. Before her exposure to the Shrine of the Black Madonna, Collins's life growing up in Detroit's east side had not prepared her to be receptive to the changes of the 1960s and 1970s, as the black consciousness movement began to take shape around the country.

Even more alien to her than the plight of black men was the rhetoric of the nationalist leadership movement during the 1970s. It was during this period that the country was riveted by the call for black power from such militants as Stokely Carmichael and H. Rap Brown. As she looks back on that era, she recalls:

> I had a very bad opinion of black militants. . . . I thought they were people who did not work, people who did not comb their hair, and people who were not very clean. This was in 1967. Although it was after the 1967 rebellion [Detroit riot], although I argued mightily with my white colleagues in the physics department supporting the rebellion, I was still angry. But I didn't want white people to know that I was angry at the militants.

It was not until she met the Reverend Albert B. Cleage, Jr., pastor of the Shrine of the Black Madonna, that she changed her opinions about black nationalism and African American men. The transformation has been so successful that today Collins is identified as one of the most African-centered members of the Congress and one of the most vocal supporters of efforts to improve the conditions and the plight of black men. The lack of political and racial consciousness resulted in part from her background growing up in Detroit's east side during the early 1940s and 1950s.

The Early Years

Born in Detroit on April 13, 1939, Barbara-Rose Collins grew up in a predominately Polish neighborhood where she was surrounded by an extended family that was accepting and warm. In later years, it would be baffling to hear her white colleagues at Wayne State University describe her neighborhood as a slum or a ghetto, because her memory of home was much different. "I lived in a Polish neighborhood and consequently all of my friends were Polish at that time. When I started going to school, I started to meet black kids like me. The Polish kids went to Catholic school," says Collins, attempting to retrace the roots of her early childhood. "It was a lovely neighborhood on the east side. I would call it middle class; when I was at the university I was told it was a ghetto or a slum. I never thought that. Every year everybody would rush to paint their houses, and we were always proud."

With a wistful look, the congresswoman describes her childhood as one in which she not only gained a lot from her working-class mother and father but also gave a lot back. The eldest of four children, even as a child she would go to school, come home, and teach her newly learned lessons to her parents and siblings. Her vision of those early years is a mixture of a supportive family where she was given assurances of self-worth, options, and opportunities and a neighborhood where there were preferences but not necessarily racism.

As the Polish kids went off to parochial school, Barbara-Rose Collins began her foray into the black world outside of her neighborhood. This time she was the preferred one. She kept a neat and well-groomed appearance, and her father constantly checked with the teacher to make sure she was doing all right. She feels the teachers had a predilection for kids with lighter skin and that she was singled out for special attention. Indeed, even today, Barbara-Rose Collins, in her soft, almost singsong voice, still evokes an image of the teacher's pet:

> Teachers picked their favorites. Unfortunately I believe now that their favorites depended on how you looked. At that time I was fairly light skinned compared to some of the other children, and I had pretty little dresses. I was a part of the little core group of teachers' pets. And because of that I got to go to the symphony every week. Everyone in the school was supposed to take turns, but I got to go every week. I started my piano lessons at the age of four. So I already had a proclivity toward classical music. I got a very well-rounded education at that school.

As the years have gone on, she sees that special attention as having exposed her to opportunities that the other children did not have, such as attendance at concerts, learning to appreciate classical music as well as learning to play an instrument. Today, in addition to an enjoyment of classical music, she plays the harp and paints for relaxation. This special treatment and exposure Collins also credits with giving her the kind of confidence she needed to move forward and achieve. What Collins began to realize later was that her special treatment came at the expense of the other black kids who did not receive it because of the arbitrary standards of the teachers.

According to Collins, even though her special nurturing home and school environment undergirded her success as a member of the larger society, it also stunted her understanding and awareness of her own African American heritage and its import in the United States. Collins believes that on this score she was cheated. Instead of forming her own opinions about the intense dynamics and diversity of the civil rights movement, which was in full swing during her early adult years, she relied instead, she says, on the mainstream white media and the majority culture to define what was acceptable and what was not. It is through this filter that she grew to be suspicious of black nationalism and the black-power movement, leading her to join in the condemnation of black men.

Undoing the miseducation about the black experience began while Collins was working at Wayne State University and after she had separated from her husband, Gary. Gary and Barbara-Rose Collins were married in 1958 and had two children—Cynthia and Christopher. The couple separated in the late 1960s. In 1972, Gary Collins died. Before her husband's death, Collins had already become a single working mother, holding a job as a purchasing agent in the Physics Department of Wayne State University in Detroit.

Working at the university was prestigious for a black person in a city where most were blue-collar factory workers. So that even though Collins was not a college graduate, she was considered to be middle class by blacks in her community. She lived near the campus, having moved away from the neighborhood where her extended family remained. Separated from her husband and dating on occasion, Collins recalls one particular Christmas Eve party in the home of a couple who belonged to the Pan-African Orthodox Church, the Shrine of the Black Madonna.

> All these militants came into this house who had been on television and the house was so middle class. And the owner had an African room that he was very proud of. And I was thinking what kind of people were these. Because they didn't fit the stereotype that I had acquired from reading the newspapers. They were just such normal people and so then at midnight they were giving gifts. And saying I will see you in church. I said, "Is this a church party?" And it was a church party. They invited me to the Shrine of the Black Madonna.

The Shrine of the Black Madonna is a Pan-African Orthodox Church in Detroit that has a historic place in the Afro-centric movement of the 1960s and 1970s. Started by the Reverend Albert Cleage, Jr., the church was founded as a result of a movement by the pastor to reaffirm and reclaim the presence of Africa in the early Christian Church and in so doing to reflect on that relationship with the African American journey through Christianity.

In the early 1960s, the church attracted many of the major militant and black power leaders, such as Stokely Carmichael and H. Rap Brown, who would come and chastise the black middle class for moving away from the community. It was a unique situation. Very few avenues were open for the mingling of the militant leaders of the time with the black middle class. What Cleage was able to do was to bring together the resources of the black community with its problems in an effort to find internal solutions. He did it through religion and historical perspective.

In his 1968 book, *The Black Messiah,* Cleage writes: "Basic to our struggle and the revitalization of the black church is the simple fact that we are building a totally new self-image. Our rediscovery of the Black Messiah is a part of our rediscovery of ourselves. We could not worship a Black Jesus until we had torn off the shackles of self-hate. We could not follow a black Messiah in the tasks of building a black nation until we had found the courage to look back beyond the slave block and the slave ship without shame."[2]

It was this message that Barbara-Rose Collins heard while attending the Shrine of the Black Madonna, and it was this message that she fought against accepting as a part of her personal philosophy, because it went against everything that she had believed about herself and about black people. "Mentally, I fought him all the way as I was getting educated. Finally I did join the church and finally I did get angry at the fact that I had missed out on so much. I never saw Malcolm X because I let the newspapers tell me that he was a violent man and evil. I just started putting my life in context and my eyes were opened."

Collins was in the right church. The Shrine of the Black Madonna was not just talk. It was an activist church with political clout that defined social justice and change and worked for it. The church was and remains involved in the lives of the community through support of grassroots organizing and involvement in the body politic. It also serves as a powerful base as well as a strong spiritual foundation for supporting political candidates and progressive change.

For Collins, the Shrine of the Black Madonna became one of the single most significant aspects of her life in public service—from her first seat on the Detroit School Board to her congressional bid, the church has been the impetus for her decisions to run for office and has been the reason that she declined to run in other cases, when Cleage was not supportive of her.

The Political Odyssey

Her first foray into political life was to run for a seat on Region I of the Detroit School Board. The school board was a natural for Collins. She had been battling with her daughter's school from the time she moved back into her old community and transferred her daughter from a private school to a neighborhood school—the same school that Collins had attended as a child. However, where she had been nurtured and given a broad and strong education, her daughter was being given a remedial compensatory education. Collins expressed interest in her daughter's education. But instead of treating her like a concerned parent, the administrators looked upon her as an intrusive, unwanted nuisance. One school official went so far as to contact her employer, Wayne State University, to see how it was that she could afford to take so much time away from her job to visit the school. It could have cost her the job, but rather than being intimidated, she was emboldened and politicized.

"That would have done one of two things: gotten me fired or reprimanded, but it would also remove a concerned parent from the school system. So when they asked me to run for school board, I didn't want to, but I did." It was 1971, and Barbara-Rose Collins, with the urging and support of Cleage, started her political career. Hers was a classic first campaign. She hand-printed her first campaign materials, walked door-to-door seeking out voters, and she won the election.

Once on the school board, she made changes. She helped institute community-based parent involvement, required that children have homework and that the school remove the comic-book-style reading material from the classroom. Using the knowledge of purchasing gained from Wayne State, she refuted arguments waged by the school administration that they could not gain adequate textbooks. It ruffled some feathers with the teachers, but Collins wanted to restore the schools to the standards of excellence that she remembered from her childhood.

The pace and energy required by Collins to hold down a job, rear two children, and spend long nights deliberating on the school board took its toll on her health. And as she was entering her third year on the board and still working in the purchasing office, she lost her eyesight, the result of stress. It was a condition she says was caused by a lack of oxygen to the brain. It also was enough to frighten her, and for the time being enough to keep her from seeking reelection. That was in 1973.

She regained her eyesight, however, and was once again being encouraged by Cleage to run for public office. This time he suggested that she run for Detroit City Council. She did and won the primary but lost the general election. "Then, I ran for a couple of special elections and two months later I won the state legislative seat. I went door-to-door. I pulled an upset and beat the incumbent."

Although Cleage had been responsible for getting her interested in politics, by now she was hooked on elected office and wanted to move as far as possible. It was 1975, and Collins was headed for the Michigan House of Representatives. When she speaks of her days in the Michigan legislature, it is an opportunity to tell one of her favorite stories:

> My first victory was to defeat a bill that the speaker put in. It would change the time and I spoke against it because it meant that kids would be going to school in the dark. And I was very much against that because a dear friend's daughter had been raped and it was in the daylight. And I went to the speaker and told him that I would not support him. I drafted this horrible speech that said, "Did you know that your daughters and mothers would be raped on the streets, if this bill is passed."

Collins recounts how the legislators, who were usually not accustomed to heated debates on such a minor issue, became angry with the Speaker for even offering the bill and defeated it. It began a string of legislative successes for state representative Collins. She includes in her list of successes a fair housing bill, sexual harassment legislation, and a bill to equalize treatment of women with that of men receiving pension benefits. The latter bill became the law of the land when the U.S. Supreme Court ruled favorably, upholding the Michigan law.

Six years in the statehouse and three on the school board had transformed the former concerned parent into a politician who had now set her sights on higher office. Saying that she always looked for the office that was the next highest with increasingly more power, Collins, bored with the state legislature, set her sights on Congress.

Her first attempt was during the term of Congressman Charles Diggs of Detroit.

Diggs, the son of a prominent Detroit family, was being investigated by the U.S. Justice Department for fraud. The investigation eventually ended up with an indictment resulting in his imprisonment. Once the indictment was handed down, Collins made it known that she wanted to run for the seat. This time she ran into an unexpected roadblock.

"I wanted to run, but Coleman Young and my minister had a man they wanted in office; it was George Crockett. I thought I could beat him and I was going to run anyway," says Collins of her dashed ambitions. George Crockett, a Democratic stalwart and labor lawyer, was supported by the powerful Detroit mayor, Coleman Young, and by Collins's own mentor, the Reverend Albert Cleage. It was a rude awakening for the woman who had entrusted her political ambitions and future to her religious leader.

Disillusioned by the lack of support from her political mentors, she did not run for Congress. Instead, in 1982 she decided to run for the Detroit City Council. It was closer to home, and she could cultivate her ambitions to move to Washington from a different vantage point. It was also a time of political liberation for her. She came up against Mayor Coleman Young again.

While on the city council, she decided to make changes to the power paradigm, making the council a stronger and more accountable body. The first thing that she worked on was the development of an accounting mechanism so that the council would not remain a rubber stamp for the wishes of the mayor, but rather would act more responsibly as the oversight entity for the mayor's expenditures and collections. Mayor Young was not at all enthused about her innovations, but she insisted on continuing to improve upon the system of checks and balances, creating an ongoing friction between herself and the mayor.

"When I got on the city council, I found that it was a weak city council. So Coleman Young and I had clashed immediately," she has said. Collins claims that even though the newspapers called her a puppet for the mayor, it was not true. She respected him, but she fought against having the council rubber stamp his actions without some form of accountability. As for the newspapers, at that time she says that the *Detroit Free Press* had "been an enemy" of hers for a long time. "To them," says the representative, "I was an abomination." Whatever the paper thought of Collins, it was undeniable by this time that the voters wanted her. She had a strong grassroots base in the community and she was a formidable political opponent.

Collins served on the Detroit City Council from 1982 to 1991. During that time two significant events had an impact on her life and her political career. In 1988 she decided once again to make it known that she wanted to go to Congress. This time she refused to take "no" for an answer. Saying that she was "tired of waiting for Crockett to retire," she went up against the congressman in 1988 and lost by only eight points. She warned him that she would be coming back in 1990 without the "velvet gloves." In the meantime, she ran for reelection to the Detroit City Council, but was almost derailed by a personal tragedy. In 1989 her son was arrested and sent to prison for armed robbery. It was a personal setback that Collins finds difficult to talk about. But what she does talk about is the support she received from women in the city of Detroit who prayed her through her reelection bid.

> I ran into trouble with my son, which I promised him I would not speak about any longer. . . . But that devastated me and I was running for re-election. I could not speak; I had lost my voice. The women in the community got me reelected. They would come to my apartment and pray over me. They prayed me back into office.

Collins was returned to the city council, where she patiently awaited the next chance to run for Congress. It came in 1990, when Crockett announced his retirement. She immediately became the front-runner in the Democratic primary. With a firm constituency base and a hands-on political style, the familiar politician was expected to win and win with a mandate. She received 81 percent of the vote in the general election, taking her place in history as the first African American woman elected to Congress from the state of Michigan.

The Congressional Years

In 1991, when Barbara-Rose Collins entered the 102d Congress, she along with Delegate Eleanor Holmes Norton (D-D.C.) and Congresswoman Maxine Waters (D-Calif.), joined veteran Representative Cardiss Collins (D-Ill.). It was the largest group of black women in Congress since the early 1970s. Collins entered with an ambitious legislative agenda. Announcing her intention to "save the black male," institute an urban agenda, and create economic opportunities for Detroit, she set forth a broad and unattainable legislative program.

While she never achieved the first two objectives, she did manage to get some funding into Detroit during her first term in Congress. As a member of the Public Works and Transportation Committee, she was able to successfully get funding for Detroit when it was designated as a federal empowerment zone.

During the 103d Congress, Collins introduced the "Unremunerated Work Act of 1993." The legislation, which was applauded by major women's groups, was lampooned by financial writers, who felt that it was an unenforceable and unrealistic endeavor to try to attach value to work in the home. The legislation called for an economic mechanism for calculating housework, which was primarily performed by women, as a part of the gross national product. The bill, which received ample press coverage, never made it out of committee.

Collins was a lot more visible in the 103d Congress, the year that the number of black women in the House expanded to nine. She was a part of the loyal Democrats who supported most of the bills put forth by first-term president Bill Clinton. Although she initially voted against the administration's omnibus anti-crime bill–because of the provisions that expanded the number of offenses covered by the death penalty and a controversial provision that would send away to prison for life anyone who was convicted of three felonies–she eventually supported a revised version. She voted against the North American Free Trade Agreement, and along with the other black women in Congress, she voted against the Hyde Amendment, which would prevent poor women from having abortions using Medicare funds.

When Collins went back home for reelection to her third term in 1994, her old Thirteenth Congressional District was now the Fifteenth and included a new blue-collar, black constituency. Detroit was depopulating, as it were, causing her to lose a considerable portion of her original district following the 1990 census and subsequent reapportionment because people were leaving the depressed urban center of the city.

As a result, her former congressional district was redrawn and relabeled the Fifteenth Congressional District, adding the sections of River Rouge and Ecorse—both blue-collar, black communities—to the predominantly white Grosse Pointe and Hamtramck. Collins's district was still predominately minority, with a 26 percent white population, 70 percent black, and most of the remainder Hispanic. With the new communities added, however, future elections would depend upon Collins's ability to engage a new constituency unfamiliar with her early political beginnings. Although she won her third term handily with 84 percent of the vote, serious accusations about her competency were raised during the primary by challenger Tom Barrow. These were added to other potentially damaging accusations that would plague Collins throughout the 104th Congress. From the very beginning of her tenure in her long-sought congressional seat, she had a hard time gaining the momentum she needed to become an effective legislator. Her first scandal came shortly after being sworn in to her first term, when she confessed to campaign financing irregularities. She admitted her wrongdoing and paid the requisite fine.

Collins was known for having a disproportionately high staff turnover, and one incident that occurred during the 104th Congress seemed to spotlight her vulnerability on that issue. It concerned an allegation that she had fired a gay staff member after finding out that his roommate had died from AIDS. In the process of his official complaint to the Office of Fair Employment Practices, the staffer accused the congresswoman of using astrology as a determinant of employment suitability.

The latter claim was not acted upon, but the first one was settled by the Office of Fair Employment Practices for less than $50,000. However, on the heels of the settlement, the congresswoman received additional bad news. The Justice Department was investigating an alleged misuse of scholarship funds designated for inner-city students. Collins was accused of using the funds for personal use. As the Justice Department moved forward, she quietly engaged private counsel to fight the charges and set her sights on pushing forward a five-prong legislative program and bringing into focus a more realistic agenda for issues affecting the urban centers and the restitution of the black male.

"I came to Congress to get money for Detroit and I did that in my first year," said Collins about her congressional accomplishments and future objectives. "When I came here I said I wanted to save the black male. Well that was rather superfluous. Now I want to save the black family. I formed a caucus to do that. If you save the family you have the children all in one. Regrouping now is what I am doing to get back again."

Collins's biggest challenge was trying to balance such an ambitious agenda while cooperating with the investigations into her finances by the Federal Elections Commission, the U.S. Attorney's Office, and the House Ethics Committee, a cloud that threatens any legacy that she might leave. In the summer of 1996, she lost the Democratic primary.

Part Three

The U.S. Senate

Chapter 10

Carol Moseley-Braun

Moving from Symbol to Substance

I have a special interest in racial issues. I'm African American. It goes without saying that I have a special interest in gender issues. I'm a female. And there's precious few of us on the Senate floor at this point. So, if anything, I think, part of what I'm here to do is to be a legislator, a top-drawer legislator and, in so doing, give this body, the benefit of the experiences and knowledge, frankly, that I bring to the Senate.

Résumé

Carol Moseley-Braun

Personal

Born August 16, 1947
      Chicago, Illinois

Family Divorced; one child

Religion Catholic

Party Democrat

Took office Age 45, January 5, 1993

Education

B.A. University of Illinois, 1969

J.D. University of Chicago, 1972

Professional/Political Background

1972–1977 Prosecutor, Chicago

1978–1988 Representative, Illinois House of Representatives

1989–1992 Cook County recorder of deeds

1993– U.S. Senate

Selected Awards/Organizational Affiliations

U. S. Department of Justice Special Achievement Award; Best Legislator, Independent Voters of Illinois; Alpha Kappa Alpha Sorority.

Congressional Data

Committees: Banking, Housing, and Urban Affairs; Judiciary; Finance

103d Congress: 1993–1994

1992 general election results: 55 percent of the vote

104th Congress: 1995–1996

105th Congress: 1997–1998

Carol Moseley-Braun

The First African American Woman Elected to the United States Senate

Illinois
Democrat
103d Congress–present, 1993–

Carol Moseley-Braun, the first African American woman elected to the U.S. Senate was the quintessential symbol of the 1992 Year of the Woman. She had the right background as a former Illinois state representative; the right opponent, Senator Alan Dixon, a pro-Thomas Democrat; and as a crossover candidate with proven interracial appeal, she had the right constituency. The feminists and the African American women's political movements emerged as strong supporters of the Chicago attorney-turned-politician.

Chicago machine politics had produced more African American political firsts than any other city, primarily due to its strong ward politics and politically active black community. Its first black mayor, Harold Washington, who was a political mentor to Moseley-Braun, was one of a dozen African Americans from Chicago who had been elected to the U.S. House of Representatives. Among the others, there were other historic claims. Cardiss Collins, elected to the House of Representatives in 1973, had served in Congress longer than any other African American woman—twenty-three years. Oscar DePriest, a Republican, was elected to Congress in 1929 and was the first black to be elected following the end of Reconstruction. Senator Moseley-Braun had a tremendous political legacy behind her own historical achievements.

The Early Years

Moseley-Braun was a Chicago success story. Born to Joseph and Edna Moseley in Chicago on August 16, 1947, she had a mixed economic experience growing up. She was the oldest of four children, and her father, who had dreams of being a successful jazz musician, worked instead as a Chicago policeman. Her mother was a medical technician. It was a childhood that created a reservoir of desire for something more. It was also the stuff of legends. When her mother and father were together, she enjoyed the working middle-class lifestyle that the two parents could provide her. However, money was not enough. Her father took out some of his own frustrations on Carol, and although she does not openly talk about the nature of his actions toward her, she does say, "I had to grow up fast."[1]

In her mid-teens, when her mother and father had separated, she moved with her mother and the three other siblings to live with her grandmother. The neighborhood was markedly different, earning its nickname "bucket of blood," because of the fights and stabbings that occurred routinely.

A graduate of Chicago public schools and colleges, Moseley-Braun received her undergraduate degree from the University of Illinois in 1969 and her J.D. from the University of Chicago in 1972. While in law school, she met and eventually married, Michael Braun, also a lawyer.

Following law school she went to work as a prosecutor in the U.S. Attorney's Office from 1972 until she entered politics. In 1977 she gave birth to Matthew, her only child, and a year later, with the encouragement from her Hyde Park neighbors, she launched her first campaign.

The Political Odyssey

In 1978, Moseley-Braun ran for a seat in the Illinois House of Representatives and won. Victorious on her first foray into elected politics, her political career from that point on had only a few setbacks, which were quickly overshadowed by successes. She served for a decade in the Illinois House, where she was known for her legislative leadership in sponsoring progressive bills on education and her ability to build successful coalitions.

She introduced legislation that barred the state of Illinois from investing funds in South Africa until apartheid was abolished. She filed and won the reapportionment case that affirmed the "one man, one vote" principle in Illinois and sponsored bills to ban discrimination in housing and private clubs. For her legislative leadership she earned for each of her ten years in the legislature, the award for "Best Legislator" given by the Independent Voters of Illinois–Independent Precinct Organization.

Her political ally while in the state legislature was Mayor Harold Washington of Chicago, who selected her in 1983 as the city's floor leader in the legislature, a position that required her to spearhead legislation that supported the city's housing, education, budget, and other municipal needs. On her own, she became the first black and the first woman to serve as assistant majority leader in the Illinois House. During her ten-year stay in the legislature, her accomplishments were significant, but so were her setbacks. In 1986 she mourned the death of her brother, who died of a drug overdose. That same year her interracial marriage to Michael Braun ended in divorce and her mother suffered a stroke that would eventually lead to nursing home care. On the political front, she looked to expand her horizons and sought the post of Illinois lieutenant governor, but her ambitions were eclipsed by Washington, who blocked her selection. Despite her past performance on behalf of the mayor and her party loyalty, he refused to endorse her.

In 1987, after a brief period of political mourning and what she calls a religious experience, she ran for Cook County recorder of deeds. She won and became the first African American to serve in a countywide elected position. As impressive as her victory, was her ability to head a crossover ticket with appeals across racial and ethnic lines. The ticket was dubbed the "Dream Team" because of its unique character, emerging from Cook County's highly segregated politics.

As her star began to rise, so did her political tribulations, which were magnified by increased publicity and press exposure. While serving as recorder of deeds, for example, she moonlighted as a lobbyist and lawyer, thus giving her critics cause to look beyond her novel election success. They claimed possible impropriety when she received a lucrative municipal bond contract from the city of Chicago. It was the kind of dichotomy that would haunt her throughout her political career. For all of her freshness as a politician of the new school, she looked as though she were a politician of the old school of perks and privilege. Some viewed her as a politician with a dual agenda—one was the successful identity candidate and politician who espoused progressive ideas and represented the ambitions and aspirations of women and of blacks; and the second was that of an age-old Chicago pol who took advantage of her political position for personal ends.

When Moseley-Braun launched her campaign for the U.S. Senate, she began with great promise and minor problems, which would overshadow an otherwise remarkable movement into national political office. She embodied the change that the country sought following the Clarence Thomas confirmation hearings, and she was seen as one who represented the struggle of feminists and the yearning of African Americans for a presence in the Senate. Heavily courted by the feminist movement and spurred by her own political ambition, she threw her hat into the ring for the seat held by Democratic incumbent Alan Dixon. Looking back on the event, she is a lot more coy than political observers are about her decision-making process.

> I was going to leave government and go into the private sector when, literally, a draft started for me to run. People started calling me and writing me letters, even sending unsolicited checks for me to run following the Senate going on television around the confirmation of Justice Thomas. This was even before we knew about Anita Hill and the sexual harassment issue.
>
> From the very beginning, I started getting calls from people who were concerned that the Senate was not representative of America, and they asked me to run. And at first, I kind of resisted the call, I resisted the draft. And then one day, I was sitting with my son over dinner, and talking with him about it, because, you know, any time you run for office, it affects your family. And I asked him what did he think. And after he asked me what my credentials and qualifications for office were. He was fifteen. After he took out his yellow pad and started asking me questions, "Well, what's your platform?" He then said, "Well Mom," he says, "I think you

should go for it, because you know, your generation has left this world
worse off than you found it." And when he said that, I was like, stunned.
And it was like, oh no, that's not true.

And so we sat over dinner, talking about whether or not my generation had left things worse off than we found it. And every time I would
point out something that we had done that was positive and good, he
would come back with something that was messed up. And the more he
talked, the more it occurred to me that if I'm going to be in government, then I ought to try to make a contribution, I ought to try to be
relevant, I ought to try to make a difference. And so I decided at that
point to go for it.[2]

Not everyone was as encouraging as her son. Doubts expressed by an Illinois
Democrat, Senator Paul Simon, were probably the most troubling because of his liberal
reputation and his public calls for diversity in the Senate. Simon told her that she
should "wait until either Al [Dixon] or I retire, then it will be time for you to run." After
she won the primary, Simon publicly apologized for his statements, but it stood as a
reminder to her that she had an uphill battle even within her own party.

Her victory in the primary was remarkable. With 38 percent of the vote, she
defeated Dixon (35 percent) and Al Hofeld, a Chicago attorney (27 percent). The momentum created by the primary swept her into the general election and onto the national political scene. In November, in spite of campaign mishaps and a serious scandal involving a
reimbursement owed to the state Medicaid program, Carol Moseley-Braun defeated the
Republican candidate, Richard Williamson, a prominent Illinois businessman.

The Congressional Years

A tidal wave of goodwill and optimism from around the country
followed when she was sworn in to the 103d Congress on January 3, 1993. She became
one of six women serving in the U.S. Senate during that session, and along with
Dianne Feinstein (D-Calif.) opted for a seat on the Judiciary Committee, more out of
symbolism than desire. Because the previous, all-male Judiciary Committee had
questioned Anita Hill during the Clarence Thomas hearings, the presence of two
women, one an African American, was good for the new image of the more diversified Senate.

Soon the senator from Illinois captivated the nation with a rare show of political
passion and courage. With tenacity and persuasive oratorical skills, she moved the Senate beyond ordinary debate on July 22, 1993, when she launched a filibuster over the
passage of the United Daughters of the Confederacy (UDC) amendment to the National
Service bill. It was long to be remembered as the event that introduced Senator Carol
Moseley-Braun to the nation and introduced the Senate to the meaning of diversity.

The UDC filibuster was a defining moment for her because it marked the distinction between Carol Moseley-Braun the symbol, an icon of the 1992 Year of the Woman, and the substance of Carol Moseley-Braun, the U.S. senator.

When asked what was her most significant moment during her first session of Congress, she readily admitted that it was the UDC debate:

> There was a real positive, almost euphoria among the body, among the members of this body immediately following that vote. And that sense of goodwill, that sense of "we've done the right thing," really kind of hung around for awhile. I wound up thanking my colleagues in the Democratic caucus a couple of days after the vote, thanking them for their support. They were just beaming. They just felt so good about what transpired there. They felt good about the fact that it really had been an extraordinary moment.

It was an extraordinary moment, indeed, and an emotional one, not just on the floor of the Senate but behind the scenes as well. In this one event the converging influences of a hostile press and powerful lobbyists intersected with the shifting political climate of the Senate, producing a moment that was best described by New York's Democratic senator, Daniel Patrick Moynihan.

"An epiphany," explained Senator Moynihan, "is a sudden shining through of a hidden truth."[3] Moynihan was not addressing a religious convention, nor describing a biblical phenomenon. Rather, he was standing in the chamber of the U.S. Senate giving definition to the transformation taking place in front of him. A normally stoic Senate debate had just turned into a passionate confrontation on the historical remnants of America's most divisive era—the Civil War. The debate was made all the more poignant because of the active presence and evident heartfelt oratory of the Senate's first black member in over a decade, Moseley-Braun.

> I really had not wanted to have to do this because in my remarks I believe that I was restrained and tempered. I talked about the committee procedure. I talked about the lack of germaneness of this amendment. I talked about how it was not necessary for this organization to receive the design patent extension which was an extraordinary extension of an extraordinary act to begin with. What I did not talk about and what I am constrained to talk about with no small degree of emotion is the symbolism of what this vote means. . . . So I turned to my colleague, Dianne Feinstein. You know, I am really stunned by how often and how much the issue of race, the subject of racism, comes up in this U.S. Senate, comes up in this body and how I have to, on many occasions, as its only African American here, constrain myself to be calm, to be laid back to talk about these issues in very intellectual non-emotional terms, and that is what I do on a regular basis. That is part and parcel of my daily existence.[4]

Moseley-Braun's angst had been aroused because the Senate had just voted 52 to 48 to continue the practice of placing its seal on a logo that contained the Confederate flag.

The freshman senator naively thought that she had squelched the amendment in the Judiciary Committee but was outmaneuvered by the arch conservative senator Jesse Helms (D-N.C.), who strategically attached the United Daughters of the Confederacy amendment to President Bill Clinton's popular National Service Act.

The amendment, introduced by Helms, renewed the patent for the insignia for the UDC. Traditionally, every fourteenth year since the 1800s, the Senate voted on the UDC's petition to extend its design patent so that the nonprofit organization could continue its practice of using the Senate seal. The UDC was a twenty-five-thousand-member organization composed of white women who traced their roots and ancestry back to Confederate soldiers in the Civil War. Southern senators consistently supported the petitions throughout the years, winning approval each time with little or no opposition. This year, Helms, working in tandem with another avid southern supporter, Senator Strom Thurman (R-S.C.), first tried to introduce the amendment in the Senate Judiciary Committee; but Senator Moseley-Braun blocked the bill and kept it from moving out of the committee into the full Senate.

This was the second incident in one day in which Moseley-Braun had to engage in debate about race. In addition to the UDC debate in the afternoon, that morning she forced her Republican colleague on the Judiciary Committee to apologize for his comments regarding slavery. Both incidents were around issues that most people thought would never be discussed in much detail in the U.S. Senate in 1993—slavery and the Civil War.

For Moseley-Braun it was a day to challenge symbolism and tradition around the country's unhealed wounds of racism. Although her very presence as a black senator representing a predominantly white state was a sign that healing, however slow, was taking place, there was still a lot of work to be done in the Senate. Almost every image that day carried the symbolism of the breaking away from tradition, whether major or minor. She was at the center of that change. Even the pantsuit she wore was a victory of sorts. Earlier in the year, she had made news when she became the first woman to wear a pair of pants on the Senate floor, rejecting the dress code of the few women who served in the upper chamber. This moment was the latest snapshot pointing to the erosion of the traditions brought about by the 110 newcomers to the 103d Congress (1993–1994). Among them were the six women and one Native American who had already changed the gender and racial composition of the once exclusively white male club. Here she was on the verge of changing another senatorial tradition.

"When the issue of the design patent extension for the United Daughters of the Confederacy first came up, I looked at it. I did not make a big deal of it. It came as part of the work of the Judiciary committee," said Moseley-Braun, giving some background in the prelude to the debate, "I said, well, I am not going to vote for that. When I announced I was not going to vote for it, the chairman, as is his due, began to poll the members. We talked about it, and I found myself getting drawn into a debate that I frankly never expected. Who would have expected a design patent for the Confederate flag?"[5]

As she recounted the history of how the amendment made its way from the Judiciary Committee to the floor of the Senate, Moseley-Braun watched as senators began converging on the chamber, meandering from desk-to-desk asking each other about the sudden caustic tone of the debate. Focused on the issue and determined to maintain control of the filibuster, she refused to yield to any of her colleagues, except for those discussing the United Daughters of the Confederacy amendment. An uncharacteristic hostility pervaded the normally civil Senate chamber when Helms accused Moseley-Braun of being confused about the flag on the insignia. He implied that the flag was not the Confederate flag. Placing a poster on his desk with an enlarged representation of the insignia, Helms criticized her for mistakenly identifying the flag on the design as a Confederate flag, although he knew she was correct.

> And there are those in this body who say this really is not the Confederate flag. I did my research, and I looked it up as I am wont to do, and guess what? That is the real Confederate flag. The thing we see all the time and are accustomed to is the battle flag. In fact, there is some history on this issue. . . . This flag is the real flag of the Confederacy. If there is anybody in this chamber, anybody, indeed anybody in this world that has a doubt that the Confederate effort was around preserving the institution of slavery, I am prepared to and I believe history is prepared to dispute them to the nth. There is no question but that the battle was fought to try to preserve our Nation, to keep the States from separating themselves over the issue of whether or not my ancestors could be held as property, as chattel, as objects of commerce and trade in this country. And people died.[6]

An exasperated and incredulous Carol Moseley-Braun was challenging another colleague for the second time in one day over the issue of slavery. Just hours earlier, she had a heated exchange with Senate Judiciary member, Republican Orrin Hatch of Utah. Hatch attempted to engage Judge Ruth Bader Ginsburg—President Clinton's nominee for associate justice of the U.S. Supreme Court—in a debate about abortion. A prolife senator, Hatch used the Senate Judiciary Committee hearings as a platform for espousing his views on abortion. He was not unique in this respect; senators from both sides of the aisle tried to force nominees for the courts to reveal a position on abortion.

However, Moseley-Braun's attack on Hatch was not about his political position or posturing, but about the example he chose to use to make his point. Hatch started comparing *Roe v. Wade* to the *Dred Scott* decision. The comparison held that each decision established a right that had no basis in the Constitution. *Roe v. Wade,* according to Hatch, established a false right to choose abortion, just as *Dred Scott* gave slave owners a false right to own human beings as property.

Before Hatch could finish his statement, Moseley-Braun called for a point of personal privilege, a procedure that allows a senator to depart from the official protocol and introduce a personal statement for the record. She called the line of questioning personally offensive and said that it was difficult to sit in the committee and hear an intellectual defense of slavery. Hatch attempted to restate his position and protested that he was misunderstood by Moseley-Braun. He said what he really meant was that he described the *Dred Scott* ruling as the worst case in the history of the court and likened it to the false interpretation of the constitutional rights implicit in the *Roe v. Wade* abortion decision.

Hatch, whose urbane rhetorical style was last used to vilify Anita Hill, protested that his was a simple example that had no overtones of pejorative racial animus, but Moseley-Braun would not accept his explanation, only his apology. Once again, the sedate setting of the red-carpeted committee room was shattered by a rancorous discussion of race. Except this time the debate was behind the Judiciary Committee table, not in front of it, as it had been during the Clarence Thomas nomination hearings. Eventually, Hatch recanted, closing out what had the potential of becoming a protracted debate on slavery. As it turned out, the protracted debate took place in the Senate Chamber not the committee room, and with Helms not Hatch.

It was shortly after the Hatch encounter that Moseley-Braun, while still in the Judiciary Committee meeting, received the message about the Senate's vote on the United Daughters of the Confederacy amendment. With the Hatch encounter still fresh in her mind, she left the Judiciary Committee and rushed over to the Senate Chamber.

Now, as she confronted Senator Jesse Helms, she was pushing to reverse the vote to give the UDC the distinction and prestige derived from the use of the Senate's stamp of approval. To reverse the decision, she went beyond the banality of politically correct speech—and to the fundamental issue of the Senate's position on the racially explosive and divisive issue.

The Senate should have been forewarned of the potential for this kind of clash of cultures. The diversity sought and brought about by the 1992 election meant that "business as usual" on race and gender issues was a thing of the past. Gender, race, and ethnicity were issues that the Senate would have to confront and deal with in order to maintain the civility it was used to as a result of homogeneity. This was the change sought by the 1992 election—the creation of a more diversified Congress that would integrate in a constructive and healing manner the experiences of marginalized Americans.

Thus, it was not just the insignia or the right of the UDC to exist and continue to carry out its mission; it was the credibility and integrity of the U.S. Senate that was at stake. Would it continue to be a vehicle for sanctioning a symbol of racial divisiveness that still resonated with the painful experiences of three-and-a-half centuries of slavery; or would it abandon tradition and reverse the vote in deference to the Senate's new African American presence? As she said in a louder than normal voice:

> More Americans died in the Civil War than any war we have ever gone through since. People died over the proposition that indeed these United States stood for the proposition that every person was created equal without regard to race. That we are all American citizens. . . . I am getting excited, because quite frankly, that is the very issue. The issue is

whether or not Americans such as myself who believe in the promise of this country, who feel strongly and who are patriots in this country, will have to suffer the indignity of being reminded time and time again, that at one point in this country's history we were human chattel. We were property. We could be traded, bought and sold.[7]

As is evident, her deliberations addressed not only the subject of racism, but of inclusion and quality of citizenship for black Americans. The historical import of Moseley-Braun's filibuster is found in this statement. The profound response to the question: when will African Americans become unquestioned and unquestionably American? was the dialogue underlying major issues traversing the nation in the early 1990s. From the rollback of civil rights gains to the debate over multiculturalism and affirmative action, her indignation spoke to a nation of patriots—African Americans—who wanted to know when they would become real Americans. It was a highly moral question being posed around a seemingly innocuous amendment. However, there was more to the UDC amendment than just the hopes, aspirations, and marginalization of African Americans.

Notwithstanding her principled argument, there was another side to the UDC imprimatur story—one that did not include the high moral tone that she extolled. Yet, it had a direct bearing on the outcome of the UDC patent extension vote. That admixture of democracy and capitalism that melded into uncomfortable but sometimes compromising alliances between congressmen and women and lobbyists was also present.

The United Daughters of the Confederacy generated a higher level of visibility than is normal for essentially a ceremonial piece of legislation, and while Carol Moseley-Braun's unique response was one of the reasons, another came from an unlikely source, Procter and Gamble, the multibillion dollar food conglomerate. Ceremonial resolutions and amendments occur daily in the U.S. Senate. They range from resolutions declaring a particular day for a person or event in the member's home state to a senator taking time out from legislation to read a letter from a constituent and having it inserted into the *Congressional Record*. They have no news value, as a rule; but rather this common touch gives senators something to send to constituents shoring up their grassroots support. Over time, another aspect of this practice had emerged—putting the Senate's seal or imprimatur on the trademark or a logo of a corporation or manufacturer. Whereas, for nonprofit organizations such as the UDC, the imprimatur meant congressional legitimacy and contributed to the potential for charitable donations, for corporations, it meant protecting millions of dollars in profits.[8]

Following the debate, the *Legal Times*, a Washington, D.C.–based trade newspaper, reported on the behind-the-scenes lobbying of Procter and Gamble supporting passage of the UDC amendment. It was the potential loss of profits that drove the Procter and Gamble lobbyists to get involved in the United Daughters of the Confederacy debate. Procter and Gamble (P&G) had sought and received, over the years, an imprimatur for its trademark symbol for Olestra. Olestra is the trade name under which P&G marketed its low-calorie potato chips. Plans for expanding its multimillion dollar profits by including other low-calorie snacks were also at stake with the potential loss of its imprimatur. The Olestra imprimatur would expire in 1997, prompting P&G to institute a quiet lobbying effort by its representatives in Washington. Since few people knew about the P&G imprimatur, the lobbying efforts went virtually unnoticed, except for the clamoring of a few senators and consumer groups, who objected to the 1997 renewal on grounds that it gave unfair commercial advantage to the corporation. Linking its fate to the outcome of the UDC petition, Procter and Gamble began monitoring the Senate's actions and lobbying senators who opposed renewal.

Because they are diligently focusing on one issue, lobbyists are generally ahead of staff and the public on legislation—providing background information to Senate staff, polling senators for vote projections and tracking bills from committee to the floor of the Senate. They are invariably the most informed sources on the legislative status of their chosen topic. Consequently, while the rest of the country and the media were startled by Senator Moseley-Braun's filibuster over the imprimatur for the UDC, P&G lobbyists had worked behind the scenes preparing for this day ever since she refused to vote for it in committee.

As a part of their attempts to gain support, the lobbyists sent out literature on the nonpartisan, charitable work performed by the UDC and talked with senatorial staff about the significance of renewing the patent design. Perhaps thinking that they would influence Carol Moseley-Braun, some of the supporters went so far as to say that if a black woman could trace her ancestry to the Confederacy, then she would be eligible to apply for membership in the organization.

The debate progressed, and P&G's prospects for victory seemed more remote as Moseley-Braun won over more senators. By the end of the day, the Procter and Gamble lobbyists were joined by the American Legion representatives, whose pending imprimatur was also threatened by the UDC vote. After the filibuster, neither P&G nor the American Legion could take for granted that the tradition of routinely extending the U.S. Senate's imprimatur would continue unchallenged.

If Carol Moseley-Braun was aware of this lobbying effort and the threat to Procter and Gamble, she did not show it; nor apparently did she care about it. As the filibuster progressed, she picked up more and more support as senators began to recognize that this was an issue that would not go away and that the longer Moseley-Braun held rhetorical sway over the Senate, the more at risk they were of appearing to be insensitive to the racial issues underlying the debate. It did not help that the cable channel C-SPAN was broadcasting the filibuster around the country.

C-SPAN was the fourth estate at its best. The impact of a virtually neutral media that gave coverage without comment appeared to heighten citizen interest in and understanding of the legislative process. There is some indication that the C-SPAN presence also has a bearing on the senators' responses and votes. At least in this instance, it meant that while some may have voted for the amendment quietly at first, now they had to declare their vote and offer constituents and the viewing audience a clear statement on their position.

Of course, for southern senators this was critical. If not a racial issue, the issue of the Confederate flag and the United Daughters of the Confederacy was certainly a strong cultural one. So much so that while the pathos inherent in Moseley-Braun's deliberations was indeed memorable, it quickly gave way to another more powerful sentiment— southern pride.

Alabama's Democratic senator, Howell Heflin, as if responding to the ecclesiastical pronouncement of Moynihan's epiphany experience, spoke eloquently in his southern drawl about the tragedy of holding onto a past that had come to be anathema in the present. Heflin was known as an astute statesman with political integrity and strong support for southern interests. So when he spoke of his ancestors and their commitment and sacrifices while fighting under the Confederate flag, it carried a tremendous amount of credibility and political currency. He spoke of his longstanding respect for his forebears, who withstood the indignities resulting from the Civil War in the years that followed. Acknowledging that his family was rooted in the Confederacy and that they might "be spinning in their graves," Heflin reversed his vote for Helms's amendment and voted for Moseley-Braun's motion to table it. Heflin's vote was not only the most dramatic but also the most symbolically significant, capturing in one act the operative forces throughout the debate.

For it was not that Moseley-Braun's filibuster on the Confederate flag ended the debate—nor began it. What she was able to do was to set the parameters for future debates and discussions in the Senate on racially sensitive issues. She had done, with persuasive oratory, what customarily would have been accomplished through back-room negotiations and arm twisting. She won a reversal of the previous action with a vote of 75 to 25 in favor of tabling the Helms Amendment.

The final vote as well as the filibuster and the Hatch confrontation in the Judiciary Committee hearings were front-page news on July 23, 1993, in *USA Today,* the *Washington Post,* the *Chicago Tribune,* and newspapers around the country. The July 22 evening network news coverage was replete with clips from the dramatic moments on the Senate floor.

The media aftermath for Moseley-Braun was a major departure from the negative coverage she had been receiving and complaining about following her campaign. She enjoyed a newfound national reputation as a spokesperson for the issues affecting African Americans—not necessarily a title that she sought, nor one that she was used to having, but one that gave her high visibility in black and white communities around the country.

In reality, she was still out of character as a politician concerned with race. Her political constituency was predominately white, and her Senate votes generally reflected those interests. According to some of her critics in the Congressional Black Caucus, her reliance on white support sometimes meant that her votes had a detrimental impact on black interests. When questioned about her designation as a spokesperson for the interests of African Americans, she deflected those questions by focusing on her broad appeal and, as was her technique with the press, she controlled the press conferences so that she shifted the topic toward something less racial and thus less threatening.

Ever since her arrival at the Senate, Moseley-Braun had tried to stay away from controversial topics in her press conferences. In fact she had not given many partly because the press was still carrying stories about the campaign scandals that plagued the last days before the general election. In particular, she tried to avoid discussion of the Medicaid story and the sexual harassment story about her former campaign manager and then fiancé, Kgosie Matthews.

The Medicaid story started during her campaign, when it was reported that she owed the state Medicaid office $15,000 as reimbursement for her mother's stay in a nursing home. Funds paid to her mother from royalties on land that she owned out-of-state had been disbursed in the care of Moseley-Braun. The funds were divided up between Moseley-Braun, her sister, and her brother, who had since died. However, the funds were legally required to go toward her mother's care. During the campaign, Moseley-Braun denied any wrongdoing, but after continued negative press coverage decided to "voluntarily" give the state the $15,000.

The Kgosie Matthews story also plagued the senator well into her tenure in the Senate. Matthews was Moseley-Braun's campaign manager, making $15,000 a month. Staff members had accused him of sexual harassment and mismanagement. The former complaint was taken up by Moseley-Braun at the end of the campaign, when she asked a friend of hers to investigate the complaint. According to the senator, no wrongdoing was revealed as a result of her friend's investigation.

Moseley-Braun and Matthews then left the country after the campaign, flying on the expensive Concord airplane to tour South Africa, Matthews's home, and other parts of Africa. Before leaving, the senator-elect purchased a new car and moved into a new condominium apartment on the fashionable North Side of Chicago. The story might have gone unnoticed had it not been for the timing. It just so happened that the rest of the freshmen senators were undergoing orientation and getting settled into the Senate while she was on vacation. This gave the media a reason to discuss the propriety of such a trip and the purchase of the condo and the car by a candidate whose campaign coffers were in the red. The senator-elect had raised over $6 million in campaign funds but now had a half-million-dollar campaign debt.

Carol Moseley-Braun felt, probably more than any other senator, that her press coverage had not been fair with regard to these events. As a consequence, she developed, as most politicians do, a way of deflecting the questions and otherwise avoiding the reporters. Generally, it was through folkloric anecdotes that included adages from her father, quotes from her son, or other less racial, less topical responses. Other times, as when fending off inquiries about Matthews and Medicaid, she would dismiss the questions as nonsensical or personal and undeserving of an answer.

The United Daughters of the Confederacy changed her attitude, at least for the time being. Now she found herself with more than five hundred invitations for speaking engagements each week, according to her appointments secretary. She also developed a new strategy for handling the press. Her press secretary was now courting the media, calling press conferences weekly. The media responded in different ways to this new press strategy and newfound access. Some welcomed an opportunity for an audience with the senator. The pundits and commentators stayed aloof but were critical of Carol Moseley-Braun's attack on the Senate for violating politically correct language codes. One First Amendment columnist described her speech as an attempt at revisionist history.

Others populating the senator's press conferences were special interest press, the black press, and Illinois newspapers, but rarely any members of the Senate's radio and television gallery. Moseley-Braun's popularity did not spread to the Senate's fourth estate, especially not in the gallery. Were it not for the fact that the senator's electronic media coverage was directly dependent on the attitudes of the members of the Senate's television and radio gallery, this aside would not be necessary. However, the gallery stands out as an example of how the behind-the-scenes press operations were sometimes as reticent as the senators to embrace diversity either in the U.S. Senate or within its own ranks.

The prestigious Senate radio and television gallery, along with the White House assignment, represents the zenith in the careers of most broadcast journalists. It is an institution not too unlike the Senate—predominately white and male. So while the U.S. Senate had much adjusting to do to accept the first African American woman in its ranks, so did the gallery. The gallery is devoid of any history of diversity. A few women populate its ranks, but the lack of African Americans or other minorities is in stark contrast to the changing times. In addition to its normal neglect of black members of Congress, the gallery members in general engendered an unusually mean-spirited attitude toward the freshman senator from Illinois.

The UDC filibuster brought the issue of race out in the open, not only in the Senate but also behind the scenes in the Senate press gallery. Many of the reporters in the Senate radio and television gallery had a difficult time giving Moseley-Braun the respect that they reserved for other senators. Contributing to the disrespect may have been an early confrontation between members of the gallery and her press secretary, who made the mistake of storming into the television gallery and, with a few choice words, accusing the broadcast journalists of not giving her boss enough positive press. The incident's lasting impact was that it created a strained relationship between the senator and the press corps.

Suspicious of the media because of her campaign travails, Moseley-Braun generally stayed away from individual requests for interviews. American Urban Radio Network's George Wilson was one of the few exceptions. Whether it was the tension and bad relations with the press secretary or a press gallery not ready for the changing 103d Congress, a potentially explosive incident ignited some simmering feelings of racism and sexism.

In August of 1993, a few weeks after Moseley-Braun's UDC victory, a *Washington Times* article carried a front page picture of Moseley-Braun standing next to, smiling, and talking with Haiti's president, Jean Bertrand Aristide. The members of the gallery cut the photo out, placed it on a legal-sized sheet of plain white paper and asked for suggested "headlines." Even though such chicanery is rampant in newsrooms, this one took a turn for the worse. The request was not out of the ordinary, but the response was. For example, one said: "Can we go to bed together, tonight?" Another was handwritten with large print saying, "Oh, I thought you were Bishop Tutu." Although the dozen or more comments were more sexist than racist, the act itself was more reflective of the latter.

The actions of the reporters infuriated the few regular black members of the Senate radio and television gallery and tarnished the reputation of an otherwise respected press corps. Of course, with the newsmakers engaging in the improprieties of racism and sexism, there was no one to report the incident. In addition, the unspoken code of loyalty kept the black reporters from reporting it as well. Even though they had been privy to an inordinate amount of sexist and racist comments about Moseley-Braun, the African American journalists complained little and generally avoided confrontation. This time was different; the tensions were so high in the gallery that one black journalist had the sheet taken down from the wall and thrown into the trash.

America's first African American female senator may have changed the way the Senate conducted some of its routine business and also established herself as an orator in the tradition of America's major debaters, but there was no salvaging of her relationship with the press. It was on a downward spiral, leaving very little opportunity for her to overcome the lingering scandals of her Senate race and prompting a continuous flow of follow-up stories on aspects of her campaign. Her momentary hope of rising beyond the negative campaign press coverage was soon dashed as reporters nearly broke the glass door of her Hart Senate Office Building suite in early November.

Once again, the Medicaid story had been revived. This time it was by the *New Republic* magazine. The reporter—who had previous and subsequent reported instances of inaccurate reporting—alleged that she had received information from disenchanted campaign workers about evidence that Carol Moseley-Braun had knowingly prevented her siblings from reimbursing Medicaid for her mother's care, and that there was evidence to prove it.

The old Medicaid story was taking on new life, causing Moseley-Braun once again to retreat from the press by staying away from the Senate for three days. One of the days required a critical vote on sexual harassment charges against Senator Robert Packwood (R-Oreg.). Because the vote was so critical, all senators were required to be on the Senate floor or risk being subpoenaed. Carol Moseley-Braun called in to say that she would not be in that Monday—her mother was ill.

In the final round of the revived Medicaid story, Moseley-Braun's successes from the UDC debate overshadowed the story and its impact on her image, causing short shrift in the coverage on the major television stations.

As she moved toward the end of her first session in the Senate, she could look back on an active legislative agenda her first two years. She shepherded through the nomination of the controversial Dr. Joycelyn Elders as U.S. surgeon general and sponsored the amendment to the 1993 omnibus anti-crime bill that gave the courts the right to treat violent juveniles fourteen and older as adults. She also cosponsored the bill to create community development banks and supported unfunded mandates and the North American Free Trade Agreement (NAFTA).

The press could not erase the memory nor the import of July 22, 1993, because it was a debate that resonated as a historic reminder of the new rules of engagement brought about by the cultural, racial, and gender symbolism stemming from Carol Moseley-Braun's rhetoric on the Senate floor. It was a defining moment for the senator. She was no longer an icon for the 1992 Year of the Woman, nor had she languished in her status as the first African American woman in the Senate. She was an active legislator, a skilled debater, and a survivor who would create her niche in the U.S. Senate.

Part Four

The Southern Women of the 103d and 104th Congresses

Chapter 11

Corrine Brown

*Political Savvy Wrapped Up in a
Homespun Package*

I represent fourteen counties, thirty-one cities and fifty cities that
are not incorporated. So I have 250 miles and I have four major populations, Jacksonville being one. The area that I have the second largest
population of Haitians in is the Orlando area. And then I also have
Daytona Beach and I have the city of Gainesville.

Résumé

Corrine Brown

Personal

Born   November 11, 1946
Jacksonville, Florida

Family   Single; one child

Religion   Baptist

Party   Democrat

Took office   Age 46, January 5, 1993

Education

B.A.   Florida Agriculture and Mechanical University, 1969

Ed.S.   University of Florida, 1971

Professional/Political Background

1977–1982   Counselor and professor, Florida Community College

1982–1992   Representative, Florida House of Representatives

1993–   U.S. House of Representatives

Selected Awards/Organizational Affiliations

Honorary doctor of laws, Edward Waters College; first woman elected chair of the Duval County legislative delegation; consultant to Florida Governor's Committee on Aging.

Congressional Data

Third Congressional District: Jacksonville and Orlando

Committees: Veterans' Affairs; Transportation and Infrastructure

103d Congress: 1993–1994
1992 general election results: 59 percent of the vote

104th Congress: 1995–1996
1994 general election results: 58 percent of the vote

Corrine Brown

*One of the First African American Women
Elected to Congress from Florida
(Jacksonville)*

Third District, Florida
Democrat
103d Congress–present, 1993–

I hurried back to Eatonville because I knew that the town was full of material and that I could get it without hurt, harm or danger. . . . So I rounded Park Lake and came speeding down the straight stretch into Eatonville, the city of five lakes, three croquet courts, three hundred brown skins, three hundred good swimmers, plenty guavas, two schools and no jail house.

—Zora Neale Hurston, *Mules and Men*[1]

In 1993, the beginning of her first term in office, Corrine Brown beamed with pride when she discussed the hundreds of writers, artists, and tourists who annually converge on Florida's Third Congressional District in search of the town of Eatonville. Once there, they pay homage to the life, works, and achievements of the hometown writer and anthropologist Zora Neale Hurston. Hurston cut her literary teeth on the same Florida soil that prepared Brown for public office, and with pride she considers herself a part of the tradition of women whose attributes have been celebrated and archived by the prolific writer and folklorist.

When Zora Neale Hurston wrote more than a half a century ago about the women of Florida and her hometown, the race colony of Eatonville, it was at a time when the state was the "least populous in the South with 1.4 million people. It was swampy, isolated, disease-ridden, bigoted, with no mineral resources but phosphate mines, not much agriculture outside its citrus groves and hardly any manufacturing at all."[2]

Yet, what Hurston was able to do was to enshrine an Eatonville, both mythic and authentic, that was fixed in time and rooted in American history. It was one of more than a hundred settlements of its kind, founded in the 1880s by blacks who purchased land, built schools and churches, and established cities and townships. Hurston's classic novel, *Their Eyes Were Watching God,* the story of Janie Crawford, the wife of Joe Clarke, the real-life founder and mayor of Eatonville, is a mixture of fiction, fact, anthropology, and love story about the settlement of the first black incorporated town in America. One historian describes the founding of Eatonville in this way.

African American settlers first came to the northeast section of what is now called Orange County, Florida, because of the work opportunities in Maitland, a town being built by Northern whites, many of whom were Civil War veterans.

Coming from neighborhoods and enclaves in the surrounding counties and towns as well as from West Florida, Alabama, Georgia and South Carolina, these African Americans provided the necessary work force to build a town where whites never had lived. In 1885 Joe Clarke, originally from Georgia, was the first African-American to acquire land [in Florida]. Clarke later acquired additional property from Lewis H. Lawrence and Josiah Eaton, of Maitland. The latter gave the town its name. With land deeded from Lawrence, the St. Lawrence African Methodist Episcopal Church was built and the initial property sold by Eaton was subdivided and sold to other blacks. In 1887 on August 18, Eatonville filed for incorporation as a town in Orange County.[3]

The story of Eatonville is particularly significant because it gives a frame of reference for assessing the spirit of independence and the sense of ownership exhibited by black Floridian leaders—one that affirms their stake in the state and entitles them to the exercise of the complete franchise. Hurston's unmatched writing paints pictures of the strong charismatic and boldly audacious men and women who take control of their destiny. With a certain style and flare, using a dialect stemming from the unique blend of African idioms and borrowed American English, her characters establish themselves as a part of the rich historic landscape of Florida.

Today, as Florida takes its place as the country's fourth largest state, with 13 million people, perhaps it is Hurston, the folklorist, who provides the backdrop for an introduction to the Third Congressional District's representative, Corrine Brown—a woman who could easily have found her way onto Hurston's pages. She traces her ancestry and that of Congresswoman Carrie Meek (D-Fla.) back to the same small Georgia town. Brown, like the early settlers of Eatonville, has a "never say no" attitude and a fierce civic commitment expressed with a refreshing candor. Plain speaking and possessed with "get to the point" shorthand phrases, Brown brought to Capitol Hill her own rhetorical style, replete with dialect and syntax. Although it took a while to get used to, her responses to reporters and interviewers eventually became good thirty-second sound bites for radio and television and quotable copy for newsprint.

Just being in her presence can produce flashbacks to the memorable Hurston women. A Corrine Brown sampler includes:

- After winning the 1992 Democratic primary during the "Year of the Woman": "This is the year of the woman, so get out of the way, men."
- When asked by a network anchor right after her election to Congress if she supported term limits: "Yes. The person that represented most of my district was here for forty-four years. I want the same term—forty-four years."

- When asked about her position on the North American Free Trade Agreement: "It's a job killer. Kill it before it multiplies."
- On getting ready for her first session of Congress: "Let's stop talking and let's get it on."
- On teen pregnancy: "We have too many babies having babies."
- On the black vote in her district: "I get maybe 40 percent of the white vote and 98 percent of the black vote. If black people don't come out to vote, I'm dead meat."

And yet, no matter how charming or engaging, there should be no mistake that Congresswoman Corrine Brown is anything but a serious legislator and consummate politician. The deceptively guileless exterior is a veneer that masks a woman with the political toughness to ensure that black Floridians received all of the minority districts to which they were entitled, who fought to keep military bases open, who intervened to make certain that the rights of black youth were being protected from an overzealous police department, and who refused to back the president when the economic well-being of her constituency was at risk. In short, Corrine Brown is a seasoned politician who thrives on the bread and butter of elected office—constituent services.

Nowhere is the adroitness of her political instinct more apparent than in the battle she waged during Florida's redistricting following the 1990 census. Brown constantly reminds interviewers that it was her efforts that resulted in the final redistricting plan that produced three majority black congressional districts, rather than the original plan for only one.

First, acknowledging that her district includes the historic Eatonville, with equal measure she describes the remainder of the Third Congressional District. "My district includes fourteen counties, thirty-one cities, and fifty cities that are not incorporated. I have 250 miles and I have four major populations, Jacksonville being one. The area that I have the second largest population of Haitians in is the Orlando area. And then I also have Daytona Beach, and I have the city of Gainesville."

The Third Congressional District, Congresswoman Carrie Meek's Seventh, and Congressman Alcee Hastings's Twenty-third are the majority black districts that elected Florida's first African American members to Congress since the two aborted terms of Republican Josiah Walls in the nineteenth century. Until 1993, he was the only black to have been elected to Congress from Florida. His is another story of the Reconstruction era's miscarriage of power exercised by white men in Congress.

By 1870, when Walls, a schoolteacher, ran for and won a seat in the U.S. House of Representatives, he had already been enslaved, forced to fight in the Confederate army and had volunteered to fight in the Union army. The Republican ran for and won a seat in the U.S. House of Representatives, becoming a duly-elected member of the Forty-second Congress (1871–1873). His papers approved, he was given committee assignments, only to be unseated by white Democrats who invalidated his election. In 1872, he ran again for the Forty-third Congress (1873–1875) and won with a vote margin of nearly four hundred. Claiming voter fraud, Democrats unseated Josiah Walls a second time, giving his seat to his white Democratic opponent. Cheated out of a seat legitimately earned through the electoral process, and with an irrepressible political ambition, Walls eventually was elected and seated in the Florida Senate.[4]

The political continuum beginning with Walls's Reconstruction battles, however, would be ruptured more than a century, until Brown and other black state legislators waged an offensive against white Democrats to gain more seats in Congress during reapportionment after the 1990 census. This time, Corrine Brown, as a member of the Florida legislature, had no intention of having blacks cheated out of representation again in 1992.

"It was a lonely time for me," she says, reflecting back on the time when she decided to fight the Florida redistricting plan. "Whites would not speak to me because they were mad and blacks would not speak to me because they were afraid."[5] In spite of the slights, Brown stood firm in her conviction that blacks deserved three of the four seats approved for the state of Florida.

At issue was the fact that Florida had gained four seats following the 1990 census, expanding its delegation in the U.S. House of Representatives from nineteen to twenty-three. Many black members of the state legislature were at odds with the Democrats, led by senate president Gwen Margolis, because they objected to a redistricting plan that gave Florida's fourteen percent black population only one of the four seats. But their protest did not extend as far as Brown's, which was to challenge it in court.

Corrine Brown remembers how the minority legislators were called into a meeting and told by the leadership that they wanted to avoid any "public battles that might prove embarrassing" and that they had made the decision to give blacks only one seat and Hispanics three. To which state representative Corrine Brown responded, "We [African Americans] have been here for more than one hundred years, they [Hispanics] have been here for only thirty. I am not going to let you get away with that."

She joined with a group that included a Tulane University professor who drew up a map that carved out three congressional districts for blacks and one for Hispanics. The plan won court approval in May of 1992.

The Early Years

Corrine Brown's passion for protecting the interests of black Floridians in many ways was as parochial as it was political. She had spent her entire life in Florida under political domination of white men in Congress and the state legislature. She was born in 1946 in Jacksonville. When she was just two years old, the city's voters—those who enjoyed the free exercise of the voting franchise—elected a Democrat who would be in office until 1992, retiring only months before her own election.

Charles Bennett was elected to the House of Representatives in 1948, representing all of Jacksonville along with the adjacent counties. His tenure was indicative of the stranglehold on politics and Congress that southern white men enjoyed following the expulsion of blacks in the post-Reconstruction era. Until the actual implementation of the 1965 Voting Rights Act after the 1970 census, white politicians were an immovable force and an accepted fact of life in the South.

Jacksonville, Florida's largest city with a population of around 650,000, was carved up into two sections during the 1992 redistricting. Rather than run for reelection in one of the districts, Bennett—aging and an early victim of polio—retired. The large black population of the city was attached to Corrine Brown's Third Congressional District and the remainder was placed in the Fourth Congressional District, which elected Republican Tillie Fowler.

A political base since Brown's first days in office in the state legislature, Jacksonville holds one of the keys to Brown's past. When asked about her young life, without hesitation she says: "I was born and raised in Jacksonville, Florida. I went to elementary school there and high school. I was the class homecoming queen and all of that. It's Jacksonville, Jacksonville, Jacksonville."

A child of the South and proud of it, her fondest memories go back to a time when the biggest event in the summer was the "big meeting." Once a year she would go to the country and meet and greet an extended family of cousins, brothers, aunts, and uncles. Even today, she relishes being one of the three generations of women—her mother, her daughter, and herself—who go home every August for the "big meeting." Brown smiles when she thinks back to the days when her relatives would convene on this one weekend out of the summer to go to church service, cook food, and catch up on the latest family gossip.

"I remember when I used to come from Jacksonville, they thought that I was from the big city. I wouldn't work in the fields like the other kids. I was clearly meant to be a house Negro." She smiles at the unintended double entendre. "So, I had a grandfather who didn't like my 'city ways,' and he would say to me, 'You don't see me and I don't see you. You don't talk to me and I don't talk to you.'" And with that he would ignore her during the whole event. Brown continues, "That was his way of letting me know that I thought I was too good for the country people and he didn't appreciate it."

What the memory of her grandfather does for Congresswoman Brown is to remind her of the distance between the "little people" and those that have been blessed to serve them—a lesson she would take to heart while building a strong constituent-service track record in the state legislature and in the Congress.

Before heading into a life in public service, however, Corrine Brown took some detours. Her daughter, who is now a successful lawyer, was born in 1965. Brown began college that same year. After graduating from Florida A&M University, where she received a bachelor of science in education, she went on to get a master's degree in education from the University of Florida. From 1977 to 1982, Brown went to work as a professor at the Florida Community College, where she would later work as a guidance counselor. She tried her hand as an entrepreneur and began a travel agency, but later sold when it became part of a protracted controversy surrounding her congressional campaign.

The Political Odyssey

Meeting and becoming friends with a sorority sister, Gwendolyn Sawyer-Cherry, would eventually change the course of Brown's vocation and avocation. Sawyer-Cherry, politically committed, active and well-respected in Florida politics, fostered an appreciation for public service in her friend and sorority sister. As a professional educator, Brown had always been active in civic activities in Jacksonville, but the inspiration to go beyond her initial field of education and into public life was the consequence of Sawyer-Cherry's influence. One of America's truly unsung heroines of the South, Sawyer-Cherry was the first black woman to serve in the Florida Senate. Any black woman active in southern politics during the 1960s and 1970s could not help but to have encountered and been encouraged by her progressive stance on political empowerment for women. It is Sawyer-Cherry whom Shirley Chisholm credited with having advanced her presidential primary bid in Florida.

In *The Good Fight,* Chisholm's book about her 1972 Democratic presidential primary bid, she mentions Sawyer-Cherry as the one person who stood by her during the difficult days of the Florida primary and who gave her direction on campaigning in the state. Needless to say, both black women who now sit in Congress representing Florida, Carrie Meek and Brown, named Gwendolyn Sawyer-Cherry as their political mentor. Brown goes so far as to say that Sawyer-Cherry bequeathed her a special gift of guidance.

With a far-away look in her eyes, Brown recounts how she first got into politics at Sawyer-Cherry's urging. After one unsuccessful attempt at running for a seat in the Florida state legislature, Brown was about to give up, but Sawyer-Cherry prompted her to try again.

"It was the night before a fund-raiser and Gwendolyn Sawyer-Cherry and I were talking on the phone about politics and strategy"—Brown glances down—"and I wanted to get off the phone, because I knew that I would see her in a little while, but she just kept on talking. Telling me all kinds of things about running for office. Finally, we said goodbye and that was the last time we talked to each other." Sawyer-Cherry was killed in a car accident that night. "I just think that she was trying to give me everything that she knew about politics so that I would be successful." It was a consoling thought that helped her endure the loss of a good friend, mentor, and political ally.

Brown's luck did change. She went on to win a seat in the Florida House of Representatives in 1982, where she served for nearly a decade, gaining a reputation as a champion for low-income people, housing, education, job training, and the elderly. Her ten years in the Florida House of Representatives proved to be a strong foundation from which to launch a congressional bid. So when she threw her hat into the ring for the 1992 congressional race, she had a pretty good handle on the constituency that she would serve, if elected. The Third Congressional District was 50 percent black, according to Brown, although the statistics say that the voting population was between 55 and 58 percent black.

Culturally, demographically, and economically diverse, it has a large poor population in both urban and rural areas, combined with the economically dynamic Orlando, in Orange County, where Disney World keeps the tourism market alive and a significant number of blue collar workers employed. A senior citizen population that is slightly multiracial but predominantly white also populates the area. After fighting for the creation of this amalgam known as the Third Congressional District, Brown decided that she might as well run to represent it in Congress.

With the slogan "Corrine Fights, Corrine Works, Corrine Delivers, Corrine Makes It Happen," Brown entered into a field with three other Democrats—Andrew Johnson, Arnett Girardeau, and long shot Glennie Mills. Girardeau, a black state senator, came in third in the primary with 18 percent of the vote, forcing a run-off with the two leading candidates, Brown (43 percent) and Johnson (31 percent). As with other sunbelt elections in newly created minority districts, Brown's closest competition, former state representative Brown, was white. In a self-defeating theme, Johnson spent much of his time running for a district that he felt should never have been created, criticizing its shape, its purpose, and directing that criticism toward his opponent, Corrine Brown.

Either to mock the majority black district voters or to grab headlines, Johnson called himself the "blackest candidate" in the race. By labeling himself as the candidate with the best interest of the African American community at heart, he castigated Brown as not possessing that interest. But even with such a bizarre charge, the run-off election, like the primary, showed Corrine Brown to be the better campaigner as well as the people's choice. Not one of her opponents could match her success on the stump. She went from door-to-door campaigning, hands-on style, touching the flesh, and making commitments to be accessible and accountable.

Although she won the run-off with 64 percent of the vote, a threat of scandal soured an otherwise sweet victory. Johnson accused Brown of financial improprieties, saying she used her state employees to work in the travel agency she owned. He followed up his accusations later by filing charges with the Florida Commission on Ethics. Rather than pursue the probe, Brown eventually agreed to pay the state $5,000; however, she denied any wrongdoing. She went on to win the general election against Republican Don Weidner, an attorney for the Florida Physicians Association, receiving 59 percent of the vote to Weidner's 41 percent. Observers agreed and Weidner conceded that Brown was the better campaigner with a stronger media strategy and a style that was more personable and appealing to voters.

The Congressional Years

Shortly after Brown was sworn into the U.S. House of Representatives in January of 1993, one of her hometown newspapers, the *Orlando Sentinel Tribune*, issued a word of caution to the newly elected member of the Florida delegation.

"Her campaign treasurer resigned this week. He said that someone signed his name to a campaign finance report submitted to the Federal Elections Commission. . . . all of Ms. Brown's work with citizens and elected officials throughout her district is undermined when there are questions about the judgment and honesty of her staff and supporters."[6]

Although Corrine Brown responded to the allegations with the explanation that it was an unfortunate act by an overly anxious staff person who wanted to get the finance report in on time, the ethics issue remained a central criticism of her public life. Indeed, it was a reminder that the cloud of scandal still hovered over her horizon, a threat that very well could account for her redoubled effort to make her presence felt in Washington and appreciated at home.

Brown promised and delivered on her pledge to make herself accessible to her constituents by holding periodic town meetings and visiting her district's remote rural areas with greater frequency. Hers was the fulfillment of expectations for the "little people" that more established representatives often overlooked. To demonstrate, she tells the story of the elderly constituent who came to her office in Florida to get help in having his Medicaid prescription filled.

"I had a person in my office; I'll just call him Mr. Hall. I had to help him go to the doctor and get his medicine and get his prescription filled. You may think a Congressperson's office should not be doing that kind of personalized service, but there are many Mr. Halls out there that need that kind of help and assistance. It's a very important part of health care, helping seniors to be able to afford their medicine."

While it may be conveniently anecdotal for Brown to point to the incident of the "little person" getting help from Congress, the story nonetheless makes the point that her range of constituency stretches from the corporate giant of Disney World to the senior citizen trying to make ends meet, each holding a key to how she needed to conduct her legislative business while in Washington in order to get reelected. Her Florida base was both sophisticated and unsophisticated about the workings of Congress.

Personally, Brown was also discovering that in many ways she was as unaccustomed to her new status as her uninitiated constituents. A heavy-set woman about five feet, five inches without heels, with caramel brown skin and reddish undertones, her full face had an easy-to-come-by smile—a smile she flashed in angst as well as joy. Candid sometimes where others might finesse, Brown complained to a reporter about the high cost of living in Washington, D.C. "I can't believe it—I could own a place on the water for what they're asking up here. An efficiency costs $600," said Brown, who was used to paying $514 monthly for a three-bedroom home in Jacksonville.[7]

But lack of sophistication about life in the city did not translate into the same thing in Congress. When it came to the politics of the House of Representatives, Brown was in her element. She had a decade of Florida politics behind her, and that was her strong suit. She used it to her advantage. When she decided to lobby for the committees of her choosing—Public Works and Transportation and Veterans' Affairs—the freshman congresswoman went to every committee member and the Democratic leadership lobbying to get her choice of committee assignments. She wanted to prevent military base closings, protect entitlements for seniors, and get jobs and job training for the unemployed and the underemployed. It was not glamour that she sought in committee assignments, but the meat and potato, pork barrel assignments that would show up in the headlines of the hometown newspaper.

Once landing the committee assignments, however, her legislative initiatives got off to a slow start. She found herself in Washington dealing with a local Florida issue that had international implications. In a state where tourism is one-fifth of the state's economy, two incidents of carjackings and murders of foreign tourists created a panic back home in Brown's district, as well as abroad, since one of the tourists was German. Given a description of the perpetrator as a young black male, Florida's overzealous police went into high schools and rounded up black youth, pulling them out of classrooms and questioning them. They held young men in prison without due process. It did not take long before Brown's phones were ringing with irate calls from Florida parents.

"I got on the phone," the congresswoman said, describing her response. "That's why you have African American congresspersons. I got on the phone with Janet Reno [the U.S. attorney general], who is from Florida, and she contacted the Sheriff and my office worked very closely with that. Because, basically, if you're going to arrest people, or if you are going to question people, you should have some probable cause. You can not do as the Sheriff was doing there, go into the school and take all males and just pick them up and take them downtown and question them."

Brown took delight in her access to the Washington power structure, which could be used as a tool to solve local problems in Florida. Her intervention may or may not have resulted in quelling police actions, since such actions may also have been affected by the arrests made shortly thereafter. Nevertheless, with the headlines dying down on the tourists' murders, Brown was able to turn her attention to the issues of the 103d Congress, such as the North American Free Trade Agreement (NAFTA), Haitian refugees, health care, budget reconciliation, and the omnibus anti-crime bill.

One issue looming large in 1993 was that of Haitian refugees and the return to power of exiled president Jean Bertrand Aristide. The Haitian refugee policy of the U.S. government had a direct impact on Brown's district. In 1993 America's support for President Aristide could cynically be labeled contradictory or euphemistically be said to have been in a constant state of evolution. Ever since the democratically elected leader secured asylum in the United States, he had been using funds impounded in America to pay American lobbyists, public relations firms, and lawyers, including a former Maryland congressman, Michael Barnes, to put pressure on Congress and the White House to support his return to Haiti. He openly denied wanting U.S. military intervention, but hinted that the use of the U.S. military might prop up democracy in his homeland.

Just as Aristide was ambivalent about U.S. involvement, so too was America ambivalent about him. Republicans and conservatives considered him a Marxist, and many were familiar with the role that the Central Intelligence Agency had played in the politics of Haiti. They had no intention of supporting his return. In the meantime, Haitians were leaving the country, risking their lives on makeshift boats headed for the Florida coast, where the state complained of financial hardship in providing support for those who landed on its shores.

Democratic president Bill Clinton had criticized his predecessor, George Bush, for sending Haitians back home, where they could in all likelihood expect imprisonment or death. Once elected, however, he continued the Bush policy. Brown's district, which contained a large Haitian American community, had a stake in the government's eventual position on Haiti, and she worked behind the scenes with the White House and the U.S. State Department to help formulate a policy that would be fair to the Haitian people while not overburdening the resources of Florida. Black leaders in the Congress joined forces with other human rights groups to bring more attention to the plight of Haitian refugees. Brown and other Congressional Black Caucus (CBC) members went to Haiti to see first-hand the conditions that had caused thousands to risk their lives to come to America. They came back with a report on unstable economic and political conditions of the military government and the deaths and economic destitution among Haitian citizens.

The visit confirmed Brown's suspicion that the government had not taken the Haitian situation seriously. "We in Florida suffer from the fact that the government has not had a fair policy pertaining to Haiti. And one of the issues of discussion in Florida especially for African American people has been the treatment of Haitians." Then, with unpretentious and perhaps unintentional understatement, she said, "We kind of think part of this has been the fact that Haitians are people of color."

Brown's pronouncement was shared by many African American leaders. Pressure from the activist lobby Trans-Africa opened the floodgates and literally shed the light of media attention on the administration's policies when its president, Randall Robinson, went on a well-publicized hunger strike to bring attention to the plight of Haitian refugees. The concerted efforts of the CBC and Trans-Africa, as well as other groups, did force the Clinton administration to use the resources of the U.S. government to begin a process toward ending the Haitian crisis.

The former chairman of the Joint Chiefs of Staff, Colin Powell, and former president Jimmy Carter went to negotiate with the Haitian military regime, headed by Gen. Raoul Cedras. If all else failed, they told Cedras on behalf of the U.S. government, a military attack would be imminent. The message brought results. The military government disbanded and American troops were deployed to maintain order during the transition and return of Aristide.

America eventually returned Aristide to power and oversaw a flawed but relatively peaceful democratic election in 1995 that reinstated Aristide as president. However, even though the flow of refugees had halted, the plight of those still in refugee camps off the coast of Florida in Guantanamo Bay, Cuba, continued to be an issue for Brown. Relatives of her constituents were lost in a legal limbo: would they be returned to their country or be allowed to enter the United States to live with family members? The resolution of the Haitian military situation did create a small victory for Brown, but after ten years in the Florida legislature, she could understand the need for small victories. Small victories in legislation, however, would prove more elusive.

Jobs and the creation of job opportunities were an integral part of her platform. With major military bases closing, Florida would lose jobs. With NAFTA, Brown saw the hope of jobs becoming more remote for her poverty-ridden pockets of economic morass. When the Clinton administration began lobbying members of Congress to support NAFTA—a measure that would open Mexico and Canada to American business with fewer regulations and a chance for low-wage workers—she remained resolute, answering with a resounding "no." She considered NAFTA a threat to job creation and a detriment to her constituency. She said: "I want to support the Caribbean, Mexico, and other places and help them toward economic development in that area, but not at the expense of hard-working Americans. I feel very, very strongly about that. And in fact, all of the studies indicate that NAFTA would hurt Florida more than any other state. So, I don't see how any member from Florida could vote for NAFTA."

Her steadfastness was a mark of Brown's independence and left political pundits puzzled about classifying her as either a surefire liberal or a centrist. Brown's voting pattern, while not politically predictable, did generally benefit her constituents in tangible ways.

She could cite the following legislative accomplishments at the end of her first term. She secured a $100 million federal courthouse for Jacksonville, helped keep a defense contractor in the city and added an additional two thousand jobs to the economy, introduced legislation to transfer the Orlando Naval Training Center Hospital to the Department of Veterans' Affairs, with an annual $22 million operating budget and four hundred new jobs for the district. A supporter of capital punishment and a strong law-and-order proponent, Brown supported $3.5 billion for additional police officers and voted for the Brady bill, a handgun-control measure.

She had an opportunity to test how well her efforts had been received in Florida when she ran for reelection in 1994. The strength of her incumbency was tested in the Democratic primary by Alvin Brown, a federal bureaucrat, who lost handily when she defeated him with almost 70 percent of the vote. The general election was not as easily won, although she received 58 percent of the vote in the race against black Republican Marc Little, a talk show host.

But Brown returned to a less kind, less gentle 104th Congress (1995–1996), one that was now controlled by Republicans. She found that her seat was one of those targeted by the Republican National Committee for elimination or defeat. All of a sudden, she was a lot less certain about the durability of the Florida redistricting plan. The redistricting ruling that created the most anxiety after the *Shaw v. Reno* decision was the eagerly awaited

Georgia Eleventh Congressional District ruling, scheduled for June 1995, before the U.S. Supreme Court's recess.

The whole month of June had almost passed without a ruling from the Supreme Court. June 29, 1995, the last day of the court's session, was the day after the Democratic minority in the House of Representatives orchestrated an all-night session, fighting the majority's desire to place another Republican on the powerful Appropriations Committee. The wisdom of the all-night session was questioned, but Democrats, although unsuccessful, felt good about their endurance and unity. Walking into the House dining room, Brown was not her normal ebullient self. She wore a red suit with a black and white striped top. An auburn wig framed blurry eyes and a face with a weary countenance. Some of her fatigue resulted from the all-night session of Congress, but the rest had to do with the decision that was just a few hours away.

"Today is a historic day," she said. "I am afraid of what might happen." Afraid was an unusual term for the determined and daring Brown. But she was no different from a number of professionals, primarily blacks and women, who used terms such as frightening, afraid, and disturbing to describe the actions of the 1995 U.S. Supreme Court. Civil rights laws were constantly coming under attack, being reinterpreted, and reversed. Earlier, Brown herself had commented about the number of black, middle-class managers with major corporations who now called on her to help them through some of the traumas of corporate downsizing and rollbacks in affirmative action.

By midday her earlier fears were confirmed. She stood on the podium with other members of the Congressional Black Caucus denouncing the Supreme Court's decision of *Miller v. Johnson,* which invalidated Georgia congresswoman Cynthia McKinney's Eleventh Congressional District because it *complied* with the U.S. Justice Department's requirement that the state take race into consideration in the creation of minority districts. In short, the new standard of the Court threatened the existence of Corrine Brown's hard-won Third Congressional District as well as those of her 103d Congress minority freshman class members.

It had been an exhausting day for the congresswoman representing the town that produced mythical Zora Neale Hurston women with "spunk." Corrine Brown was now up against the same system that cheated Josiah Walls out of his seat in Congress with outright raw grabs for power. The challenge she faced was more subtle, legalistic, and would probably be more protracted. She would have to draw out of herself some of the traits of the Hurston women in order to persevere, but that was not a talent that she did not possess. It just had to be summoned up from the deep recesses of her Floridian history—a history that said she had a right to be in Congress if she won a seat fair and square.

Chapter 12 **Carrie Pittman Meek**

*A Protégée of Mary McCleod Bethune
Enters Congress*

I don't say it's the only mission, but it is my main one—to push job creation, economic development. When I say that, I don't say that as a platitude. I want more opportunities for business for African-Americans, particularly in Florida. You will note that youngsters who get their degrees in Florida usually go someplace else to get a job. I want those youngsters who are trained there, to have jobs that they can go into as professionals. There's a brain drain in Florida. A big brain drain.

Résumé

Carrie Pittman Meek

Personal

Born   April 29, 1926
          Tallahassee, Florida

Family   Divorced; three children

Religion   Baptist

Party   Democrat

Took office   Age 66, January 5, 1993

Education

B.S.   Florida Agriculture and Mechanical University, 1946

M.S.   University of Michigan, Ann Arbor, 1948

Professional/Political Background

1949–1958   Physical education and health instructor, Bethune-Cookman College

1958–1961   Physical education and health instructor, Florida A&M University

1961–1968   Professor, Miami Dade Community College

1968–1979   Associate dean, Miami Dade Community College

1979–1982   Special assistant to president, Miami Dade Community College

1979–1982   Representative, Florida House of Representatives

1982–1992   Senator, Florida Senate

1993–   U.S. House of Representatives

Selected Awards/Organizational Affiliations

Distinguished Service Award from Frontiers International Miami Club; Florida Democratic Black Caucus, Morris W. Milton, Sr., Political Achievement Award; named by Florida newspapers as the "Best in Senate Debate," 1990; member, Metro Miami Action Plan Board; Dade County Housing and Urban Development Housing Resource Team; Florida Democratic Black Caucus; Afro-American Democratic Club (founder and past president); Phi Delta Kappa; National Organization for Women; League of Women Voters; National Association for the Advancement of Colored People; Miami-Dade Chamber of Commerce; Urban League of Greater Miami; Delta Sigma Theta Sorority.

Congressional Data

Seventh Congressional District of Florida: Tallahassee

Committees: Appropriations; Budget; Government Reform and Oversight

103d Congress: 1993–1994
1992 general election results: 100 percent of the vote

104th Congress: 1995–1996
1994 general election results: 100 percent of the vote

Carrie Pittman Meek

*One of the First African American Women
Elected to Congress from Florida
(Tallahassee)*

Seventh District, Florida
Democrat
103d Congress–present, 1993–

"God sent me here," Carrie Meek—the granddaughter of slaves—told the politically sophisticated African American audience. In 1993, Meek brought to the 103d Congress wit, wisdom, and a beguiling political acumen, wrapped in a package of boundless energy and unapologetic religious fervor. Captivating a national audience with her impressive path from sharecropper's daughter to congresswoman, her life story proved irresistible to the media. Impressive too, were her maneuvers to land a seat on the powerful Appropriations Committee. Although an unlikely starting point for a freshman, it was a sure testament to the political savvy of the veteran state legislator.

Carrie Meek was, indeed, a political enigma. At the age of sixty-six, she was the oldest woman elected to Congress during the 1992 "Year of the Woman," and though she described herself as "old as rainwater," she was more energetic—perhaps due to her early athletic career—than many of her younger colleagues. Her own best press secretary, she regaled the media with her unpretentious recollections of her life and its poignant and sobering twists and turns.

Her early career in teaching and a more recent productive tenure as a Florida state legislator framed a life as a single parent and a survivor of America's segregated past. Now, she was one of three history-making blacks elected to Congress to represent Florida. Meek, House Democrats Corrine Brown, and Alcee Hastings were the first African Americans to serve in the Florida congressional delegation in the twentieth century. Josiah Walls, a Republican, was the first African American to represent Florida in 1871.

Indeed, Congresswoman Meek did not have to wait to get elected to Congress to make history. She never tired of letting listeners know that she saw history being made and was already a part of it. "I heard Paul Robeson sing when I was a girl. I heard Marian Anderson sing. I heard Countee Cullen recite his poetry," she told an audience at the Congressional Black Caucus (CBC) legislative weekend. "I saw George Washington Carver as he spoke to us about the peanut. So I have been there and I have heard all of the legendary heroes."[1]

The Early Years

Now she was becoming one of those legendary heroines herself.

"Who is Carrie Meek?" was the rhetorical question asked of the short, bespectacled, pleasingly plump, brown-skinned woman on stage at the CBC forum. It was really an invitation that was too open-ended to be true, because Carrie Meek would waste no time answering. So the woman who was born Carrie Pittman on April 29, 1926, to William and Carrie Pittman began her story:

> I was born one of twelve children. My father was a sharecropper. My mother was a domestic worker and everything else. She used to wash clothes with a battle ax, make her own soap. She was one of fourteen children. Never thought I was poor. I guess you would say I was poor. But I didn't know it. We had lots to eat. I stayed little for a long time but it finally got through. Some of that food that I had way back there finally came through. But anyway, I had a most enjoyable childhood. I was working since I was about ten or eleven years old in Miss Ann's kitchen, anyone's kitchen where I could get a job. I was watching them [white people] closely.
>
> And I grew up in Tallahassee. I went to school at Florida A&M University, elementary school, high school and college at a black university. I finished Florida A&M, taught school for many, many years, married two men, outlived both.
>
> So, it's amazing, my background. My background is in education and social work. I've been doing some of everything all my life. I have three children and they're grown now and doing good things. So about fourteen years ago [1979], I was elected to the House of Representatives of the State of Florida. And from there, the next two years, I was elected to the Congress—not to the Congress, I'm way ahead of myself—to the [Florida] Senate.
>
> I was in the Senate of the State of Florida for about eight years. So I grew to know all of the constituency of what you call elected bodies. I had some pork choppers. I had some rednecks. I had some of everything. So I saw how they make government work. And I swear if you see it, you wouldn't like it so much. You wouldn't like it a lot. But I saw it. My major areas of expertise in the Senate were education and housing. And I learned a lot about those things.
>
> One thing I never forgot, and that was civil rights. I was on the case from the minute I got there until when I left. Because, you know, they just don't understand. They don't understand. You have to help them understand. And that's what Carrie Meek was about, helping them understand. In my own inimitable way, I taught them how to understand that black folks deserve a space on this planet. And that we deserve our rights. And we deserve our privileges. And we need some of that money. So, that's what I was all about.
>
> And I came to the Congress. And I met nice academic people like Eleanor Holmes Norton. And she had never forgotten yet, when we met. I

have been a great admirer of hers throughout the years, when she was in the civil rights commission, and I always admired her because she has a scholarly acumen. I have a little bit of that too. But it's only—but mine kind of fades on the periphery of things until I have to call on it. Otherwise I use these other resources which are within my body.[2]

Carrie Meek's rendition of her life in nonstop prose, while engaging and entertaining, misses some of the true emotions, good and bad, that went along with the events that she recounts. Take education, for instance. In more serious dialogues, Congresswoman Meek talks about how she worked on the farm with the livestock and wanted to become a veterinarian. She speaks of the importance of education to her uneducated mother and her grandmother, who was born into slavery. It was the kind of encouragement that led to her taking advantage of her athletic prowess and using it as an entrée into college.

Long before she was a congresswoman, Meek was a track and field star as an undergraduate at Florida A&M, where she graduated in 1946 with a bachelor of science in biology and physical education. She was serious about continuing her studies; however, the South's segregated state education system meant that she could not attend graduate school within Florida. But under the separate but equal ruling, the state provided funds for her to seek an education somewhere else. As with many other blacks seeking graduate-level studies in the 1940s, she headed for the Midwest, where she found the University of Michigan to be more receptive to black graduate students. At Michigan, she received a master's degree in physical education and public health in 1948.

Some of the joy that Congresswoman Carrie Meek received from teaching at Bethune-Cookman College in Daytona Beach, Florida, also is unrecorded in her account. She was one of the few people living today who had an opportunity to work closely with the school's founder, Mary McCleod Bethune—the outstanding educator and human rights advocate, adviser to presidents and founder of the National Council of Negro Women. If any one person could be said to have had a tremendous impact on the life of Carrie Meek, it was Dr. Bethune.

By her very stature and prestige, the founder of Bethune-Cookman College brought guests to the campus who were the influential people of their time. Meek was exposed to such people at a young and impressionable age. While at Bethune-Cookman, she met first lady Eleanor Roosevelt, played basketball with famed tennis champion Althea Gibson, and met political leader Madame Nehru of India. Most of all, Meek received immense satisfaction from her role as a shaper and molder of young minds. She would often remember how young people, whose lives she changed, would approach her and remind her that she had been the teacher who made a difference.

Again, at the same time that she is low key about her marriages, closer examination reveals the hardship of being a single mother, not having any support to fall back on, recognizing that the least little deviation could mean the difference between eating dinner or not. All in all, Meek persevered and reared three children and endured the hardship of two divorces while still making a contribution to the Dade County community. Ambitious and talented, she moved up in the ranks of the college system, gaining the reputation as a hard worker and conscientious and frank administrator. By 1960 she was involved in the Model Cities program in Florida. For many people close to the needs of the poor and the urban centers, the Model Cities program represented an antipoverty program that put very little back into the communities they were designed to serve. Meek felt the same, but was more candid. She called those who abused the program "Ghetto hustlers" because she saw the program's wasteful spending and misguided direction under corrupt leadership. Meek decided to get involved.

The Political Odyssey

With Carrie Meek, as with other women in politics in Florida, one woman is often mentioned as having a tremendous influence on her political career— Gwendolyn Sawyer-Cherry (1923–1979). The Florida state representative died in an automobile accident, leaving behind a number of women who credit her with having encouraged and supported their political ambitions. Both congresswomen from Florida —Meek and Corrine Brown—speak of how she mentored them through the labyrinth of Florida politics. Sawyer-Cherry, a graduate of the University of Miami Law School, was the first black woman in the state legislature. When she died while in her fourth term in office, it left a void in the legislature and a missing presence that Meek was encouraged to fill. She accepted the challenge and faced twelve opponents. She was considered by pollsters as having no chance of winning. Entering the primary as an underdog, she emerged as the victor. She served in the Florida House from 1979 to 1982. That year she ran and was elected as the first black state senator since Reconstruction. In the Florida Senate, she chaired the Education Appropriations Subcommittee and established herself as a skilled debater and one of the legislature's most effective members. As a state senator, Meek developed much of Florida's current housing finance policy, established a broad array of public policy guidelines that included legislation that facilitated home ownership for working-class people, and sponsored legislation that created opportunities for the construction of more than one thousand affordable rental units. She also sponsored legislation that promoted minority business enterprises, education programs that encouraged literacy and prevented dropouts, and economic development in the inner city and blighted areas.

Meek was content in the Florida Senate, but when the issue of reapportionment arose, supporters encouraged her to run for Congress.

> I had gotten to the place in the Senate that I was in a position of leadership. I was chairwoman of the education subcommittee on appropriations, and had several other substantive committee assignments. So I thought about it, and my answer to myself was, how can I best serve the

people I represent? And I figured that if I were to come to Congress, which perhaps would have broader issues and broader policy levels, that I could help the most. Then, I decided that I would run. And that's why I did it.[3]

Her election was nothing short of a landslide. The only obstacle that she faced was the weather. Florida had just been hit by the devastating Hurricane Andrew, and election day had to be called off. Meek's campaign staff rented sound trucks and drove through the voting district announcing the instructions for the new election day. It was one of the major expenditures in her $400,000 campaign—an expenditure more than ten times that of her two opponents combined. Weather notwithstanding, she won the Democratic primary with 83 percent of the vote over candidates Darryl Reaves and Donald Jones, going on to the general election in 1992, where she received 100 percent of the vote. It was a pattern she would repeat in 1994 when she was reelected to a second term.

The Congressional Years

Thus, Meek came to Congress with a clear understanding that her 100 percent vote was a mandate to bring jobs and opportunity back to Florida's newly created Seventh Congressional District. Her strong stand on economic development and jobs for Floridians stood in stark contrast to her support for one of the major and most controversial trade agreements of the 103d Congress—the North American Free Trade Agreement (NAFTA). The legislation would eliminate barriers for American businesses who wanted to move to Mexico and take advantage of its low wages and lack of environmental regulations.

Economists were not in accord as to what impact the agreement would have on American jobs, but there was a school of thought that said that NAFTA would cost jobs for American workers. With Meek's strong stand on job creation, it was surprising to her supporters that she voted to pass NAFTA. One of the few criticisms raised about her first term was her shift in position on NAFTA, which she defended. It was her position that NAFTA did mean jobs, even for Florida. However, eighteen months after its enactment, even the Clinton economists noted that the treaty had cost Americans almost eighty thousand jobs. Meek's supporters say that she was an unwitting victim of the extreme pressure put on freshman members by President Bill Clinton.

She was an otherwise very loyal voter for progressive politics. She voted along with the Congressional Black Caucus more than 80 percent of the time.[4] She supported a ban on assault weapons, safeguards for access to abortion clinics, approval of the crime bill, President Clinton's budget—which raised taxes and cut spending—handgun control and the Clinton administration's position on lifting the ban on homosexuals in the military.

During the 103d Congress she was a constant presence on the floor of the House. Her high visibility was in part due to that first month in Congress, when she accomplished something few freshmen had—she landed a seat on the powerful Appropriations

Committee. With her background in the Florida legislature and her personal resolve and determination, she visited every member of the committee asking for their support. Her success and political acumen were testaments to a determination that would be equally as powerful when she was at odds with the House of Representatives.

The time for that test would come in 1995 during the 104th Congress. Smooth sailing with the Democrats in the 103d Congress was soon followed by the whirlwind of the Republicans of the 104th. Meek lost her seat on the Appropriations Committee under the Republicans and was given a seat on the Budget and Government Reform and Oversight Committees instead. The loss was devastating, given the lengths she had gone to get on the committee. Of course, Meek was a pro and she knew the politics of power and its transient nature. Even though it was a tough new Congress, it could not contain the spirited, sixty-eight-year-old congresswoman.

In January 1995 she refused to be muzzled by Republican leaders any longer. Congressman Newt Gingrich, the Republican Speaker of the House had contracted with Rupert Murdoch—one of the leading media moguls, who had business before the Congress—for a $4.5 million book advance. The House Ethics Committee was looking into the matter, the newspapers had given the lucrative deal headlines, but the tightly controlled Republican Congress refused to let members speak on the issue. Meek refused to be censored.

On January 19, 1995, she rose to make her one-minute speech for the day, and as the House quieted down, she was given permission to speak. In remarks that would be expunged from the *Congressional Record,* Meek questioned the Speaker's lucrative book publishing deal, saying that the allegations about Gingrich's book deal troubled her and that she was not satisfied with the answers. She was halfway through her comments when the gavel began to rise and fall, the Speaker pro tem called the House to order, the Republicans raised loud objections, and the sergeant-at-arms was poised to bodily carry Congresswoman Meek off the floor of the House, but she would not stop talking:

> News accounts tell us that while the Speaker may have given up a 4.5 million dollar advance, he stands to gain that amount and much more in royalties. Where I come from that's a lot of dust [money]. If anything, now, how much the Speaker earns has grown much more dependent upon how hard his publishing house hawks his book.
>
> Which leads me to the question of exactly who does this Speaker really work for. . . . Is it the American People or his New York publishing house?[5]

With calls to strike her remarks, the Republicans succeeded in having them expunged from the official *Congressional Record* of the session. It was another of those unbelievable occurrences, like the possible specter of having the House police literally carry away a woman who was old enough to be their grandmother. Meek, a grandmother and the granddaughter of slaves, barely missed being physically removed from the floor of the House of Representatives.

She boldly challenged the Republican-led House of Representatives on other occasions during their control, because she knew that she was engaged in a new battle. She needed all of the old tools of perseverance, faith, and courage to win. More importantly, the religious Meek also knew where to get those tools when she needed them the most.

Speech Excerpt: Congresswoman Carrie Meek at the 1993 Congressional Black Caucus Legislative Weekend on Women in Politics Workshop on Women in Congress

I thought about what Mary McCleod Bethune taught me. I worked at Bethune-Cookman College for ten years, and she always talked about the day would come when we would be known not for the color of our skins. She said this before Martin said it. But she said, "You'll be known for your character. And you'll be known for how well you're able to do a job." And when my good Senator here [Senator Carol Moseley-Braun] was elected, I almost died, almost died. I watched her election, and I used a term which Mary McCleod Bethune always used. "What has God wrought?" What has he wrought that I would be sitting here today at a table with Eleanor Holmes Norton and my good Senator from—she's from Illinois, from Chicago, big city lady.

But anyway, to be here with Senator Braun and Eleanor Holmes Norton, is to me, I think it is a part of history to be here, to know that I'm the oldest woman, even though I try to act 39, I'm the oldest. I try to act 39, but I'm old as rainwater. So, to be here, with them, in the Congress, is to me, an affirmation of what God has wrought. And I'm really, really loving it. I'm having a good time here with these folks. A great time. I'm getting some things done. I'm supporting everything the Black Caucus does. And when Eleanor stood on the floor and told them something, and I was there when Eleanor was talking about the District of Columbia. I was right there. I was up all night sleepy, but I was there with her because that personified what Carrie Meek is all about. When black folks are doing something, I'm there. And I'm going to be there and I'm going to push it.

I like white people too. But I think first of what is in this that's going to push black America. We need that push. We needed it since we came over here packed like spoons in the slave ship. And here we are now sitting in the halls of Congress. What has God wrought? What has he wrought? What has he wrought?

Source: Carrie Meek, Official Taped Proceedings, Congressional Black Legislative Weekend, 103d Congress, September 1993.

Chapter 13 **Cynthia Ann McKinney**

*Waging the Battle against the
Reversal of the Voting Rights Act*

Well, if you listen to my dad, he says I didn't learn enough. But
certainly, one of the things that I have learned is determination and
perseverance. Those things that are worth fighting for are often times
very difficult to achieve. And so we can't just try once or twice. But
we have to be dogged in our determination to see our results
achieved. And so, we take on the tough issues and we do real public
service, really without expectation of reward.

Résumé

Cynthia Ann McKinney

Personal

Born   March 17, 1955
Atlanta, Georgia

Family   Divorced; one child

Religion   Catholic

Party   Democrat

Took office   Age 37, January 5, 1993

Education

A.B.   University of Southern California, 1978

Professional/Political Background

1984–1985   Diplomatic fellow, Spelman College

1985–1988   Instructor, Clark Atlanta University and Agnes State College

1988–1992   Representative, Georgia House of Representatives

1993–   U.S. House of Representatives

Selected Awards/Organizational Affiliations

Metro Atlanta HIV Health Services Planning Council; National Council of Negro Women; National Association for the Advancement of Colored People; Sierra Club; freshman class secretary, 103d Congress.

Congressional Data

Eleventh Congressional District, Georgia: parts of Dekalb, Burke, and Butts Counties

Committees: Agriculture; International Relations

103d Congress: 1993–1994
1992 general election results: 73 percent of the vote

104th Congress: 1995–1996
1994 general election results: 66 percent of the vote

Cynthia Ann McKinney

*The First African American Woman
Elected to Congress from Georgia*

Eleventh District, Georgia
Democrat
103d Congress–present, 1993–

Reapportionment, the redistribution of the 435 House seats among the states to reflect shifts in population, and redistricting, the redrawing of congressional district boundaries within the states, are among the most important processes in the U.S. political system. They help to determine whether the House will be dominated by Democrats or Republicans, liberals or conservatives and whether racial or ethnic minorities receive fair representation.[1]

The Eleventh Congressional District was virtually carved out by Cynthia McKinney, who moved into it in 1992 so that she could run for the seat that she had created. The former Georgia state legislator sat on the Reapportionment Committee and fought hard for the Eleventh—the third minority district in the state. The scars endured in that battle were probably running through McKinney's mind as she stood on the platform alongside her colleagues in the congressional press room three years later, on June 29, 1995, when the U.S. Supreme Court handed down the decision declaring her congressional district unconstitutional.

McKinney, with a white pantsuit, her trademark braided hair, and an upturned chin stared beyond the cameras and remained resolute until asked about her next plan of action. Flanked by other members of the Congressional Black Caucus (CBC), it was evident that the decision had rendered her temporarily speechless. She stepped to the microphone, swallowed hard and spoke in a hesitant voice.

> No, there is nothing planned. There have been many of us trying to get something planned. But the fact that there is nothing planned speaks a whole lot about where we are as a people, as a community, who understood what this could mean, but whose priorities quite frankly were someplace else. Now we are confronted with this problem and I am sure we are going to come together and will respond in such a way as to not totally decimate our numbers of elected officials across this country who are at all levels of government.[2]

Fighting back tears, she then abruptly left the press conference. If there was one moment that gave insight into the complex political persona of Cynthia McKinney, it was this day, when her congressional career appeared to hang in the balance. Often called tenacious and uncompromising to a fault, she appeared vulnerable and exposed in an age-old political process in which she had been outmaneuvered by a conservative U.S. Supreme Court.

McKinney had just lost a fight that could cost many of the black members of Congress their seats. She had fought so hard for a third black congressional district in Georgia that she ignored the advice of her most trusted adviser and colleague, her father, state senator Billy McKinney, who cautioned her about pushing the reapportionment issue to the limit.

McKinney realized her ambition of becoming the first black woman to be elected to Congress from Georgia in 1992. That year she pressed for the creation of the Eleventh Congressional District, won the battle in the state legislature and then moved to Decatur, Georgia, so that she could run for the seat she had helped create. McKinney was a fighter.

McKinney had a history of defiance that included standing before the conservative Georgia state legislature and denouncing the Persian Gulf War and opposing her father and others in the state legislature on the issue of gay rights. While in Congress she had on a number of occasions debated major conservatives on abortion rights. But on the day of the ruling, she was saddened but surprisingly resigned to the Supreme Court's decision.

Known as *Miller v. Johnson*, the decision invalidated McKinney's Eleventh Congressional District because, in the Court's opinion, race was the overarching determinant in the district's creation, resulting in the abridgment of the constitutional rights of the five white plaintiffs. In their lawsuit, the white Georgians alleged that their Fourteenth Amendment right to "equal protection under the law had been violated" by the state's drawing of the congressional district's lines to maximize black voter participation. The Supreme Court's decision meant that the Georgia state legislature had to redraw the Eleventh Congressional District, and perhaps the other two minority districts as well, if they were proven to have been drawn with race as the major consideration. The state complied by eliminating McKinney's district and that of Congressman Sanford Bishop. The action eventually left only one minority black district, that of moderate civil rights veteran John Lewis.

Civil rights activists and black and minority legislators knew that the implications of the ruling would be far-reaching, with the worst case scenario being the elimination of not only McKinney's seat but of most seats held by African Americans and Hispanics representing minority districts.

Speculation that the decision could conceivably reverse the success of three decades of a qualitative voting franchise for African Americans and other minorities was heightened because the chances for a different Supreme Court with a more progressive temperament was so disturbingly remote. Georgia's Eleventh Congressional District had caused the Court to go further than many expected by reinterpreting the legislative intent of the Voting Rights Act of 1965 as it related to the creation of minority districts. In its opinion the Court stated:

> Our presumptive skepticism of all racial classifications . . . prohibits us as well from accepting on its face the Justice Department's conclusion that racial districting is necessary under the Voting Rights Act. Where a State relies on the Department's determination that race-based districting is necessary to comply with the Voting Rights Act, the judiciary retains an independent obligation in adjudicating consequent equal protection challenges to ensure that the State's actions are narrowly tailored to achieve a compelling interest.[3]

This reinterpretation, which in essence called into question whether the establishment of minority districts was in line with the intent of the Voting Rights Act, appeared to give further grounds for challenging all such districts.

Unprecedented numbers of black and other minority representatives were elected to Congress through the creation of these minority districts, with the largest contingent being members of McKinney's 103d congressional freshman class (1993–1994). Between 1985 and 1995, African Americans elected from predominantly black congressional districts rose from seventeen to thirty-two, and the increase for Hispanics was from nine to twenty. The statistics point to the potential threat the Supreme Court ruling posed—one that could decimate the first truly diverse and representative Congress that America had ever elected.

Needless to say, it was a tragic blow to voting rights and that is why more than resignation was expected from Congresswoman Cynthia McKinney, whose reputation as a confrontational and uncompromising politician was earned in no small measure from her efforts to create the minority district in question. In an apologia more than a call to arms, McKinney told an eager press corps hours following the decision: "I know that there is no burden too heavy to bear. This is a burden today but one that with all of these shoulders that are here we bear with dignity and grace and also with a redoubled effort to bring this country together rather than tear this country apart."[4]

McKinney's losing battle to save her congressional seat began on January 13, 1994, a year into her first term in the U.S. House of Representatives, when the white voters filed their racial gerrymandering lawsuit. That year, she joined other black members of her freshman class from North Carolina, Louisiana, Texas, and Florida who faced similar challenges. The protracted court battles would rack up millions of dollars in legal fees—drawing on dwindling resources of the NAACP Legal Defense Fund, the American Civil Liberties Union (ACLU), and private finances in an effort to combat the well-funded conservative legal organizations supporting the white litigants.

Alleging Fourteenth Amendment rights violations, the basis for the lawsuits themselves made a mockery of the hard-fought and hard-earned rights of American blacks.

The Fourteenth Amendment was ratified because of the violation of the rights of African Americans and the issue of white racial gerrymandering, which for more than half a century had diluted the black vote. These issues formed the foundation for the enactment of the 1965 Voting Rights Act.

Under the jurisdiction of the U.S. Department of Justice, southern states covered by the act were required to have any major legislation or change regarding voting, including the drawing of congressional districts, reviewed and precleared by either the U.S. Justice Department or the District Court of the District of Columbia. A vigilant Justice Department under Republican president George Bush had forced many of the states drawing districts after the 1990 census to maximize the majority black districts by placing high concentrations of blacks in a congressional district. Where the black population was spread across a large geographical area, the lines were drawn to include them.

Cynthia McKinney was not a hapless victim in the redistricting battle. She lobbied long, hard, and successfully for a third district that would have a majority black voting population. However, her efforts were in many ways both augmented and overshadowed by a larger strategy. This strategy had two major benefactors—the predominately white southern Democrats and the Republican party, eagerly awaiting an opportunity to expand in the South.

On the one hand, the majority white Democrats in state legislatures drew bizarre congressional districts that safeguarded white incumbents. And although in essence they legally tried to comply with the law, they had no intention of giving up any occupied seats. On the other hand, the Republican party also gained in the long run. Of course, they would not see the benefits from the 1990 redistricting until 1994, when the newly carved out black majorities created enclaves of white conservative congressional districts that provided fair game for Republican candidates. This seemed to be inevitable, since there were few black votes to boost the numbers in the Democratic party in those areas after the districts had been carved out. With the Republican gains in the House of Representatives in the 104th Congress (1995–1996), there was no longer a need to continue to maximize black districts, leaving state legislators with the responsibility now of essentially protecting what remnant of Democratic control they had.

It was this analysis that the ACLU's director of the Voting Rights Project, who supported McKinney, referred to when he said outside of the U.S. Supreme Court on the day of the ruling, "White Democrats who control the legislature would bleach out the majority-black districts in Georgia and further the interests of the Democratic Party by electing more Democrats—probably white—to Congress."

McKinney, as a former representative in the Georgia legislature and a member of its Reapportionment Committee, knew all too well that redistricting was nothing other than a preferential system for determining who controlled the state's politics. She had participated in the politics of redistricting just as the old-line Democrats had done, and she perhaps knew that hers might be a temporary victory. Her initial hope hinged on the possibility that the Supreme Court would stay above politics and respond, as it had done historically, to reapportionment by choosing not to enter into the fray of state governance. Recent history, of course, had not supported that assumption. In fact, this Court was not just indifferent. It was actually hostile to the Voting Rights Act and other civil rights remedies designed to level the playing field for blacks and other minorities.

Historically, the whole issue of redistricting and reapportionment was always wrought with race, ethnicity, party preference, and economic advantage. What the Court did was to leave all of those other determinants in place and eliminate race.

Being well-versed in the technical dynamics of how congressional districts are created was not necessary to understand the more fundamental message underlying the Supreme Court's ruling—that this was another in a string of setbacks to civil rights from the conservative U.S. Supreme Court. Dorothy Gilliam, a champion of women and civil rights and a columnist for the *Washington Post,* wrote what many blacks including McKinney believed, "A decision by the Supreme Court on Thursday was only the latest and most obvious signal that a period that has been called the Second Reconstruction is coming to an end."[5]

Gilliam's label, the "Second Reconstruction," had already become a part of the lexicon of African Americans as they witnessed the rolling back of civil rights gains through Supreme Court rulings supported by Republican members of Congress. African Americans had been whispering what Gilliam was saying out loud, and even though they had hoped that it would not happen, many recognized its inevitability given the conservative Court.

Not all African Americans felt uncomfortable with the rulings. Two, in particular, stand out as openly supporting them, actively participating in the effort, and creating a defining moment in philosophical differences in black political thought. McKinney's fellow Georgian, and the only black on the Supreme Court, Justice Clarence Thomas, joined with the other conservative Republican-appointed justices, Antonin Scalia, Sandra Day O'Connor, Anthony Kennedy, and Chief Justice William Rehnquist in the 5 to 4 ruling. In addition to *Miller v. Johnson,* which opened virtually all race-based electoral districts—those created in response to the 1965 Voting Rights Act—to constitutional challenge, they also prevailed and handed down decisions during the same term that limited the scope of school desegregation programs and made it tougher to uphold federal affirmative action programs and minority business set-asides.

In lockstep with Thomas's actions in the Supreme Court was the reaction of the black Republican congressman from Connecticut, Gary Franks. Franks may have taken particular pride in the defeat of McKinney. A year earlier, in 1994, when Congresswoman McKinney was holding hearings in her district on the threat the lawsuit posed, Franks went to Atlanta to testify in favor of the lawsuit, at which time the congresswoman's father, state senator Billy McKinney, chased Franks out of the meeting, verbally threatening bodily harm. For this the elder McKinney was fined $500—a fine he said was worth it because of Franks's stance.

Even before the hearings, each time the court ruled to roll back gains in civil rights,

Franks positioned himself in the House of Representatives to codify the judicial ruling. One example that baffled black and white leaders was his response to the first attack on the Voting Rights Act—*Shaw v. Reno*. In this case, the Supreme Court ruled in favor of the complainants, and Franks drafted legislation to codify the ruling. The ruling declared that the Twelfth Congressional District, represented by Mel Watt, was unconstitutional because it was drawn with race as the primary consideration. Thus, white voters were denied equal protection under the law. The first ruling remanded the case back to the state for resolution. In essence Franks's bill would have made law the claim that the irregular shape of North Carolina's Twelfth Congressional District deprived white voters of their Fourteenth Amendment rights because the district was created with race as a major consideration. Although the legislation had at least one hundred white Republican sponsors, the proposed bill died in committee.

On the day of the Georgia ruling, Congressman Franks called a press conference ahead of the CBC, in which he applauded the work of the Supreme Court and proclaimed vindication for his failed legislative effort:

> On June 30, 1993, I introduced a bill on racial gerrymandering of districts. It prohibited the creation of legislative districts based on race. I received over one hundred co-sponsors, all Republicans back in 1993 and obviously the Supreme Court agreed with this position.
>
> It is my belief that those with a different opinion on this issue were inadvertently asking for a return to a segregated society or an apartheid-like society. They were attempting to put as many blacks into one district to so-call guarantee an election of blacks to Congress. In my opinion, if the Supreme Court had ruled any differently it would have been a significant setback to race relations.[6]

Indeed, the position of most of the black people with historical perspective and the civil rights experiential ethos was summed up in the words of the Reverend Jesse Jackson: "The decision is disastrous because it strikes at the very heart and soul of the 1965 Voting Rights Act, the most important piece of social legislation of this century for people of color. The legal precedent that was upset by the court's action is critical, because political rights are preservative of all other rights."[7]

McKinney's case carried major implications for all of the black members of the House of Representatives with the exception, perhaps, of Republicans Gary Franks of Connecticut and J. C. Watts of Oklahoma, and Democrats Eleanor Holmes Norton, delegate from the District of Columbia, and Ronald Dellums of California. For different reasons these members were out of danger, the two Republicans because they were not in minority districts and Norton because the nation's capitol lacked voting representation in the Congress—Delegate Norton was Washington, D.C.'s only representative in the Congress and she represented the entire city. Dellums was in a majority white district, which included Berkeley, California. Thus, McKinney was the first casualty of the new attack on minority representation in Congress.

The Early Years

Cynthia Ann McKinney, was the youngest of the African American women to enter into the class of the 103d Congress. When she entered in 1993, she was thirty-seven years old and by far the most striking example of a new political generation: garbed generally in bright flowing dresses, sporting a braided hairstyle and golden tennis shoes, the single parent of one, openly worried about her dual role as mother and congresswoman. Rather than upset the schedule of her son, Coy, who was in elementary school during her first and second terms, McKinney left him in the care of her mother, Leola, a former nurse at Atlanta's Grady Memorial Hospital and her father, a Georgia state representative, J. E. "Billy" McKinney.

McKinney did not become the first black woman to be elected to Congress from Georgia by accident. She was groomed by her father. She went to St. Paul of the Cross, a Catholic high school in Georgia, and later to the University of Southern California, where she received an A.B. in 1978. In the early part of 1980, McKinney married Coy Grandison and moved with him to his home in Jamaica. In 1985 they had a son, Coy, Jr. A year later her name was placed on the ballot to run for the Georgia state legislature. Actually, when Cynthia McKinney's name was placed on the ballot, she was still living in Jamaica with her husband.

The Political Odyssey

Her father, who was a tremendous influence on her political life and aspirations, felt that she could run for the state legislature and win. Agreeing with him, McKinney returned to the States after separating from and eventually divorcing her husband, to run for office. Upon her return she campaigned in the 1986 election for the Georgia state legislature and lost. Her father had missed the mark this time. She did not win the election, but she was encouraged by the results and considered the defeat as a temporary setback at most.

> One of the things that I have learned is determination and perseverance. Those things that are worth fighting for are often times very difficult to achieve. And so we can't just try once or twice, but we have to be dogged in our determination to see our results achieved. And so we take on the tough issues and we do real public service, really without expectation of reward. . . . The very moment that you expect to be rewarded for public service is the very moment that you're willing to compromise on very important issues. We just have to understand that we're here for a mission, we're here for a purpose. And one of those purposes is not to compromise those areas that are of vital concern to our constituents.[8]

The editorial "we" is ever present in McKinney's discourse, as though she is still a partner with her father in the Georgia state legislature, where the two served together after she eventually won a seat in 1988 to represent Fulton County. The father-daughter legislative team was rare, and for the young McKinney it offered the protection of an ally against potential falls. Considered uncompromising in her challenges to the status quo, she was also considered by her critics to be a recalcitrant state legislator, which may account for her very limited record of actual legislative accomplishments in the Georgia House. Not noted for her ability to compromise, she was identified instead by her outspokenness on issues not normally challenged by the conservative Georgia state legislature.

In 1991 McKinney received national attention when she used the floor of the Georgia House to announce her opposition to the Persian Gulf War. Two-thirds of its members walked out on the speech in protest. Her father stayed and listened and then defended her against the opposition, who took to calling her "Hanoi Cynthia," a throwback to the days of actress Jane Fonda, whose outspoken position against the Vietnam War earned her the label "Hanoi Jane."

But it was that dogged determination and readiness to speak out on topics better left alone, that got McKinney elected to Congress. When redistricting became an issue in Georgia, she made it her issue by fighting for an expansion of the minority districts from two to three. The Georgia legislature presented two plans to the Justice Department for preclearance after it gained one seat resulting from the 1990 census reapportionment. It was the first seat in this century gained by the state, and it would change the composition of the solidly Democratic congressional delegation of nine Democrats and one Republican, Newt Gingrich.

The white Democrats in control of the Georgia state legislature had two major objectives and one standing requirement in drawing the new 1992 congressional district map. They wanted first to place Gingrich's seat in jeopardy, shifting it so that it would make it more difficult for him to get reelected. Gingrich had been a thorn in the side of the Democratically controlled House of Representatives since his election to Congress in 1979.

Second, since they knew that the expanding suburban Atlanta population of affluent whites would probably vote Republican, they would in all likelihood have to resign themselves to the fact that two districts would be lost. Their major constraint, however, was that they were required to maintain the minority Fifth Congressional District, and a shift in the black population gave them the Second Congressional District, another minority seat. It was the creation of the third minority district—McKinney's Eleventh Congressional District, which included the suburbs of Atlanta, Augusta, and nineteen rural counties— that the legislature was reluctant to include in the redistricting plan presented to the Justice Department.

In 1992 McKinney won her battle for the third district. Turning from crusader to politician—just as the "good old boys" had done in the past—as soon as the state legislature adjourned, she moved out of her Fulton County state district and into the Eleventh Congressional District so that she would qualify as a candidate for the 1992 election. With the help of her father, a three-time unsuccessful candidate for the U.S. House of

Representatives, she launched her campaign for Congress. With the elder McKinney, her major strategist, campaign manager and treasurer, close at hand, Cynthia McKinney joined four others in the crowded Democratic primary. The major competition came from the one white candidate, George L. DeLoach, and the alleged favorites, black state senator Eugene Walker and state representative Michael Thurmond, chairman of the state house black caucus.

The father-and-daughter team's strategy was to attack the two leading black candidates because they were the strongest and to treat them as a part of the old system of Democratic machine politicians. With almost two decades in the Georgia House, Billy McKinney had a better handle on the vulnerability of the two black candidates and thus could better focus the younger McKinney's tactics. As for her opponents, both Walker and Thurmond attacked McKinney's integrity. They charged that she had abandoned her constituency in Fulton County by moving into the Eleventh just to run for Congress.

McKinney countered by painting herself as a champion for the people who fought to get the additional district and fair representation for blacks. Besides the normal ugliness of the campaign, another cloud hung over the trail. There were places that the black candidates could not go because of the intense racism that still hampered the progress of the South. Even after her election, McKinney could not enter parts of the Eleventh District because of threats of violence.

The results in, McKinney received 31 percent of the vote, DeLoach 25 percent, Walker 22 percent, and Thurmond 16 percent. A required run-off produced another victory for McKinney, who received 56 percent to DeLoach's 44 percent, virtually assuring her of a win over the Republican challenger in the general election, Woodrow Lovett. Indeed, she did win, by a landslide vote of 73 percent to Lovett's 27 percent.

The Congressional Years

The briefly held victory was Cynthia McKinney's reward for winning the battle for another minority congressional seat. The elder McKinney took his bows for staging a successful campaign, and his daughter took her place in history as the first African American woman elected from the state of Georgia. When McKinney was sworn in to the 103d Congress in 1993, she selected and received assignments on the International Relations and Agriculture Committees.

But just as in her four years in the state legislature, it would be her confrontations that would bring her recognition in the press and not her legislative agenda. This time it was the Hyde Amendment, an amendment that forbade government funds being used for abortions for poor women. The debate was a catalyst for mobilizing the forty-eight women in the House, and it was a headline grabber for the Georgia congresswoman.

If there was one legacy shared by black women who have served in Congress, it is opposition to the Hyde Amendment, which usually comes attached to the appropriations bills for Health and Human Services. Congressman Henry Hyde (R-Ill.) is considered by some political analysts to be one of the few "intellectually honest" members of Congress. The Catholic congressman represents "one of the most heavily Republican districts in the nation."[9] And yet, in the perception of prochoice women, there is no stronger foe, no larger villain than the tall, gray-haired veteran congressman.

He has been identified as one of the most ardent antiabortion members in the Congress. Taking every opportunity to promote his cause, he uses a technique perfected by the former African American congressman from Harlem, Adam Clayton Powell, Jr. Powell would attach a nondiscrimination amendment—called the Powell Amendment— onto every appropriations bill that came through the House. His success is legend in creating opportunities for blacks in education, access to public accommodations, and publicly supported services.

In similar fashion, in the early 1970s Congressman Hyde used the same tactic to block federal funding of abortions, which he considered murder. The first amendment was proposed while the inimical Barbara Jordan was still in the House of Representatives. Former congresswoman Jordan's account of her battle to eliminate the Hyde Amendment is quoted in *A Woman's Place,* by former congresswoman Marjorie Margolies-Mezvinsky.

> I had the misfortune to be in Congress when the Hyde Amendment was introduced and passed in 1977. I even served with Henry Hyde on the House Judiciary Committee. He pursued his legislation with an unusual enthusiasm and stridency that was as shocking as it was eye opening to me. I used all my influence with the Texas delegation to get these representatives to vote against the Hyde Amendment.... Although I was discouraged to see legislation pass which was sponsored by men and designed to limit women's freedom, I was pleased to help Jim Wright switch his influential vote. And yet, sixteen years later, the Hyde Amendment, incredibly is still being flaunted by men over the desires of the women it tyrannizes.[10]

Even with such past valiant and spirited opponents as Barbara Jordan, Hyde could not get over the anger and the outrage exhibited by the women of the 103d Congress. His own behavior notwithstanding, he participated in the House of Representatives shouting match between supporters and opponents of the amendment, which included a very caustic Cynthia McKinney. Hyde, known for his vitriolics, insulted Representative Cardiss Collins when he implied that she did not know what was happening with poor people in her district.

Collins, a twenty-one year veteran of the House at the time, demanded that he retract his statement, which he later did. However, if anyone captured the moment and the essence of the debate, it was the freshman McKinney. After listening to the banter of white men talking about abortion for poor women who were disproportionately women of color, she approached the floor for recognition, and after calling the Hyde

Amendment "nothing but a discriminatory policy against poor women who happen to be disproportionately black," she added, "Quite frankly, I have just about had it with my colleagues who vote against people of color, vote against the poor, and vote against women."

Hyde turned the tables on McKinney: "We tell poor people, 'you can't have a job, you can't have a good education, you can't have a decent place to live. . . . I'll tell you what we'll do, we'll give you a free abortion because there are too many of you people, and we want to kind of refine the breed.' "[11]

The exchange was significant in that it was the first to actively point out the militant and strident tone of the new African American women in Congress, and it also separated their agenda from that of the white women feminists in the House. House Speaker Tom Foley was called in to quell the fiery debate that ensued. For the first time, enough women were in the House of Representatives to demand respect and a different approach to the deliberations that centered around women's issues. The Hyde Amendment passed the House by a vote of 255 to 178, causing some major divisions in the Women's Caucus between minority women and prochoice and prolife congresswomen.

The schism was further exacerbated when Senator Carol Moseley-Braun (D-Ill.) refused to vote for the Freedom of Choice Act, which would codify the Supreme Court's decision in *Roe v. Wade,* providing the right to chose abortion. Moseley-Braun in solidarity with McKinney and the other black women in the House, let it be known that if poor women could not exercise their right to abortion, she would not vote for a bill that would allow women with means to have abortions.

It may have been a victory for Henry Hyde, but the Hyde Amendment debate had moved women of the House to a new relationship—one that ostensibly gave more respect to the role of African American women in defining the lives of the people they represented. For McKinney, it meant more visibility and resulted in calls for her to expand her leadership opportunities within the House. She was later called upon by the House leadership to head the Women's Caucus Task Force on Children, Youth and Families and continued to work within the confines of the Women's Caucus and the Progressive Caucus and to serve as the secretary for the 103d freshman class of Democrats.

Less than two weeks after the Supreme Court decision, McKinney was back to her old fighting posture. She was wearing a T-shirt with the slogan, "You Can't Keep a Good Woman Down, Cynthia McKinney—You Go Girl." Her father was beside her loudly criticizing the fifth vote on the Supreme Court, Clarence Thomas, as a "handkerchief-headed Uncle Tom," and McKinney's legislative staff was preparing a bill to bring back cumulative voting, which would eliminate winner-take-all elections. She hinted at starting a third-party campaign and persuaded the American Civil Liberties Union to challenge the state's redrawn map, which eventually eliminated the Eleventh Congressional District in accordance with the ruling. Congresswoman Cynthia McKinney had rebounded. She was not going to repeat history, her apologia was gone, and her call to arms had begun.

Excerpts from
Miller v. Johnson
Supreme Court
of the United
States
June 29, 1995

In *Shaw v. Reno,* 509 U.S. . . . this Court articulated the equal protection principles that govern a State's drawing of congressional districts, noting that laws that explicitly distinguish between individuals on racial grounds fall within the core of the Equal Protection Clause's prohibition against race-based decision making, that this prohibition extends to laws neutral on their face but unexplainable on grounds other than race, and that redistricting legislation that is so bizarre on its face that it is unexplainable on grounds other than race demands the same strict scrutiny given to other state laws that classify citizens by race. Georgia's most recent congressional districting plan contains three majority black districts and was adopted after the Justice Department refused to preclear under [subsection] 5 of the Voting Rights Act, two earlier plans that each contained only two majority-black districts. Appellees, voters in the new Eleventh District—which joins metropolitan black neighborhoods together with the poor black populace of coastal areas 260 miles away—challenged the District on the ground that it was a racial gerrymander in violation of the Equal Protection Clause as interpreted in Shaw. . . . Appellants cannot refute the claim of racial gerrymandering by arguing the Legislature complied with traditional districting principles, since those factors were subordinated to racial objectives. Nor are there tangible communities of interest spanning the District's hundreds of miles that can be called upon to rescue the plan. Since race was the predominant, overriding factor behind the Eleventh District's drawing, the State's plan is subject to strict scrutiny and can be sustained only if it is narrowly tailored to achieve a compelling state interest. . . . In utilizing [subsection] 5 to require States to create majority-minority districts whenever possible, the Department expanded its statutory authority beyond Congress' intent for [subsection] 5; to insure that no voting-procedure changes would be made that would lead to a retrogression in the position of racial minorities with respect to their effective exercise of the electoral franchise. The policy also raises serious constitutional concerns because its implicit command that States may engage in presumptive unconstitutional race-based districting brings the Act, once upheld on a proper exercise of Congress' Fifteenth Amendment authority, into tension with the Fourteenth Amendment. . . . affirmed and remanded.

Source:
U.S. Supreme Court Syllabus, *Miller et al. v. Johnson et al.,* appeal from the United States District Court for the Southern District of Georgia, no. 94-631.

Kennedy, J., delivered the opinion to the Court, in which Chief Justice William H. Rehnquist, Associate Justice Sandra Day O'Connor, Associate Justice Antonin Scalia, and Associate Justice Clarence Thomas filed a concurring opinion. The dissenting Justices were Associate Justice John Paul Stevens, Associate Justice David H. Souter, Associate Justice Ruth Bader Ginsburg, and Associate Justice Steven Breyer.

Chapter 14

Eva McPherson Clayton

*The First Woman to Chair a
Democratic Freshman Class*

I think there is a higher expectation of us as Afro-American women
because there have been so few of us. And once we are here in some
mass, then they will see us as a group and we will not have to be just a
Barbara Jordan or just a Shirley Chisholm, but we would be looked
upon as individuals. . . . So, I think the expectation is, in my judgment,
a little too high.

Résumé

Eva McPherson Clayton

Personal

Born September 16, 1934
Savannah, Georgia

Family Married to Theaoseus Clayton; four children

Religion Presbyterian

Party Democrat

Took office Age 58, January 5, 1993

Education

B.S. Johnson C. Smith University, 1955

M.S. North Carolina Central University, 1965

Professional/Political Background

1974–1976 Executive director, Soul City Foundation

1977–1981 Assistant secretary for Natural Resources, North Carolina Office of the Governor

1981–1992 Technical Resources International (TRI), Ltd.

1982–1990 Commissioner, Warren County Commission

1993– U.S. House of Representatives

Organizational Affiliations

Fair Housing Commission and Judicial Compensation Commission; member, Association of County Officials.

Congressional Data

First Congressional District, North Carolina: parts of Warren, Washington, and Wayne Counties

Committees: Agriculture; Small Business

103d Congress:	1993–1994
1992 special election results:	57 percent of the vote
1992 general election results:	67 percent of the vote
104th Congress:	1995–1996
1994 general election results:	61 percent of the vote

Eva McPherson Clayton

*The First African American Woman
Elected to Congress from North Carolina*

First District, North Carolina
Democrat
103d Congress–present, 1993–

"I wanted to be a missionary and I don't share this too much, but Albert Schweitzer was a model for me," confided Congresswoman Eva Clayton of North Carolina in an almost conspiratorial tone.

> Not that I thought I was as brilliant as he, nor could I play the piano, nor did I have a love for philosophy nor was I a theologian. But I was interested in medicine and I was interested in theology and I took a lot of philosophy courses in college. My initial interest came from people who served their lives in the fields of Africa. . . . I think that the desire that I have to serve and be engaged in people's lives is why I am serving in Congress and it is what gives me the impetus to serve with the depth that I do.[1]

Eva Clayton—while not following her original path as a physician and missionary in Africa—did find an outlet for her penchant for service, first as an active civic leader and eventually as an engaged and effective legislator. It was service that she considered equally as fulfilling and personally rewarding. Never more so than in 1992 when—with the support and encouragement of her husband and four adult children—the 58-year-old Clayton made her imprint on American history.

She held the dual distinction of being the first woman elected to serve a full term in Congress from North Carolina and, along with Melvin Watt (D-N.C.), she was one of the first African Americans elected to the House of Representatives from her state in the twentieth century. Actually, because she won a special election to serve out the remainder of the 102d Congressional term of the deceased Walter Jones, Sr., Clayton was technically the first black from North Carolina to be elected in the post-Reconstruction period.

In January 1993, after her swearing in as a freshman member of the U.S. House of Representatives in the 103d Congress, she became the first of her gender and race to be elected president of a Democratic freshman class. With sixty-three members, it was the largest Democratic class since the post-Watergate elections in the 1970s. Thus, in a short span of three months, Clayton became a leader in what was to have been the last session of a forty-year stint of Democratic leadership in the U.S. House of Representatives.

The Early Years

Born September 16, 1934, in Savannah, Georgia, Clayton moved to Augusta when her father, an insurance man, was relocated to the city. It was there as a child in Augusta that she decided to pursue a career in medicine and missionary work. Two incidents ignited the young woman's ambition and fired her imagination.

Clayton grew up in the Methodist church and later became a Presbyterian—both reformed denominations with strong social-activist components. Like many young people, she was impressionable and began to envision a life in service to a people in need. After befriending a neighbor who was stricken with polio, she came to the conclusion that it was medicine that would give her that special edge as a missionary. The thought became more than the musings of a young woman. It carried her through a Presbyterian high school and into her college years at Johnson C. Smith University in North Carolina. There, as a premed student, she majored in zoology. While in her freshman year, she met Theaoseus T. Clayton, a senior and prelaw student. Theaoseus Clayton was a native North Carolinian. Born in 1930, he graduated from Johnson C. Smith in 1955 and went on to law school in 1958. After graduating, he began a legal career that would eventually establish him as one of North Carolina's prominent lawyers and civic workers.

The two married (and have stayed married for nearly four decades) and remained in North Carolina. Eva Clayton completed her course work at Johnson C. Smith, graduating in 1955 with a bachelor of science in biology. In 1962 she earned a master of science degree in biology and general science at North Carolina Central University. Although she had invested academic time in the premed sciences, by the late 1960s she abandoned her idea of becoming a physician, studying for a law degree instead. The Claytons were on the cusp of the emerging new politics of North Carolina. By 1968 they were involved in voter registration and education projects that led to her first foray into national politics— seeking a seat in the U.S. House of Representatives.

The Political Odyssey

One account of Clayton's first race reported: "As a graduate student that year, she went door-to-door in the black community in an effort to unseat Democratic Representative L. H. Fountain, who black leaders felt was unresponsive to their concerns. She received 30 percent of the vote, though Clayton says she knew she had embarked on a long shot when none of the men who had criticized Fountain decided to challenge him."[2]

The political neophyte's impressive 30 percent showing was enough to make the political establishment take notice of her and the community for which she spoke. Although unsuccessful, she was respected for her political courage, her hard work, and a good showing in the polls—all of which became a part of her reputation as a formidable leader. Even though Clayton still views her first campaign as a bit quixotic, she has never regretted the attempt. She did later regret, however, that she dropped out of law school.

With her fourth and youngest child in tow, school was more than she could handle. "I wasn't super enough to be a super mom," Clayton told a *New York Times* reporter in May of 1993, "I left [law school] to be a mom. My husband was supportive, but I felt enormously guilty. I think I would do it differently now. I think I would know how to demand more of my husband."[3]

What she did take to fruition was her political career, however. The 1968 taste of politics kept her anxious, heightened her political ambitions, and started her on a path that would eventually lead to Congress. In the ensuing years, she continued to work as a community leader and combined those efforts with various executive and administrative positions. She served as executive director of the Soul City Foundation from 1974 to 1976—a black new town development founded by civil rights activist Floyd McKissick. She was appointed by Governor James Hunt to serve as assistant secretary for natural resources for North Carolina from 1977 to 1981. Leaving government, she launched her own company in 1981, Technical Resources International, Inc. (TRI), a consulting company specializing in economic development. Its clientele included local and state governments, small businesses, nonprofit organizations, and regional banks. She continued as president of TRI until her election to Congress in 1992.

Most significant politically was her election to serve as a member of the Warren County Commission in 1982. In many ways her political odyssey paralleled the journey of North Carolina from a sleepy southern state to a progressive Sun Belt attraction. Clayton gained high visibility as a Warren County commissioner, in part because of her role in the county's transition, characterized by the changing of the guard in local politics and economic development that spurred growth in the county. For example, in 1982, when she was elected as chair of the Warren County Board of Commissioners—a position she held for nearly a decade—there were two African Americans on the once all-white five-member commission. By the end of her tenure as chair, the commission was majority black and a major political force in Warren County and in the state's transition.

Clayton oversaw economic development, delivery of health care, and maintenance of roads and infrastructure for the growing county. The North Carolina Research Triangle, a respected academic center, was both a magnet that brought in high technology businesses and an amalgam of intellectuals, technocrats, and professionals, many of whom were attracted by southern lifestyles that were less costly and more environmentally appealing alternatives to northern cities.

A major shortcoming of an otherwise forward-looking state was its congressional representation, which for many was exemplified by its most visible senator—arch-conservative Republican Jesse Helms. Although there were still some hard-line Jessecrats—white Democrats who voted for conservative white Republicans based on racial protectionism—blocking racial progress in the state, the nearly successful senatorial campaign waged by the black Democratic former mayor of Charlotte, Harvey Gantt, offered a glimmer of hope for possible change. In a racially charged campaign, Gantt lost to Senator Helms by a vote of 53 to 47 percent. The 1990 senatorial race drew national attention, and the close vote meant to some that change was inevitable and that the stigma of the state's regressive politics would soon subside. One analyst concluded the following about the Gantt-Helms race:

> Gantt fell in the polls, and there was reason all along to think some of the Helms vote was hidden, concealed by conservative voters who would not speak openly to pollsters of the hated liberal media. Gantt carried young voters and Helms, the elderly—the opposite of partisan patterns elsewhere in the nation that year—and Gantt won solidly in Charlotte but ran behind in much of east Carolina. It was said by some that Gantt lost because of racism. But what is remarkable is that North Carolina's polarized politics has developed to the point that a black candidate can compete on an equal basis with a white—something that would have been astonishing 20 years ago.[4]

Despite the fact that Gantt's political showing was encouraging, North Carolina would not get black representation in Congress until 1993. When it came, it resulted in part from the welcoming economic climate of the 1980s that brought an unprecedented population growth to the state. So that by the 1990 census, North Carolina—under the requirements of the Voting Rights Act of 1965 and its 1982 amendments—had to create two new minority congressional districts.

The reluctance to create the first new seats in sixty years was evident in the unsuccessful configurations that the state senate initially mapped out. Each congressional map drawn by the state legislature had as its purpose the preservation of white congressional seats with minimal compliance with the Voting Rights Act. The final map, which was approved by the U.S. Department of Justice included two irregularly shaped congressional districts—the First and the Twelfth. The districts—which would eventually put two African Americans in Congress for the first time in the twentieth century—came under scrutiny and court challenge almost as soon as they were created.

One of the districts, the First Congressional District, with a 57 percent black majority, included Clayton's Warren County political turf, giving her an opportunity to renew her quest for a seat in the U.S. House of Representatives. As she prepared to run, the incumbent in the old First Congressional District—Congressman Walter Jones, then 78—announced his retirement. It was speculated that one reason was to take advantage of the law allowing him to keep his campaign treasury and the other was so that he could shift his political support to his son.

Walter Jones, Jr., a state senator, would run in the new minority district. As the younger Jones prepared to capture the Democratic primary, Clayton was developing her strategy to run against him. She was one of seven candidates running in the Democratic primary—two whites and five blacks. Jones, Jr., had the greatest advantage: name recognition, his father's political machinery, and support from white Democrats—all of which would normally be enough to assure victory. Indeed, he was victorious, but did not gain the 40 percent plurality necessary to win in a Democratic primary. With 38 percent of the vote, he had to go head-to-head with the runner-up, Clayton, who received 31 percent.

Of course, the existence of a run-off made black representation a possibility, but not a certainty, which meant that Clayton's election strategy was crucial. Due to the irregular shape of the district, strategic campaigning was required for Clayton to overtake Jones's inherited political machine. In listening to her description of the First Congressional District, the difficulty she had in designing a cohesive winning strategy is evident.

> My district geographically is a very large district. It's large because we don't have a lot of people in our districts. By and large we call it a rural district. If you think of North Carolina, it would be considered the northeast and the southeast, going along the Virginia line from Vance County to Henderson to Elizabeth City. Then you move southerly down to Wilmington and again you come west over to Fayetteville. And all of those counties in between would be part of my twenty-eight counties. I have eight counties in their entirety. And I have twenty counties I share with other Congresspersons. The third district overlaps the second and the seventh. Big cities that I have that are over twenty-five to thirty-five thousand would be Fayetteville, Rocky Mount, Wilmington, Kingston. Those would be what we consider our larger towns.

It was this expansive area that the candidates had to capture to win the election. With more than twenty-five years of hands-on development and organizing experience in the community, Clayton's strategy was to capitalize on her name recognition in the areas where she had been involved in the work of county, civic, and religious organizations. She would also use her strength with the unions and national women's organizations to gain campaign funds, volunteers, and exposure. Where she was not known, Clayton relied on the historic import of a successful election to capture the grassroots vote of black North Carolinians. Giving the voters a chance to participate in history by electing the first African American in the twentieth century and the first black woman ever was a part of Clayton's campaign strategy for winning the rural pockets of black voters.

With the slogan "The Best for the First," she defeated Jones in the Democratic run-off with 55 percent of the vote to his 45 percent. As a result, in November Clayton was both a candidate for the remaining term of the elder Jones, who had died in office on September 15, 1992, and a candidate for a full term, representing the new district. She won both. On election day, with 67 percent of the vote, she defeated Republican Ted Tyler, who received 31 percent, and a minor Libertarian candidate, who received 2 percent. In the special election for Jones's seat she received 57 percent of the vote to Tyler's 41 percent, with the Libertarian candidate maintaining the same percentage as before.

In the meantime, Melvin Watt, an attorney, also won a seat in the U.S. House of Representatives, representing the newly created Twelfth Congressional District. Both Clayton and Watt gave North Carolina black representation for the first time since Republican congressman George White (1897–1901) left the House of Representatives.

Because White's departure was an enduring symbol of the end of Reconstruction, the press, primarily the African American press, gave historical significance to the victories of Watt and Clayton by repeating the history of the demise of Reconstruction. As with most of the blacks who were elected in 1992 from the new minority districts of the South, they were the first post-Reconstruction representatives in Congress from their states. North Carolina was a special reference point for the historical analysis, because White's departure officially sealed the political gains made by blacks in the nineteenth century.

It was the political compromise between Republican president-elect Rutherford B. Hayes and Democratic presidential challenger Samuel Tilden in 1876 that established a process that systematically stripped away the voting franchise of African Americans, withdrew federal troops from the South, and condoned vigilante violence against blacks for almost a century. It was one of the most egregious injustices inflicted upon blacks by the government since slavery. Politically, the post-Reconstruction period is punctuated by White's speech, delivered on the eve of his departure in 1901. Standing before the House of Representatives, he made these historic and impassioned remarks:

> This, Mr. Chairman, is perhaps the Negroes' temporary farewell to the American Congress. But let me say, phoenix-like, he will rise up someday and come again. These parting words are in behalf of an outraged, heart-broken, bruised and bleeding people, but God-fearing people, faithful, industrious, loyal people . . . rising people, full of potential.[5]

It would be almost three decades before another African American would serve in Congress. Oscar DePriest (R-Ill.), sworn in in 1929, would rise up phoenix-like as the first black to be elected in the twentieth century. In spite of discriminatory Jim Crow treatment in the congressional dining halls, rest rooms, and surrounding living quarters, blacks would continue to serve in Congress throughout the first half of the century, albeit at a slow pace. And they would endure the humiliation until 1945, when the bold and audacious New York Democratic congressman Adam Clayton Powell, Jr. (1945–1970) demanded better.

The Congressional Years

For White's home state of North Carolina, however, it would take ninety-one years—almost another century—to get African American representation on Capitol Hill. Even then, it would be a strange twist of fate that a court challenge to the North Carolinians' elections would be the first in a string of Supreme Court decisions that would overturn major civil rights gains and would provide the twentieth-century analogy to the nineteenth-century demise of Reconstruction. Three months into office, Clayton and Watt were hit with lawsuits that challenged the existence of their seats and threatened the future of all of the blacks elected from minority districts.

While fighting to maintain her district, Clayton was still able to begin establishing herself as a leader in the House of Representatives. She could not have entered at a more opportune time. It was 1992, the "Year of the Woman," and a euphoria swept over the House of Representatives as an unprecedented twenty-four new women entered the 103d Congress, expanding the Women's Caucus to forty-eight.

Because of the 1990 census and the 1965 Voting Rights Act, the number of new black legislators entering Congress was the largest ever at seventeen, expanding the Congressional Black Caucus (CBC) to forty (thirty-nine in the House and one in the Senate). In all, 110 new members entered the House; sixty-seven were Democrats. It was the largest freshman class since the 1974 post-Watergate election brought in seventy-five new members to the House.

The Democratic freshmen were immediately empowered because of the forty-year control that the party held over the House of Representatives, its control in the Senate, and its newly won control of the White House. With that party backing, the new members enjoyed an unusually high profile, and choice committee assignments as well as other perquisites of power. For example, for the first time there were freshmen assigned to the powerful Ways and Means and Appropriations Committees, both of which were generally the preserve of senior members.

It also put the freshman class leadership in a critical mediating position for competing interests both within the Congress and with the administration. The two strong power bases of the Democrats, women and African Americans, would converge in the freshman class. Representative James Clyburn (D-S.C.) knew that the political strength of the women in the freshman class could defeat his quest to be elected as class president, so he decided to cut a deal with them. If elected, he would place a woman in as chair for the first part of the session, and he would serve the balance. "If they agreed," he pledged, "I would defer the first year out of respect and homage to the Year of the Woman."[6]

Clayton became that woman. She was discerning, mature, and even-handed—all qualities that her colleagues agreed made her the perfect fit for the job. She added to her growing political biography the designation of being the first woman and the first black to become president of a Democratic freshman class, a designation that seemed not to faze her in the least.

> I did not come to be president of the freshman class. . . . That was not an aspiration of mine. I did come, however, to be a leader, did not know it was going to be as president of the freshman class or chair of what committee, but I wanted to be a leader for certain issues. And those issues that I was interested in had to do with the quality of life where people lived

and I wanted to find opportunities here in Congress, among committees and colleagues who shared that desire to improve the quality of life for their constituents.

Clayton had her work cut out for her. The class president is the intermediary between the new members and the House party leadership, as well as a facilitator for meetings with the president and vice president of the United States. At a time when the ambitious programs of the newly elected president, Bill Clinton, needed as much support in the House of Representatives as possible, the 103d Congress freshman class gained new significance and power—making the normally ceremonial and perfunctory role of the class president a pivotal and powerful position from which to launch a new congressional career. In assessing her 1993 role as freshman class president, she explained:

> I conveyed the intentions or the desires or the expectations of the leadership back to the freshman class. I also arranged for the Speaker, the majority leader or the President or the Vice President to speak to the freshman class, or likewise, they may have said to me, "We would like for the freshman class to talk with the president about the budget reconciliation act."

Legislation in the 103d Congress taxed Clayton's leadership skills and ability to build coalitions. Although major legislative initiatives such as health care reform never made it out of Congress, a significant number of other bills and amendments did. Many of them were rallying points for Democratic unity, while others chipped away at the fleeting idea of Democratic cohesiveness.

For example, even though investment in local police departments was virtually a unanimous and decisive vote, the same could not be said for "three strikes, you're out" legislation, which created schisms within the freshman class just as it had within the body as a whole. The omnibus anti-crime bill—which required life in prison for anyone convicted of a third violent crime—caused consternation among members of the CBC and others concerned with the potential for abuse against minority populations, whose representation in the prison population was already disproportionate. Others, even though liberals on social issues, were conservatives on the crime bill.

Bringing these disparate views to the fore and trying to maintain party strength in voting were tasks for which Clayton had to develop new skills and certainly different ones from those used in her Warren County Commission chairmanship. Many of her colleagues had experience in political negotiations gained while in state legislatures, which put Clayton at a slight disadvantage but not at a loss—she gained those skills while in office and prevailed as a strong class president.

Other highly charged and extensively debated legislation under her leadership included the Brady bill, a handgun control bill; "Goals 2000," an education reform bill; and family leave, a bill requiring some employers with fifty or more employees to provide workers with up to twelve weeks of unpaid, job-protected leave to care for a new child or a seriously ill child, parent, or spouse. These were some of the major items that required coordination and leadership.

One point at which she was called upon to exercise her mediating skills was during the controversial Budget Reconciliation Act. She facilitated at least three meetings with the White House, one with all of the freshman class and others with just the Democrats. Known as the Omnibus Budget Reconciliation Act, the legislation provided spending cuts and revenue increases needed to achieve $496 billion in deficit reduction over five years. The division came from the amount of reductions in Medicare, Medicaid, and other programs that freshmen had pledged to safeguard once in Congress.

Clinton, concerned in many ways more about his ability to achieve successful passage of a key piece of legislation than with the toll it would take on supporters, personally lobbied members of Congress, including one of the most pro-active members of the new class—Representative Marjorie Margolies-Mezvinsky (D-Pa.). Margolies-Mezvinsky opposed the legislation because she had made promises to preserve Medicaid and not support any tax increases. But after extensive lobbying from Clinton, she capitulated, which later cost her congressional seat. It was, no doubt, Margolies-Mezvinsky that Clayton spoke of as she was reminded of those members of her class who were not reelected after the tumultuous legislative battles of the 103d Congress. "Some of the things that we were able to vocalize in the freshman class are some of the things that were tools for our demise," she said in a somber reflection on the class's attrition rate. The budget was not the only pitfall for the freshman class though; another was the North American Free Trade Agreement (NAFTA).

Clayton announced early in her term that the freshman class would not support NAFTA. She was wrong. While unified, the class did not represent uniformity, and her control over consensus voting began to diminish when members began using their individual political capital to barter for votes. With an issue as volatile and politically visible as NAFTA, she found that members went their own way and could not be counted upon to vote in a bloc.

NAFTA was a trade bill that opened up the Canadian and Mexican borders to American goods and American businesses through the establishment of free trade zones, the elimination or reduction of tariffs, and the liberalizion of investment practices. The manufacturers and producers of American goods could enjoy the use of low-wage labor and fewer federal regulations by building factories and manufacturing plants in Mexico. For many congressional representatives whose districts included lower-middle-class and working-class poor, it meant the loss of an already shrinking job pool to a cheap labor market. As for environmentalist and consumer advocates, it could mean that products would be produced without federal guidelines and regulations that would ensure safety, reliability, and environmental soundness.

Proponents justified their support by citing such benefits as the potential impact that the treaty would have on stemming the flow of undocumented workers crossing the

Mexican borders and the potential for opening up new markets for American businesses through the expansion of economic buying power. The argument was that such opportunities would increase the consumer base for American goods. For the cynics, NAFTA was viewed as a deal between American corporations and the financially strapped Mexican government to use cheap Mexican labor, sidestepping the costly U.S. unionized labor force and American regulations of commerce.

When the session began, Clayton was certain that the freshman class had come to terms with NAFTA and that they were of one accord in their opposition. She went so far as to state on record their position. "By the way, our freshman class, as a class, took the position that we're not supporting NAFTA," she told an interviewer in early September of 1993.

Of course, as the battle moved into full swing toward the end of the first session, individual defections came at a rapid pace, including one of the most controversial, freshman Eddie Bernice Johnson of Texas. Johnson is said to have traded her vote for the promise of a federal facility in her home district of Texas. Two years after NAFTA, her "yes" vote had not produced any movement on that commitment. In looking back at it, Clayton views it as an early lesson in congressional deal-making and says she lightheartedly teases Johnson about progress on that facility. Clayton had to navigate a number of controversial legislative actions during her tenure. She continues to attribute some of the hard calls to the high attrition rate of her freshman class.

Of course for Clayton and others from minority districts, it was not getting voted out of office that created concern, but elimination of seats altogether. The U.S. Supreme Court handed down a series of rulings that favored opponents of the minority districts. It began with North Carolina in the *Shaw v. Reno* decision. North Carolina's First and Twelfth Congressional Districts would invariably become the target of racial protectionists—those who felt that the minority districts were racially gerrymandered in favor of blacks.

It became clear that it was not just idle speculation or talk. Throughout the South, whites were being funded by conservative groups to bring court challenges to invalidate majority black and Hispanic districts. Every member of the CBC who entered in 1992 from newly drawn districts was at risk of loosing a seat. However, North Carolina was the first challenge to reach the U.S. Supreme Court. There, five white North Carolinians filed a lawsuit against the state and federal governments for violation of their "right to equal protection under the law," by drawing the minority districts. It resulted in the ruling known as *Shaw v. Reno*, a precursor to other Supreme Court rulings that would strike down the voting rights and civil rights gains of black Americans. It was particularly poignant for Clayton and Watt, coming from George White's state of North Carolina, because many critics were describing the *Shaw v. Reno* decision as the first step in a second Reconstruction that would wipe out the twentieth-century gains of blacks.

This time a predominantly conservative Supreme Court—which included an African American justice, Clarence Thomas, voting in the majority—was in the eye of the storm as the country headed for a retrenchment from the previous three decades of gains in equal treatment of blacks. With worsening economic conditions, huge corporate layoffs of middle management, and international investment in low-wage labor markets taking jobs away from middle-class whites, the politicians, if not the courts, reinterpreted and recast previously legislated civil rights remedies as unearned preferential treatment injurious to whites. Not only were economic advancements of blacks under attack, but their voting franchise was once again being manipulated to thwart the large growth in the number of black elected officials.

The North Carolina case reached the U.S. Supreme Court after a lower court ruled against the white North Carolinians who brought the lawsuit against the state and the federal government over the state legislature's crafting of the irregularly shaped Twelfth Congressional District. Writing for the majority, which supported the complainants argument, Justice Sandra Day O'Connor delivered a strongly worded opinion that sent shock waves throughout the liberal establishment:

> This case involves two of the most complex and sensitive issues that the court has faced in recent years, the meaning of the constitutional "right" to vote and the propriety of race-based state legislation designed to benefit members of historically disadvantaged racial minority groups. The first of the two majority black districts contained in the revised plan, District One, is somewhat hook-shaped. Centered in the northeast portion of the state, it moves southward until it tapers to a narrow band, then with finger-like extensions it reaches far into the southernmost part of the state near the South Carolina border.
>
> The second majority-black district—District 12, is even more unusually shaped. It is approximately 167-miles long and for much of its length, no wider than the I-85 corridor. It winds in snake like fashion through tobacco country, financial centers and manufacturing areas until it gobbles in enough enclaves of black neighborhoods.[7]

This prelude led to Justice O'Connor's most damaging statement for proponents of minority districts, but one that gave solace to challengers—many of whom were waiting in the wings for their cases to be heard by the Court: "It is unsettling how closely the North Carolina plan resembles the most egregious racial gerrymanders of the past. . . . Racial gerrymandering, even for remedial purposes, may balkanize us into competing racial factions."[8]

When Justice O'Connor went on to compare the situation of minority districts to "political apartheid," it reflected an obvious disconnect between the history of redistricting and the practice of racial injustices that separated her rationale from the American reality as well as the opinions of her dissenting colleagues. Historically, the Supreme Court had, on numerous occasions, sidestepped making rulings on statewide redistricting plans, leaving the jurisdiction instead to the states. Although in *Shaw v. Reno,* the Court's actions had been much the same as in the past—to remand the case back to the North Carolina courts for reconsideration—it was the tone of the ruling that sent a message to white conservatives. That message raised the possibility that the districts could be redrawn, if not eliminated.

The four dissenting justices were a lot more realistic regarding the history of redistricting and disagreed with Justice O'Connor's assumption that there was something historically sacrosanct about contiguous districts and their shape. In his dissent, Justice Harry Blackmun wrote:

> The conscious use of race in redistricting does not violate the Equal Protection Clause unless the effect of the redistricting plan is to deny a particular group equal access to the political process or to minimize its voting strength unduly. It is particularly ironic that the case in which today's majority chooses to abandon settled law and to recognize for the first time this analytically distinct constitutional claim . . . is a challenge by white voters to the plan under which North Carolina has sent black representatives to Congress for the first time since Reconstruction.[9]

In essence, Justice Blackmun and the other dissenting justices concluded that they could not find where the plaintiffs had substantiated their claim of loss of rights to "equal protection under the law," and any other rationale would place the case outside the constraints of the role of the judiciary. They still maintained that the political act of redistricting was not a judicial matter, only insofar as a constitutional challenge was being legitimately waged. As a matter of fact, the districts were irregular because the states had actually tried to protect the congressional seats of incumbent white congressmen, while still trying to comply with the Voting Rights Act.

In addition, because housing patterns were dictated by long-standing real estate and lending practices, rural housing for poor blacks was proscribed by redlining practices of banks and rental discrimination by owners. It was primarily true of rural areas such as those of Clayton's First Congressional District, where a majority of the residents were poor. The First District had a median household income of $18,226 and per capita income of $8,918. With limited housing options and unequal access to the lending institutions, minorities had little freedom of movement.

Certainly from the point of view of white congressmen and their constituents, nothing had changed in North Carolina. White plaintiffs were now seeking legal remedies because they were now in districts represented by African Americans; the reverse had been true for blacks for nearly a century. The case also defied the state legislature, since they drew the lines before presenting them to the Republican U.S. Justice Department for approval. There was speculation that the Republicans approved the lines because homogeneous white conservative districts were created while carving out minority districts.

However, none of this was consolation to Clayton and Watt. The Supreme Court decision had in essence put the case back in the state's hands to resolve. However, the lower court once again ruled that the districts should remain intact. The plaintiffs attempted a second time to take their case to the Supreme Court, and this time the Court ruled in their favor. The flurry of activity around the ruling could have been distracting for Congresswoman Clayton, and although she was concerned, she was not stymied by the challenge to her seat. The reaction to *Shaw v. Reno* exacerbated tensions and divisions between black conservatives and black progressives. Surprisingly, there was a growing core of African Americans who also supported the Supreme Court's decision on *Shaw v. Reno.* One, of course, was Justice Clarence Thomas of the Supreme Court—the only black on the bench—who voted with the majority because he felt that the districts were unconstitutional. For many of those who had been a part of the civil rights struggle in the South, the most difficult and troubling aspect of the redistricting battle was the fact that there were African Americans in decision-making roles who had lost sight of the purpose and intent of the Voting Rights Act and who dismissed the history of the black voting franchise. Along with Thomas was a Republican congressman, Gary Franks. Franks attempted to codify the *Shaw v. Reno* decision by initiating legislation that would make minority districts illegal. His bill had one hundred cosponsors—all white Republicans, but he was unable to get it passed.

Despite the challenges, history will record that Clayton gracefully moved into congressional leadership and American history in 1993 and made a difference. Certainly among those women who have served in Congress she could be counted as one who transformed history by her achievements and on her own terms. Shying away from being compared to some of the stalwarts of the past, but with respect and deference, she comments on the women in Congress today.

> I think there is a higher expectation of us as Afro-American women because there have been so few of us. And once we are here in some mass, then they will see us as a group and we will not have to be just a Barbara Jordan or just a Shirley Chisholm, but we would be looked upon as individuals. I think that will happen with Afro-American men too. The more we're here, we will see the individual strength and the weakness of the group. And therefore, you are not compared to the one person who served some fifteen, twenty years ago.
>
> The comparison would be how are you comparing to the person who served five years ago. So, I think the expectation is, in my judgment, a little too high. I have had women, white and black, who have come to me and just thanked me for running and thanked me for winning. I'm not even representing them. They're from other states. They feel so much a part of the movement of seeing females here that it says something about them in their location. If we can do it here, it gives them hope that they can do it.

Reelected to her second term against little competition, Clayton returned to the 104th Congress, but this time it meant a shift in the political compass and a loss of committee assignments and status as a member of the majority party. The Republican majority made sweeping changes, including the discontinuance of the Women's Caucus and the Congressional Black Caucus—two political support systems that had given Clayton status in her freshman year.

She, however, had brought a certain maturity and reassuring leadership style to the Democratic freshman class. As its president, she set the tone and the standard for performance. It was no wonder, then, that as the 104th Congress convened, the door she had opened for women in congressional leadership admitted another African American woman. Sheila Jackson-Lee (D-Tex.) became the second black woman to serve as freshman class president. She was able to pick up where Clayton left off. As for Clayton, she was able to pass the baton, the advice, the reputation for excellence in leadership, and the high expectations to another woman whose task would be less daunting because of her successes.

Chapter 15 **Eddie Bernice Johnson**

*The Texan Who Charted
a New Course for Dallas*

I am a Texan. I came from the roots of Texas. I grew up politically in the Texas House and Texas Senate. We had very visible leadership. There was no question about where the leadership was on issues. We talked about it very above board. It's very different here [in Congress]. It's hard to identify, often, who is leading what. But, in Texas, I think it's the nature of Texans to be open, above board, very straight forward, saying without reservation and without apologies what we want and need for our areas and going after it.

Résumé

Eddie Bernice Johnson

Personal

Born	December 3, 1935 Waco, Texas
Family	Divorced; one child
Religion	Baptist
Party	Democrat
Took office	Age 58, January 5, 1993

Education

Nursing Diploma	St. Mary's at Notre Dame, South Bend, Indiana, 1955
B.S.	Texas Christian University, 1967
M.P.A.	Southern Methodist University, 1976

Professional/Political Background

1956–1972	Nurse, Dallas Veterans Administration Hospital
1972–1977	Representative, Texas House of Representatives
1977–1981	Presidential appointment: principal regional official for Region VI, Department of Health Education and Welfare (HEW; currently the Department of Health and Human Services); later executive assistant to the administrator for Primary Health Care
1982–1986	Founder, Eddie Bernice Johnson and Associates
1986–1992	Senator, Texas Senate
1993–	U.S. House of Representatives

Selected Awards/Organizational Affiliations

Distinguished Public Service Award, Prairie View A&M University, 1990; Outstanding Service Award, KKDA Radio, 1991; National Association of Negro Business and Professional Women and Clubs Achievement in Government, 1991; Outstanding Service Award, Sigma Pi Phi Fraternity, 1991; Certificate of Commendation, city of Dallas, 1991; Outstanding Service Award, the Child Care Group, 1991; "Legislator of the Year" Award, Dallas Alliance for the Mentally Ill, 1991; member, Alpha Kappa Alpha Sorority; 1993 Meritorious Award, National Black Nurses Foundation, Inc.; 1993 Award for Achievement in Equal Employment Opportunity, U.S. Department of Energy; member, National Council of Negro

Women; member, Democratic Women of Dallas County; member, National Association for the Advancement of Colored People.

Congressional Data

Thirtieth Congressional District of Texas: Dallas

Committees: Science; Public Works and Transportation

103d Congress: 1993–1994
1992 general election results: 74 percent of the vote

104th Congress: 1995–1996
1994 general election results: 73 percent of the vote

Eddie Bernice Johnson

*The Second African American Woman
Elected to Congress from Texas (Dallas)*

Thirtieth District, Texas
Democrat
103d Congress–present, 1993–

The stage in the House press gallery is small by pressroom standards. It was certainly not large enough to hold the twenty Congressional Black Caucus (CBC) members who stood huddled together responding angrily and emotionally to the U.S. Supreme Court's 1995 decision to rule minority districts unconstitutional. A reporter wanted to know just how Eva Clayton (D-N.C.) felt about the ruling and its impact on her district. But she would have to wait, because Clayton's gracious and slow movement toward the microphone was eclipsed by a quicker Texas colleague, Eddie Bernice Johnson.

"We will not go back," Johnson proclaimed angrily. "We will not be turned around. The Texas case will be decided on this afternoon," she told the press and the ever-present C-SPAN cameras. With such a national audience, Johnson had to make it clear that Texas's Thirtieth Congressional District—the one she carved out while a member of the Texas Senate and now represented in Congress—was also facing a challenge to its existence. The reporter patiently waited for Johnson to finish and once again asked for Clayton's comments.

It was yet another example of the traits that Eddie Bernice Johnson's supporters loved and her detractors loved to denounce—aggressive, no nonsense, outspoken, and propelled by political self-interest. Had she not possessed those traits, it is questionable whether the former registered nurse could have made it through the hard-driving Texas legislature let alone to the U.S. Congress. Her tactics got her message across, not necessarily in order to exclude anyone else but because her goal was to put her issue in the forefront. The articulate and decisive Texan was nothing if she was not strongly goal-directed. Explaining her approach to obstacles, she said, "I'm one who doesn't give up, doesn't give in, knows where I came from, knows why I'm here, and knows where I want to go."

Of course, following the 1990 redistricting battles in the Texas Senate, there are many Texas political pundits who would nod their heads in total agreement with Johnson's self-portrait. It was certainly the case when she carved out the Thirtieth Congressional District. After waiting for two decades, Dallas finally had a chance to have a minority district that had a 50 percent black voter base, and it was a feat that Johnson was being both criticized and praised for having engineered.

"It [redistricting] was supposed to come in 1972 and it did not. It was supposed to come and was ordered by the court in 1982. And that opportunity still did not come. But for 1992, I was in the Texas Senate, where most of the lines are drawn for congressional districts." And it was there that she created her political future.

The Early Years

Born December 3, 1935, in Waco, Texas—now known as the home of the Branch Davidian cult—Eddie Bernice Johnson left home to attend college because she was black in a segregated system and unable to attend the Texas universities or colleges. She wanted to become a nurse, but because Texas's white state schools were not open to African Americans, she had to leave the state. As with most blacks during this era, she looked toward the Midwest. There she entered the University of Notre Dame in South Bend, Indiana, where she received a nursing diploma in 1956.

When she returned to Texas from Indiana, she began her nursing career at Dallas's Veterans Administration Hospital, eventually becoming a psychiatric nurse. During this time, she married Dawrence Kirk and had a son, Dawrence, Jr., who was born in 1958. Very little mention is ever made of the marriage, which ended in divorce.

Medicine and health-care issues are Eddie Bernice Johnson's first love. Before her successful run for office in 1972, she devoted sixteen years of her professional life to nursing. As a psychiatric nurse, she gained firsthand experience in health-care delivery and health insurance, both of which would later become the topic of national debate during her first term in Congress.

The Political Odyssey

Active in community programs, Johnson's nursing career and her local involvement led to a run for the Texas House of Representatives. Considered a long shot by the pundits, she began a streak of election successes that would eventually take her to Washington. In a landslide victory for the Texas House, she made history by representing District Thirty-three as the first black woman from Dallas to win any political office.

That began a new career for the no-nonsense Johnson. A woman of about 5 feet 4 inches, she is the model of what a professional woman ought to look like—she is not so stylish as she is well-groomed, not so pretty as she is attractive. Her hair is always in place, makeup always just right, and clothes always fresh-looking. She is approachable as a public figure, yet guarded as a private person. She is, though, most of all a politician, and she never shies away from her program and her public persona—which is tough, ambitious, determined, and hardworking.

> I do work hard. I'm dedicated to that. Sometimes I wish I didn't push
> myself so hard. . . . That way I wouldn't have so many disappointments.
> But it is something that I have no control of. I am interested in getting
> things done. And I learned a long time ago that unless you're willing to
> put in the work, you don't look for the results.[1]

It was this attitude, supported by her efforts, that kept Johnson in good stead with her constituency. Almost from the time she entered the state legislature, she was being urged by her supporters to run for Congress. It may come as a surprise to some of her detractors, who consider her overly ambitious, that she resisted the call to go to Washington for fifteen years. "Well, I was first approached in 1974 about running for Congress," she said as evidence of her popularity among the voters. "I did not feel, at that time I was ready. I had just completed my first term in the Texas House of Representatives. . . . After that, almost every election time, someone mentioned it was time for me to think about Congress."

However, she deferred and stayed in the legislature. Her record in the Texas House of Representatives began to take shape. Naturally, she was interested in health care, but also she began cultivating a reputation as an advocate for women and minority business set-asides and economic development. With respect to her accomplishments in the area of health, the former nurse takes pride in pointing to her success in putting Texas in the vanguard of establishing preventative health care programs.

> I passed legislation in Texas that mandated the Texas education agency to
> develop age-appropriate curriculum from preschool all the way through
> high school for self-reliance, education for prevention. Because I think
> that's where we save the dollars, and that's where we save our lives, and
> that's where we get better health habits, by very early intervention. And
> that's where we will really impact the cost of health care. When we take
> control and take the responsibility for ourselves at a very early age.

She also used her position as a bully pulpit to quell Texas racism. Dallas, considered a city of the Deep South, carries many of the negative racial attributes that the image conjures up. While in the state legislature, Johnson found that she had to spend a lot of her time trying to eradicate racism in city and state hiring and contracting. She held high-profile hearings that highlighted the issues and also gave her exposure to the state and national Democratic parties.

An active and loyal Democrat, working for the presidential campaign of Jimmy Carter, Johnson was making a name for herself in Texas Democratic circles. In an unprecedented action during her second term, she became the first woman to chair a major committee in the Texas House of Representatives—the Labor Committee. Shortly after that, while in her third term in 1977, she was nominated by President Jimmy Carter for a political appointment. Constantly pushing herself to achieve, by then she had already taken the time a year earlier to earn a master's degree in public administration from Southern Methodist University (1976) at the age of forty-one. With a background in health care and health administration, solid Democratic credentials, and statehouse experience, she was a natural for the appointment. She accepted Carter's offer.

From 1977 to 1979, Eddie Bernice Johnson served the Carter administration as the principal official for Region VI of the Department of Health, Education and Welfare (HEW). In 1979 she moved to the main HEW office in Rockville, Maryland, as the executive assistant to the administrator for primary health care, where she stayed until the end of the Carter administration in 1981.

That year, with a résumé that included five years as a legislator and four as a presidential appointee, Johnson felt equipped to go out and create a business of her own. She formed Eddie Bernice Johnson and Associates, using her political clout and experience to get business for companies owned by minorities and women. She also expanded her operations to include career opportunities in airport concession management. In supporting other businesses, she was able to get her own business concession in the Dallas–Fort Worth International Airport.

The business world, while appealing, was not enough for Johnson. Thus, after five years as an entrepreneur and four as a presidential appointee, she was once again lured to the political arena. In 1986 she began on another history-making political journey. She ran for and won a seat in the Texas Senate, to represent District Twenty-three, with more than 50 percent of the vote. It was an impressive win for someone who had been out of elective office for nine years.

Johnson returned to the state senate, at the age of fifty-one, with the same force and energy she had at thirty-seven, when she entered the state legislature for the first time. In the early part of her term, she challenged the Dallas city government to mend its discrimination practices in hiring and treatment of employees. She had the Justice Department investigate racial harassment of black college students, and she championed the cause of minority businesses.

One of Texas's major government-sponsored research centers and major employers at the time was the superconducting supercollider (SSC) project. Following complaints from anonymous callers who described abuse by white employees of the SSC project, Johnson held an open hearing to determine why contractors were experiencing racial and gender exclusion from required affirmative action programs and why the project had not allotted its 10 percent set-aside to firms owned by minorities and women. The hearings made a dent in the entrenched bureaucracy of the project and reversed a few actions, giving some minority- and women-owned businesses access to the multi-million dollar contracting business.

State senator Johnson weighed in on a number of other issues, as well. She introduced legislation that called for substance and alcohol testing of all hospital employees, saying that the "enactment of the legislation would do more to bring down medical malpractice insurance rates than any other pending legislation." She introduced the legislation despite the angry response from the medical community.

Along with a senate colleague, she introduced Texas's first Fair Housing Act, which ensured free and equal access to housing for all citizens and a complaint resolution mechanism. Johnson continued her legislative push for health care, minority participation in contracting, and regulatory efforts at curbing health care abuses and encouraging preventative health maintenance.

But the most important assignment of her second stint in the legislature was her appointment to chair the Reapportionment Committee of the Texas Senate. As the 1990 census results were tallied, Johnson's legislative efforts took a back seat to her position as the chair of the Reapportionment Committee of the state senate. The committee would eventually become the arbiter for the new Thirtieth Congressional District. "The Lieutenant Governor appointed me as chair of reapportionment for the congressional districts. And at that time, I was enjoying the Senate, and though I still had some interest in Congress, my major point, at that time, was to ensure that the persons in that Dallas area—specifically, the black population—would have a district [in which] they could elect the candidate of their choice."

That was Johnson's assessment of her role, but her genteel description of the Texas reapportionment battle was given a different spin by Texas media, which likened her to a card shark who sat down at the table of the political hardball players and came away with a congressional district of her own.

It was the image that most journalists had of the state senator, but it was tempered by the one she has of herself. "It was such a difficult process that by the end of it, I had really decided that maybe it was not for me. But that encouragement was still there. There were so many people that would just not take 'no' for an answer and felt that I had earned that spot to run. And so, I finally decided that I would. And, of course, I was very successful."

She ran unopposed in the Democratic primary and received 74 percent of the vote in the general election. In the meantime her maneuvers in the Texas Senate had created major political enemies, with one paper labeling her the "Worst Senator of the Year" because it accused her of carving out the seat for herself. Intentions notwithstanding, the voters sent her to Washington, D.C., with a decisive victory.

The Congressional Years

She entered Congress in 1993, following the 1992 "Year of the Woman." She found herself among the majority with a powerful Democratic House of Representatives, a powerful Senate, and a Democratic president in the White House. She entered with what she called "a very commissioned mission to look out for those who have been traditionally under represented or not represented [in Congress]." She began by identifying jobs and job training as her main priority.

> The major thing is to make sure that we have jobs. To be sure that we have adequate training for the jobs, for the marketplace in the future. Because, we all know that the marketplace is changing very rapidly. . . . A lot of it has been placed on NAFTA, the North American Free Trade Agreement. That is not the case. These changes have come before NAFTA. They will continue to be after NAFTA, whether it is ratified or not. We are in a different age. We are in an age of technology where it requires upgraded skills. And I want to be sure that my constituency will be armed with those skills for the marketplace, whatever that market place happens to be.

NAFTA turned out to be a major issue for Johnson—one that would separate her from many of her colleagues in the Congressional Black Caucus, of which she had been elected to the position of CBC whip. It also became a point of criticism of her alleged political deal-making with President Clinton.

As it so happened, NAFTA was a key piece of legislation for the Democratic president, and he went to all lengths to get support for its passage, particularly in the House, where the new freshmen Democrats were easy targets. There were two sides to the NAFTA legislation. Some felt that the elimination of trading barriers with Mexico and Canada would cause businesses to run across the border for cheap labor and fewer restrictions on manufacturing. Others felt that it was a spark to stimulate the economy by giving American goods another market outlet, resulting in a long-term stimulation of the American economy. Congresswoman Johnson considered herself to be of the latter school:

> I have spent the entire time that I have been here looking at all sides of the issue, reading, researching, talking with people, having a NAFTA forum in the community. And I came to the conclusion that it is best for us for jobs for the future. . . . And researching the history, I find that when we have been protectionist and isolationists, we have suffered. And right now, I think that there is a great deal of fear because of the status of our economy. We are blaming everything negative on NAFTA. But we're in a changing economy. We are in a peacetime economy which is a very difficult time.

Her position did sound reasonable and she held fast to it. A lot of her tenacity had to do with the fact that Dallas had a special relationship with Mexico already, and she saw the treaty as keeping that relationship alive.

> In Texas, our economy right now depends almost solely on selling to Mexico. We sell $20 billion of goods to Mexico every year. They love American goods. And they love Texas goods. We are there geographically. And it produces a half-million jobs. If we shut that opportunity off now, Texas' economy would just go flatter than it is. Because, I think that if we

insult Mexico, in particular, at this time, they will turn to Japan. . . . It is
cheaper for them to buy goods from us, then to have Japan sell them
goods. They prefer our goods.

Unlike other members from minority districts, who voted against NAFTA because
they felt that it would mean a loss of low-skilled jobs, Johnson saw NAFTA in practical
not abstract terms. She tied the legislation into her continued efforts to support minority and small businesses, and felt that it would give small businesses access to the Mexican market and entrée into opportunities for expansion.

> This is the first time that small businesses, black businesses, women
> owned businesses, Asian small businesses, Hispanic small businesses
> have the opportunity of a lifetime. Because these nations now prefer to
> do business with smaller businesses. And there are a number of small
> businesses in my district that have become multimillion dollar busi-
> nesses because of the contacts that they have made through my intro-
> duction and others to these foreign markets. I intend to continue that.
> My twenty-one years of public service has been focused a great deal on
> empowering small businesses and my people, to have access to being
> independent. Because freedom is lock step with independence.

The NAFTA bill passed the House of Representatives 234 to 200. It went on to a
successful passage in the Senate and was signed into law by a triumphant president. Two
years later, however, NAFTA had displaced sixty thousand American workers, with
more leaving the labor force in the years that followed.

Johnson went on to make headway on her two committees, Public Works and
Transportation and Science. Although she was not on the committee handling health care,
she still maintained a high profile during the 1993 debate on national health-care reform,
unsuccessfully waged by Hillary Rodham Clinton. Johnson explained:

> I'm rooted deeply in my experience in the area of health care and
> social services. I'm not on any of those committees. It's frustrating to
> me because everything comes through a committee. . . . However,
> majority leader [Richard] Gephardt has asked me to work with him
> on health care. So I have attempted to do that. I'm working from
> somewhat of a position of a handicap not being on the committees
> where the legislation has been referred. But I'm not going to let that
> get in my way. Because I do feel that I bring a degree of expertise and
> experience in those areas from a state that has every possible health
> care need that we can identify. We're urban. We're rural. We're sub-
> urban. We're all of it. We're so very multi-cultural. We are the closest
> neighbor to the shore of Mexico around our border. So we have had
> to experience all of the possible health care problems that any state
> could possibly experience. We have seen it from across the board, the
> rich, the poor, the underserved, the unserved, the poorest of popu-
> lations, the wealthiest of populations, some of the best health care

facilities in the world, and some areas without any. So, I know that picture backwards and forwards, in terms of our needs. And I hope to be able to [have] an impact.

Johnson was easily returned to the 104th Congress, when she sought reelection. However, her battle had just begun, the decision to challenge all minority districts had already begun to have an affect on her congressional seat. A challenge to her District worked its way toward the U.S. Supreme Court as she was being sworn in to the Republican-dominated 104th Congress.

Eddie Bernice Johnson entered the 104th Congress ready to continue her fight to maintain a voting franchise for Dallas's minority population, and she refused to be stopped by any semblance of intrusion on that battle that she had waged since she entered the state legislature. Now she would continue to do it, not quietly but aggressively and forcibly, putting the political interests of the people of Dallas before the world by any means necessary. That perseverance and drive had a lot to do with the reason the voters kept returning her to office.

However, as the Congress was nearing its end in the summer of 1996, the U.S. Supreme Court issued a ruling that called for the elimination of Johnson's congressional district and that of Representative Sheila Jackson-Lee of Houston.

Chapter 16   **Sheila Jackson-Lee**

Entering a Hostile Congress

I like to classify myself as a problem-solver. And residents of the Eighteenth District simply were not getting their problems solved. It now places a burden of accountability on me.[1]

Résumé

Sheila Jackson-Lee

Personal

Born	January 12, 1950 Queens, New York
Family	Married to Dr. Elwyn Cornelius Lee; two children
Religion	Seventh-Day Adventist
Party	Democrat
Took office	Age 44, January 4, 1995

Education

B.A.	Yale University, 1972
J.D.	University of Virginia, School of Law, 1975

Professional/Political Background

1975	Admitted to the Texas bar
1975–1977	Attorney, Harkrader and Ross
1977–1978	Staff counsel, U.S. House of Representatives and Select Committee on Assassinations
1978–1980	Attorney, United Energy Resources
1981–1987	Partner, Brodsky & Ketchand
1987–1990	Associate judge, city of Houston
1990–1994	Council member-at-large, Houston City Council
1995–	U.S. House of Representatives

Selected Awards/Organizational Affiliations

State Bar of Texas; chairperson, Black Women Lawyers Association, 1980; president, Houston Lawyers Association, 1983–1984; director, Texas Young Lawyers Association, 1986; president, Houston Metro Ministries, 1984–1985; member, Houston Area Urban League; Episcopal Center for Children, 1976–1980; Board of Directors, American Association of Blacks in Energy, 1980; Rising Star of Texas Award, *Texas Business Magazine,* 1983; Outstanding Young Houstonian Award, Chamber of Commerce, 1984; Alpha Kappa Alpha Sorority.

Congressional Data

Eighteenth Congressional District of Texas: Houston, Harris County

Committees: Judiciary; Science

104th Congress: 1995–1996

1994 general election results: 72 percent of the vote

Sheila Jackson-Lee

*The Third African American Woman
Elected to Congress from Texas (Houston)*

Eighteenth District, Texas
Democrat
104th Congress–present, 1995–

In the fall of 1995, when the 104th Congress (1995–1996), was in the throes of the heated debates on affirmative action, freshman representative Sheila Jackson-Lee (D-Tex.), left the hearings after testifying and rushed to speak to a group of Washington, D.C., high school girls. The students were being hosted by Women in Government, a nonprofit organization that had as one of its projects the mentoring of young inner-city girls. This time the students were getting to know how the Congress worked.

As Sheila Jackson-Lee stood before the mostly Hispanic and African American audience, it was evident that they were familiar to her—perhaps as replicas of herself twenty-five years earlier. They were bright, inner-city girls from working-class poor backgrounds, without a clue as to what life held for them. The congresswoman standing before them let them know that she understood.

> I did not start out in the ninth or tenth grade knowing that I would end up in Congress. I sat in the same hard public school seats you do. I had the same teachers, who were my mentors and role models. I had the pressed hair, you may have perms. And my vision was not really beyond the very next day of survival. And so I cannot say to you that I am any different any better than those of you who are here. But I let life guide me.

The representative with the Texas address and the New York birthright had captured the attention of the young women. Their expressions, for the first time, seemed to explore the possibility that they too could stand where she was standing, because she had made it from where they were. It was the message that Jackson-Lee wanted to convey: "One thing that guided me was that I wanted to be a change maker, an agitator for good. So I defined myself by what was within me and what I could do step-by-step."

Jackson-Lee—a former congressional staff lawyer—did what most staffers dream of doing. She ousted an incumbent and became a member of Congress. The native New Yorker also did something else. She penetrated the Texas Democratic party, overcame criticism that she was an outsider, and upset the well-known and popular incumbent and Texas son,

Craig Washington of the Eighteenth Congressional District. It was a David and Goliath story, with the unresponsive, mercurial, and aloof two-term Washington campaigning against the energetic, affable and no-nonsense city councilwoman who promised constituents that she would make "constituency service" a priority.

Houston City Council member Sheila Jackson-Lee was just the opposite of the incumbent. Where Washington was flamboyant and tended toward rhetorical flourishes, she was plain and straightforward without pretense. As an underdog, she worked tirelessly, campaigned incessantly and in the end defeated Washington, causing one of the major upsets of the 1994 Texas Democratic primaries.

The Eighteenth Congressional District of downtown Houston was not typical in that it was used to strong black congressional leadership. It was the constituency that had sent former congresswoman Barbara Jordan (D-Tex.) to the U.S. House of Representatives from 1973 to 1978. Upon her retirement, the voters sent Congressman Mickey Leland (D-Tex.) to the Hill in 1979, where he served until his untimely death in a 1989 plane crash while on a hunger mission in Ethiopia.

Defense attorney Craig Washington followed, serving from 1989 to 1994. Washington started out as an able and respected legislator with an active political life of twenty-two years in the Texas Democratic party, but he had become lax in his representation in Congress during his last term. He had missed key votes and had alienated some constituencies on other votes. For example, his vote against the North American Free Trade Agreement angered Texas's big businesses, causing them to put their financial backing behind other candidates. Sheila Jackson-Lee was one of them.

As well as being the beneficiary of the financial backing of the disaffected businesses, what Jackson-Lee promised was a more stable, responsive, and responsible stewardship of the public trust, and the voters gave her that chance. In the heavily Democratic district, she was a shoo-in for the general election after her strong showing in the primaries, in which she defeated Washington with 63 percent of the vote to his 37 percent. In the general election, she won handily against Jerry Burley, the Republican candidate, with 72 percent of the vote. The transplanted New Yorker had replaced the entrenched Texan in an upset victory. The young woman who wanted to be a change maker, actually changed the course of Texas politics.

The Early Years

A woman with soft brown skin, who wears conservative suits and sensible low-heeled shoes that allow her to move at a fast pace up and down the long corridors of the Capitol and the House office buildings, Jackson-Lee possesses the kind of serious look of a best friend who has excelled in every subject. She looks smart and she is. Saying that "people have images of themselves," Jackson-Lee, born in Jamaica, Queens, New York, January 12, 1950, talks about the early image of her life growing up in the North.

> I would call us the working poor. I would say most of my life my parents worked, but there were times when my father was not working, but we were still able to make ends meet.
>
> I had a consistent roof over my head, my mother worked everyday and my father was in there battling, but he was just a product of what happened to black men in the forties and fifties. Job opportunities were not available. He was a talented artist and you don't really find your niche in that unless you are able to get on with some Madison Avenue company, or teach. . . . He wasn't able to do either, so he had to do manual labor and he did that.

For Jackson-Lee, the distinction between herself and the kids she grew up with—some of whom are either dead, strung out on drugs, or incarcerated—was that she had passion and ambition. Of course, what else separated her from the other kids was a strong family and an intellectual curiosity that kept her searching for ways to change her life. An honors student, she says that even with good grades, the Jamaica high school that she attended never provided her with college counseling. They just assumed that she would be heading toward a vocational skills occupation rather than college:

> I consider myself having truly seen the raw side of life. I got to Yale on scholarship, I sure didn't get there by my parents paying for it. . . . I had no recollection of any college interviewer interviewing me because no counselor referred them to me. And in the twelfth grade, I actually had no college to go to. I had not been advised or counseled, I was left to the wind, and I had been in honors classes. That was clearly racism in New York, in the North.

On her own initiative, she went on to Yale, earned an undergraduate degree in political science and graduated with honors in 1972. She is quick to admit that it was affirmative action that gave her access to Yale, but it was ability that kept her there, and this she sees as the fundamental flaw in the arguments against affirmative action. "I am an avid believer in affirmative action. I affirmatively was able to go to Yale, but I did not graduate on that basis."

Indeed, she is the example of what can happen when the playing field has been leveled and ability dictates outcome. From Yale, she went to law school at the University of Virginia, where she received her J.D. in 1975. The young woman from the working-class poor background was now headed toward a career path before reserved only for white males of means. After two years with prestigious law firms, she joined the congressional staff of the U.S. House of Representatives Select Committee on Assassinations, as staff counselor. From 1977 to 1978, she became a part of the hectic, high-energy congressional staff, trying to uncover the truth behind the deaths of Martin Luther King, Jr., and President John F. Kennedy. The congressional work did not assuage Jackson-Lee's thirst for becoming a change maker, it heightened it. After ending the work of the commission in 1978, she moved to Houston, Texas, the home of her future husband, Dr. Elwyn Lee.

A native Texan, Lee is an academic who serves as the vice president of student affairs and special assistant to the president of the University of Houston. With two children, the Lees are a contemporary professional family—both well-educated, committed professionals in high-profile positions, sharing parenting and spiritually intact. Jackson-Lee exudes a quiet spirituality that undergirds what for others would be a tension-filled and disruptive life. She commutes from Washington to Houston weekly, and when necessary she is back home attending PTA meetings for her two children and attempting to maintain continuity with her family. Her husband is the single parent while his wife is in Congress. Jackson-Lee is conscious of her non-Texan roots but boasts of her family ties to the state:

> My husband grew up in Texas. He is a very entrenched, popular Texan. He went to school there and played sports there. I came to Texas in 1978 and have two native-born children. I say that I am an adopted Texan because I came by choice. So my commitment and love is deep and abiding because I had to climb over mountains to get there.

The Political Odyssey

She found not only a home in Texas but a base from which she could begin her political career. After ten years practicing law with private firms, she finally got her first breakthrough in politics, when, after three unsuccessful runs for elected office, she was appointed to a seat as a municipal court judge. "I started off like most lawyers do and ran for judge. I ran for Judge first and lost. I ran again and lost. Eventually, I got appointed as a municipal court judge by a woman mayor."

From 1987 to 1989, she served as a Houston Municipal Court associate judge. At the same time her unofficial campaign for political office had already begun. She made the rounds of community meetings and professional organizations, solidifying her base of supporters and potential voters. While Jackson-Lee calls these activities an opportunity to be a good neighbor, she was also nurturing a constituency and gaining name recognition. It was a part of her "old shoe" strategy. She wanted Texans to be as comfortable with her as they were with an old shoe. In this way, they would not dwell on the fact that she was a native New Yorker.

Of her boundless energy and constant state of motion, Jackson-Lee replies: "People wanted me to come to their schools. I did it. I went to housing developments. We did a lot of fun things there. It is important to do things. I don't stop. I run 24 hours a day. I push others to run 24 hours. I don't ask people to do any more than I would do. But I always think there is something more to do."

In 1990, the "something more" was to run for public office again—this time for an at-large seat on the Houston City Council. "I resigned from the judgeship and ran for city council. I was the underdog in a six-candidate race and won." She was now in a position to make changes and she did. For example, taking up gun control in Texas is considered a courageous act. She did it and prevailed, getting a gun safety law passed by the council, a feat that some would consider nearly impossible in Texas.

She also championed the causes of human rights, homelessness, cable television regulations, and revitalization of the aviation industry. More than her legislative accomplishments, Jackson-Lee had earned a reputation for being accessible and accountable. It was a theme that would carry over as she successfully challenged the incumbent in the 1994 Democratic congressional primary. The victory, which followed a last-minute decision to enter the race, catapulted her to national attention because of her unexpected defeat of Washington.

The Congressional Years

Jackson-Lee was one of three new African American representatives elected to the 104th Congress. The others were Chaka Fattah, a Democrat from Pennsylvania, and J. C. Watts, a Republican from Oklahoma. As a Democratic freshman, Jackson-Lee came in with a handicap. She, unlike the other African American women elected to Congress, was the first to be elected to a hostile Congress, one in which her party was not in the majority.

The 104th Congress was the first in forty years to be led by Republicans. With a platform entitled the "Contract with America"—a pledge that the Republicans would cut government spending, return funds to the states in the form of block grants, generally trim social programs, and reform welfare—the Republicans gained a majority in both the House and the Senate. In the House they held 230 seats to the Democrats' 204, with one seat held by an independent. In the Senate, Republicans held fifty-four seats, Democrats forty-six.

Jackson-Lee's entry into the 104th Congress as the only freshman black woman and one of only twelve women was in stark contrast to the 103d Congress, when six new African American women entered and more than two dozen new women in all were sworn in. What this switch in leadership meant for the freshman from Texas was that preferred committee assignments would be hard to obtain as a member of the minority party. In addition to the normal adversarial encounters, however, the tension between the parties was so great that routine legislative protocols were suspended at times. Republican-sponsored bills were railroaded through the committees and onto the floor of the House without debate, while Democratic-sponsored legislation languished in committees.

Elected as the president of the Democratic freshman class, the second black woman to ever hold such a position, Jackson-Lee was immediately thrown into the fray.

> Being in a uniquely different climate from Democrats before me, certainly as a new member I did not have anything to rely upon. So the typical position that Democrats found themselves in was as a driver of legislation, a

> driver of policy. I decided early on that representation was representation.
> My constituents wanted me here to represent them on their issues because
> they could not be here. . . . I was appointed to the Judiciary Committee.
> Well it turned out that over the first 100 days there was an overwhelming
> amount of "Contract with America" legislation that came through that
> committee—what I called the "Contract on America." A lot of it came to
> the Judiciary. So I consider the issues almost given to me.

In the midst of a Congress that vowed to cut spending to aid the poor and kept
its promise through legislative initiatives that also cut aid to the elderly, Jackson-Lee
had to create opportunities for giving voice to her predominantly poor constituents,
even if that meant impeding legislation that detrimentally affected the Eighteenth
Congressional District—one of the poorest in the nation. "I had to tackle many issues, I
initially tackled the Balanced Budget Amendment. I worked to exclude from the amendment the impact on Medicaid. Early on I said that Medicaid and Medicare should be off-
line. Cuts should not be done on the backs of the poor."

Of course, the congresswoman found herself losing battles that she thought had been
fought and won decades earlier. A few times she had success. One such success was with
the crime bill.

> I strongly support the Brady bill. I support the ban on assault weapons
> and I am a strong supporter of prevention dollars. So I came on board
> with the crime bill amendment. I offered amendments on the House
> floor to keep those dollars in place. I offered an amendment that would
> utilize those dollars that would normally go to build prisons to be used
> instead for the purpose of creating boot camps. So I proceeded to act as
> an activist in areas that I could. That amendment was approved. Prison
> building dollars are too much and most are misdirected. Juvenile boot
> camps would be better use of some of that money. It was a small measure
> of success.

Even that victory was incomplete. The final legislation placed the funds in the
much-heralded Republican block grant funding—funding that would provide the states
with the final determination as to how the appropriated dollars would be spent on the local
level. The philosophy was a throwback to the old battle over states' rights, which equated
the term with southern segregationist policies. In the end Jackson-Lee voted against the
bill because of the block grant provision.

The freshman congresswoman was learning a lot from the opposition, and each lesson seemed to strengthen her resolve to press forward. Welfare and affirmative action were
key issues on which she felt she could have some realistic impact. However, even in these
two areas, her efforts were frustrated by a philosophically hard-core conservative Congress—
for whom welfare was considered a hand-out and affirmative action was reverse discrimination.

The Democratic party leadership created a task force for each of the major areas under attack by the Republicans. Jackson-Lee was the task force leader on the welfare reform legislation. Her approach was to hold hearings in her district and get answers about reform ideas from women who were on welfare. She did not accept the Republicans' assumption that women were having babies to get federal assistance. Having come from a neighborhood where she knew first-hand the plight of welfare mothers, she chose to tackle the problem differently. What the congresswoman learned after her best efforts at soliciting citizen input would awaken her to the intransigence of the Republican leadership:

> The women that we talked to needed child care, job training and most obviously they needed work. I proposed an amendment that the Welfare Reform bill have child care provisions, job training and a $10,000 tax incentive on the first year's salary of a person on welfare who secured a job. It would be an incentive for small businesses.
>
> I argued vigorously for it in the rules committee. The tragedy of that experience was that I got to see in living color the lock step mentality that the Republicans have. But still the Eighteenth Congressional District was not without leadership. It was important that I translated into legislation what people had talked to me about at home. My feeling was that if I spent time talking to those mothers, that their common sense would be included [in the final legislation].

The congresswoman from Texas was learning on the job about the frustrations that had caused so many in her party to defect or not seek reelection following the devastation of the Democratic agenda after the 104th Congress. The committee did not consider her feedback as necessary for them, because the Republican majority ignored her input.

She was not deterred. Running down a corridor headed back to the hearings on affirmative action that she had left to briefly address the high school students, the congresswoman was a model of unmatched energy. Speaking while running, giving a staff member a list of tasks to perform, she recited her vision for the future and the needs of the twenty-first century.

> What will our people be doing in the future. Certainly we [minorities] will have the opportunity to be in the catering, hotel, and restaurant industries, but it is my view that science and technology and work at the space station should also be available. I supported the space station as the work of the twenty-first century. I consider the space station as work for our young people, in engineering, technology, earth-to-space sciences, and computers.

The race through the corridors was to no avail. Returning to the affirmative action hearings, the congresswoman discovered that she was too late to respond to questions about her testimony. Slowing the pace, but not much, a short while later she engaged in another conversation that seemed to take her across the miles from the Capitol in Washington, D.C., to her home in Houston, Texas. Jackson-Lee, her elongated face tilted to one side, the loosely fitting two-piece red suit covering her petite frame now looked less like the congresswoman with a full plate of legislation and more like a mother with angst about two children—a teenage daughter and a preteen son—living miles away with their father.

> My kids are in Houston with my husband and he does a yeoman's task. It is a situation that where day-by-day we take it one day at a time. Because my children are important to me, I'm on the look out for any chinks in their armor. I fly home to go to their parent-teachers meetings. I am on the look out for anything that might be happening where my life is destroying them. We are still on an even keel, so far and we take it day by day. I live up here [In Washington] in a little band box, and I don't want any more. I don't want to get too familiar.

It was a candid response that reflected the dual consciousness of many of the women on Capitol Hill. Haunted by the traditional roles of the past, taking on the challenges of political life, many would come to the point that Jackson-Lee had. Answering the always unasked question, where are your priorities—family or career? With all of the progress of women, it was still "their" question and not one asked of men. Men were never asked, but women were expected to have an answer. For Jackson-Lee, the answer was clear. The long coveted and hard-fought battle to realize her goal of becoming a congresswoman was not as important as the maintenance of stability and security for her family. If the strain began to show, she was ready at a moment's notice to make the choice. It was her crystal-clear response to the ever-present question for women in the Congress that spoke to Jackson-Lee's distinctiveness as one of the new focused African American women on the brink of the twenty-first century.

Chapter 17 **Epilogue**

When she spoke with her Jehovah-like voice, it was like a powerful voice from on high. She was a great American patriot whose dedication to public service and unshakable faith in, and love of, the Constitution served her well, earning her national recognition during the Watergate impeachment hearings. When she spoke of the Constitution, her tremendous voice resonated and made it sound like the founding fathers themselves were speaking. She personified the principles of ethics, justice, and compassion.

Her untimely death is a major loss to the citizens of this great nation, particularly as we seek to resolve the difficult public policy questions confronting our country. We have lost an outstanding public servant. We will miss her advice and counsel. She leaves a great legacy that challenges all of us to rededicate ourselves to the principles of freedom and equality for all Americans.

With her eloquent voice, she spoke for ordinary Americans in a language that all could understand. To those who felt disheartened, she made them believe that they too were included in the American dream. She will be a constant reminder of the power of integrity and fairness. I will always remember her. The nation has lost a treasure and a powerful friend.

—Excerpt from the statement by Congresswoman
Carrie Meek on the death of Barbara Jordan

For the congresswomen profiled in this book, the last year of the 104th Congress began on a somber note with the January 17 death of Barbara Jordan. Her funeral service and memorial tributes reflected the scope, dimension, and impact of a life lived as one of the century's most exemplary public servants. Eulogized by President Bill Clinton, former presidents, congressional colleagues, neighbors, students, and friends of long standing, Jordan was remembered as one who stayed the course, maintained faith in the Constitution, and never tired of defending it. She lived long enough to see both the increase in the number of African American women in Congress and to witness the erosion of the Voting Rights Act that made her phenomenal life in public service possible.

A majority of the remaining fourteen African American women would also experience considerable personal and political transitions by 1996. When the euphoria of the 1992 Year of the Woman subsided, African American congresswomen were faced with the more sobering impact of a conservative U.S. Supreme Court—one that reversed the progress of minorities by ruling minority districts unconstitutional. The rulings were not only a reflection of the conservative Republican Congress, but they were part of a broader political climate that included the burning of black churches in the South, the rollback of affirmative action programs, a significant increase in incarcerated black males and females, large-scale corporate layoffs, and increased unemployment. Democrats faced with a hostile congressional climate retired after the 104th Congress in unprecedented numbers. On the eve of the twenty-first century, the remaining fourteen women profiled in this book stood at the threshold of change, pursuing full representation for both their gender and race with force and diligence.

Shirley Chisholm, in her early seventies, continued an active life, lecturing, conducting interviews, and counseling young politicians in how to make the system work to further progressive agendas. Retired and living in Florida, she is also a constituent of Congresswoman Corrine Brown. Proud of adding another historic African American woman to her congressional district's history, Brown joined forces with the stalwart former congresswoman, on occasion introducing her at political, educational, and motivational speaking engagements.

Yvonne Brathwaite Burke, now a Los Angeles County supervisor in her mid-sixties, continued the pace she had set as a congresswoman. Always anxious to give historical perspective on her political odyssey, Burke's institutional memory could be counted on to give substance, depth, and focus to the history of black women in Congress.

Cardiss Collins, once the dean of African American women in the House, joined the exodus of Democrats from the 104th Congress and retired at the close of the session. Having served nearly a quarter of a century in the House of Representatives, the congresswoman who came to stay for a short term was now finding that being a grandmother and enjoying life as a private citizen was more attractive than introducing legislation and conducting hearings in an antagonistic Congress.

Katie Beatrice Hall retained her seat as the clerk of the city of Gary, Indiana, after what an aide called "the political race of her life." Serving as the clerk and continuing to teach on a part-time basis placed Hall in the midst of the civic service to which she had devoted her professional and political career.

Completing their third term in Congress, the urban women of the 1990 congressional election were equally challenged. Two retained their seats and were not immediately affected by the Supreme Court rulings on redistricting; nevertheless, they were experiencing their own personal and professional trials and tribulations.

Eleanor Holmes Norton was in a constant state of crisis resolution as the District of Columbia attempted to move toward fiscal solvency. Some hopeful signs emerged. The Republican-controlled Congress eventually gave the District additional funding so that it could restore some of the basic services that had been cut as a consequence of the fiscal mismanagement and a dwindling tax base. Midway through the year, a national investment company allowed the District to borrow several million dollars, even though it maintained a junk bond rating. Norton applauded these actions as she continued to ward off other attempts by the Congress to wrest power from the District through legislative mandates.

Maxine Waters continued to battle the Republicans in Congress, gaining political strength and momentum from her resounding reelection victory. Waters—still the outsider on the inside—maintained a bold and audacious persona, which at times even caused alienation from her colleagues in the Congressional Black Caucus. Legislatively, she stayed focused and never wavered from her advocacy for jobs, job training, and opportunities for the disenfranchised.

On August 6, 1996, Barbara-Rose Collins was defeated by 20 percentage points in the Democratic primary for the Fifteenth Congressional District by another African American woman, State Representative Carolyn Cheeks Kilpatrick. As Collins ended her term at the close of the 104th Congress, the investigation by the Justice Department and the Federal Elections Commission on misuse of scholarship funds continued.

The women of the 103d and 104th Congresses had fundamental political survival issues to handle. All six members of the House had redistricting challenges that affected their political future.

Corrine Brown survived a court-ordered restructuring of her congressional district that resulted in a majority white voting population. After repeated delays in primary dates, the congresswoman finally won a chance to run in the general election for the 105th Congress.

Carrie Meek, whose district remained intact, was virtually assured a seat in the 105th Congress. Continuing her focus on jobs and job-training opportunities for her impoverished district, Meek pursued an aggressive legislative agenda in the last half of the 104th Congress, securing funding for technology projects for historically black colleges and institutions and championing the cause of Haitian Americans and Haitian refugees.

Cynthia McKinney fought a hard and high-profile battle to retain a seat in Congress after the Supreme Court eliminated her old district, which had a 60-percent-black voting population. The new district posed a new challenge. With two-thirds of its voting-age population white, McKinney's chances of winning even the Democratic primary appeared remote. Facing three white challengers in the primary, she enlisted volunteers from around the country to help get out the vote. On July 7, 1996, Cynthia McKinney won the Democratic primary, with more than 50 percent of the vote. She along with Sanford Bishop, the other African American Georgia representative whose district was eliminated, gave new hope to others who faced a similar plight.

Eva Clayton's district was spared in the *Shaw v. Hunt* Supreme Court decision, which declared unconstitutional the district of her North Carolina colleague Mel Watts. It was discovered that the white voters who filed against her First Congressional District did not live in the district, thus invalidating their claim. Her prospects for reelection to the 105th Congress were favorable.

Eddie Bernice Johnson was not as lucky. The U.S. Supreme Court on June 13, 1996, ruled in *Bush v. Vera* that three Texas congressional districts were unconstitutional and had to be redrawn—Johnson's Thirtieth, Sheila Jackson-Lee's Eighteenth, and the Twenty-ninth of Houston, a seat occupied by white incumbent representative Gene Green. The seat that Johnson carved out was now scheduled to be redrawn, with the prospect of fewer minority voters, lessening the likelihood that African American representation in Congress would be a reality for Dallas, Texas.

Sheila Jackson-Lee's response to the loss of her historic district was: "I am somber about this; I am shocked and disgusted. But, I will be a candidate for any district that is drawn." The tenacious Jackson-Lee solidified her support and began to establish her campaign staff to fight to retain a seat in Congress.

By the end of the 104th Congress, Carol Moseley-Braun's once-bright future dimmed. A major newsmagazine reported that the Democratic party was prepared to pay off her lingering $50,000 campaign debt in exchange for her withdrawal from a reelection bid. Her increasing unpopularity resulted in part from a 1996 trip to Nigeria, and her support of that country's military government. The trip drew rebukes from African American leadership, human rights groups, the State Department, and President Bill Clinton. The Nigeria trip coupled with a lawsuit by a former staff worker, claiming that Moseley-Braun had secretly used campaign funds to establish a private bank account, stirred concerns that she may have become unelectable for a second term.

The results of the 1996 elections for the 105th Congress gave rise to optimism. Three African American women were newly elected and all of the women whose seats had been challenged were victors. Congresswoman Juanita Millender-McDonald, appointed to fill out the term of a resigning representative, won her first full-term election to California's Thirty-seventh District with 85 percent of the vote. Both newcomers were former Democratic legislators. With 53 percent of the vote, Julia Carson, of the tenth Congressional District, became the second African American woman elected to Congress from Indiana. Another second was Carolyn Kilpatrick who, after defeating Michigan's Barbara-Rose Collins in the primary, went on to win the general election with 88 percent of the vote.

The returning incumbents included Maxine Waters (86 percent) who spent much of her campaign drawing attention to allegations that the CIA had participated in shipping cocaine into South Central Los Angeles via Nicaragua. Floridians returned both Corrine Brown and Carrie Meek, with 61 percent and 89 percent of the vote respectively. Putting together a coalition of women across race and class lines, Cynthia McKinney narrowly won the new Fourth District seat with 58 percent of the vote, but not before denouncing her father for remarks he made about her opponent. North Carolinians returned Eva Clayton to Congress with 66 percent of the vote. Texas voters gave mandates to Sheila Jackson-Lee and Eddie Bernice Johnson, who won with 77 and 55 percent of the vote, respectively. D.C. Delegate Eleanor Holmes Norton won with 90 percent of the vote as she battled a Financial Control Board that continued to erode the District's limited home rule.

The 105th Congress began with twelve African American women. For the first time, most were serving majority white districts, leading to an expansion of the scope of their constituent interests, with the potential of changing voting priorities and patterns. Faced with these new challenges on the eve of the twenty-first century, these women served as the bridge between the trailblazers and the future. Their decisions, their votes, and their understanding of the intrinsic realities of the American political system will determine whether they continue to be transformative agents in Congress or whether they are shaped and formed by it.

Appendix

African Americans in the U.S. Congress, 1870–1996

	Party/State	Congress(es)	Term(s)*
Senators			
Hiram R. Revels *(1827–1901)*	R-Miss.	41st	1870–1871
Blanche K. Bruce *(1841–1898)*	R-Miss.	44th–46th	1875–1881
Edward W. Brooke *(1919–)*	R-Mass.	90th–95th	1967–1978
Carol Moseley-Braun *(1947–)*	D-Ill.	103d–	1993–
Representatives			
Joseph H. Rainey *(1832–1887)*	R-S.C.	41st–45th	1870–1879
Jefferson F. Long *(1836–1887)*	R-Ga.	41st	1870–1871
Robert B. Elliot *(1842–1884)*	R-S.C.	42d–43rd	1871–1874
Robert C. DeLarge *(1842–1874)*	R-S.C.	42d	1871–1873
Benjamin S. Turner *(1825–1894)*	R-Ala.	42d	1871–1873
Josiah T. Walls *(1842–1905)*	R-Fla.	42d–44th	1871–1876
Richard H. Cain *(1825–1887)*	R-S.C.	43d, 45th	1873–1875 1877–1879
John R. Lynch *(1846–1939)*	R-Miss.	43d–44th, 47th	1873–1877 1882–1883
James T. Rapier *(1837–1883)*	R-Ala.	43d	1873–1875
Alonzo J. Ransier *(1834–1882)*	R-S.C.	43d	1873–1875
Jeremiah Haralson *(1846–1916)*	R-Ala.	44th	1875–1877
John A. Hyman *(1840–1891)*	R-N.C.	44th	1875–1877
Charles E. Nash *(1844–1913)*	R-La.	44th	1875–1877
Robert Smalls *(1839–1915)*	R-S.C.	44th–45th, 47th–49th	1875–1879 1882–1887

	Party/State	Congress(es)	Term(s)*
James E. O'Hara (1844–1905)	R-N.C.	48th–49th	1883–1887
Henry P. Cheatham (1857–1935)	R-N.C.	51st–52d	1889–1893
John M. Langston (1829–1897)	R-Va.	51st	1890–1891
Thomas E. Miller (1849–1936)	R-S.C.	51st	1890–1891
George W. Murray (1853–1926)	R-S.C.	53d–54th	1893–1897
George H. White (1852–1918)	R-N.C.	55th–56th	1897–1901
Oscar DePriest (1871–1951)	R-Ill.	71st–73d	1929–1935
Arthur W. Mitchell (1883–1968)	D-Ill.	74th–77th	1935–1942
William L. Dawson (1886–1970)	D-Ill.	78th–91st	1943–1970
Adam C. Powell, Jr. (1908–1972)	D-N.Y.	79th–89th, 91st	1945–1967, 1969–1971
Charles C. Diggs, Jr. (1922–)	D-Mich.	84th–96th	1955–1980
Robert N. C. Nix (1905–1987)	D-Pa.	85th–95th	1958–1978
Augustus F. Hawkins (1907–)	D-Calif.	88th–101st	1963–1990
John Conyers, Jr. (1929–)	D-Mich.	89th–	1965–
William L. Clay (1931–)	D-Mo.	91st–	1969–
Louis Stokes (1925–)	D-Ohio	91st–	1969–
Shirley A. Chisholm (1924–)	D-N.Y.	91st–97th	1969–1982
George Collins (1926–1972)	D-Ill.	91st–92d	1969–1972
Ronald V. Dellums (1935–)	D-Calif.	92d–	1971–
Ralph H. Metcalfe (1910–1978)	D-Ill.	92d–95th	1971–1978
Parren Mitchell (1922–)	D-Md.	92d–99th	1971–1986
Charles B. Rangel (1930–)	D-N.Y.	92d–	1971–
Walter E. Fauntroy (1933–)	D-D.C.	92d–101st	1971–1990
Yvonne B. Burke (1932–)	D-Calif.	93d–95th	1973–1978
Cardiss Collins (1931–)	D-Ill.	93d–104th	1973–1996
Barbara Jordan (1936–1996)	D-Tex.	93d–95th	1973–1978

	Party/State	Congress(es)	Term(s)*
Andrew J. Young *(1932–)*	D-Ga.	93d–95th	1973–1977
Harold E. Ford *(1945–)*	D-Tenn.	94th–104th	1975–1996
Bennett M. Stewart *(1915–)*	D-Ill.	96th	1979–1980
Julian C. Dixon *(1934–)*	D-Calif.	96th–	1979–
William H. Gray, III *(1941–)*	D-Pa.	96th–102d	1979–1992
George T. (Mickey) Leland *(1944–1989)*	D-Tex.	96th–101st	1979–1989
Melvyn Evans *(1917–1984)*	R-V.I.	96th	1979–1980
George Crockett, Jr. *(1909–)*	D-Mich.	96th–101st	1980–1990
Mervyn M. Dymally *(1926–)*	D-Calif.	97th–102d	1981–1992
Gus Savage *(1925–)*	D-Ill.	97th–102d	1981–1992
Harold Washington *(1922–1987)*	D-Ill.	97th–98th	1981–1983
Katie B. Hall *(1938–)*	D-Ind.	97th–98th	1982–1984
Major R. Owens *(1936–)*	D-N.Y.	98th–	1983–
Edolphus Towns *(1934–)*	D-N.Y.	98th–	1983–
Alan Wheat *(1951–)*	D-Mo.	98th–103d	1983–1994
Charles A. Hayes *(1918–)*	D-Ill.	98th–102d	1983–1992
Alton R. Waldon, Jr. *(1936–)*	D-N.Y.	99th	1986–1987
Mike Espy *(1953–)*	D-Miss.	100th–103d	1987–1993
Floyd H. Flake *(1945–)*	D-N.Y.	100th–	1987–
John Lewis *(1940–)*	D-Ga.	100th–	1987–
Kweisi Mfume *(1948–)*	D-Md.	100th–104th	1987–1996
Donald M. Payne *(1934–)*	D-N.J.	101st–	1989–
Craig A. Washington *(1941–)*	D-Tex.	101st–103d	1989–1994
Lucien E. Blackwell *(1931–)*	D-Pa.	102d–104th	1991–
Barbara-Rose Collins *(1939–)*	D-Mich.	102d–104th	1991–1996
Gary A. Franks *(1953–)*	R-Conn.	102d–	1991–

	Party/State	Congress(es)	Term(s)*
William J. Jefferson (1947–)	D-La.	102d–	1991–
Eleanor Holmes Norton (1937–)	D-D.C.	102d–	1991–
Maxine Waters (1938–)	D-Calif.	102d–	1991–
Sanford D. Bishop, Jr. (1947–)	D-Ga.	103d–	1993–
Corrine Brown (1946–)	D-Fla.	103d–	1993–
Eva M. Clayton (1934–)	D-N.C.	103d–	1993–
James E. Clyburn (1940–)	D-S.C.	103d–	1993–
Cleo Fields (1962–)	D-La.	103d–104th	1993–1996
Alcee L. Hastings (1936–)	D-Fla.	103d–	1993–
Earl F. Hilliard (1942–)	D-Ala.	103d–	1993–
Eddie Bernice Johnson (1935–)	D-Tex.	103d–	1993–
Cynthia A. McKinney (1955–)	D-Ga.	103d–	1993–
Carrie Meek (1926–)	D-Fla.	103d–	1993–
Mel Reynolds (1952–)	D-Ill.	103d–104th	1993–1995 (Resigned)
Bobby L. Rush (1946–)	D-Ill.	103d–	1993–
Robert C. Scott (1947–)	D-Va.	103d–	1993–
Bennie G. Thompson (1948–)	D-Miss.	103d–	1993–
Walter R. Tucker, III (1957–)	D-Calif.	103d–104th	1993–1995 (Resigned)
Melvin Watt (1945–)	D-N.C.	103d–	1993–
Albert R. Wynn (1951–)	D-Md.	103d–	1993–
Sheila Jackson-Lee (1950–)	D-Tex.	104th–	1995–
Chaka Fattah (1956–)	D-Pa.	104th–	1995–
Julius Caesar (J. C.) Watts (1957–)	R-Okla.	104th–	1995–
Jesse Jackson, Jr. (1965–)	D-Ill.	104th–	1995–

Source: Congressional Black Caucus Foundation and Congressional Research Service.

*Terms as given here are coterminous with the end of the congressional year. Breaks in terms for all nineteenth-century members are a consequence of contested elections designed to keep African Americans from entering Congress.

Notes

Chapter 1   Introduction

1. This quotation and, unless otherwise noted, the chapter epigraphs throughout this book are from a radio program written and produced by LaVerne M. Gill, "Talented Ten: African American Women in the 103rd Congress" (American Public Radio, rights reserved by McCain Media and LaVerne M. Gill, 1994).

2. Christine Stansell, "White Feminists and Black Realities: The Politics of Authenticity," in *Race-ing Justice, En-gendering Power: Essays on Anita Hill, Clarence Thomas, and the Construction of Social Reality,* ed. and with an introduction by Toni Morrison (New York: Pantheon Books, 1992), 253.

3. Ibid., 251–252.

4. Gill, "Talented Ten."

5. Pertinent excerpts from the Fourteenth Amendment to the U.S. Constitution (adopted 1868):

   Section 1. All persons born or naturalized in the United States, and subject to the jurisdiction thereof, are citizens of the United States and of the State wherein they reside. No State shall make or enforce any law which shall abridge the privileges or immunities of citizens of the United States; nor shall any State deprive any person of life, liberty, or property, without due process of law; nor deny to any person within its jurisdiction the equal protection of the laws.

   Section 2. Representatives shall be apportioned among the several States according to their respective numbers, counting the whole number of persons in each State, excluding Indians not taxed. But when the right to vote at any election for the choice of electors for President and Vice President of the United States, Representatives in Congress, the executive and judicial officers of a State, or the members of the legislature thereof, is denied to any of the male inhabitants of such State, being twenty-one years of age, and citizens of the United States, or in any way abridged, except for participation in rebellion or other crime, the basis of representation therein shall be reduced in the proportion which the number of such male citizens shall bear to the whole number of male citizens twenty-one years of age in such State.

   Section 3. No person shall be a Senator or Representative in Congress, or elector of President and Vice President, or hold any office, civil or military, under the United States, or under any State, who having previously taken an oath, as a member of Congress, or as an officer of the United States, or as a member of any State legislature, or as an executive or judicial officer of any State to support the Constitution of the United States, shall have engaged in insurrection or rebellion against the same, or given aid and comfort to the enemies thereof. But Congress may, by a vote of two-thirds of each House, remove such disability.

6. The Fifteenth Amendment to the U.S. Constitution (adopted 1870):

   Section 1. The right of the citizens of the United States to vote shall not be denied or abridged by the United States or by any state on account of race, color, or previous condition of servitude.

   Section 2. The Congress shall have power to enforce this article by appropriate legislation.

7. The Nineteenth Amendment to the U.S. Constitution (adopted 1920):

   Section 1. The right of the citizens of the United States to vote shall not be denied or abridged by the United States or by any State or account of sex.

   Section 2. The Congress shall have power to enforce this article by appropriate legislation.

8. Angela Y. Davis, *Women, Race & Class* (New York: Vintage Books, 1983), 141.

Chapter 2   *Shirley Anita St. Hill Chisholm*

1. Shirley Chisholm, "Representative Shirley Chisholm Declares Her Candidacy for the Democratic Presidential Nomination, January 25, 1972, in Brooklyn, N.Y.," *Vital History Cassettes* (New York: Encyclopedia Americana/CBS News Audio Resource Library), cassette no. 2 for February 1972, side A, code 02772.
2. "Unbought and Unbossed" was Shirley Chisholm's congressional campaign slogan in her first run for the U.S. House of Representatives in 1968. It was also the title of her autobiography, *Shirley Chisholm: Unbought and Unbossed* (Boston: Houghton Mifflin, 1970).
3. British Guiana won its independence from Britain in May of 1966 and changed its name to Guyana.
4. Chisholm, *Unbought and Unbossed,* 25–27.
5. Ibid., 37.
6. Ibid., 51.
7. Ibid., 53.
8. Ibid., 67.
9. Ibid., 70.
10. Ibid., 71.
11. Ibid., 73.
12. Elizabeth Shelton, "Our Full Share," *Washington Post,* Apr. 28, 1969, B1.
13. Beatrice Berg, "Brooklyn Freshman," *Washington Post,* Dec. 6, 1968, H1.
14. Shirley Chisholm, *The Good Fight* (New York: Harper & Row, 1973), 10–11.
15. U.S. House of Representatives, speech delivered at the Conference on Women's Employment, *Hearings before the Special Subcommittee on Education of the Committee on Education and Labor,* 91st Cong., 2d sess. (Washington, D.C.: GPO, 1970), 909.
16. Chisholm, "Representative Shirley Chisholm Declares Her Candidacy."
17. Ronald W. Walters, *Black Presidential Politics in America: A Strategy Approach* (New York: State University of New York Press, 1988), 86–87.
18. William L. Clay, *Just Permanent Interests: Black Americans in Congress, 1870–1992* (New York: Amistad, 1993), 219.
19. Associated Press, "GAO Urges Action in Chisholm Case," *New York Times,* Nov. 17, 1973, 1.
20. Gill, "Talented Ten."

Chapter 3   *Barbara Charline Jordan*

1. Background interview by author with staff of the President's Advisory Commission on Immigration, May 1995. Additional references for this section are from James Bonmeier, "Panel May Hold Key to Consensus on Immigration," *Los Angeles Times,* July 11, 1994, 1; Joanne Jacobs, "National ID Menace to Rights," *Miami Herald,* Aug. 22, 1994, A-13; and Paul Anderson, "Immigration Panel Backs Data Bank," *Miami Herald,* Aug. 4, 1994, A-1.
2. Barbara Jordan, "The House Judiciary Committee's Impeachment Debate, July 25, 1974, Washington, D.C.," *Vital History Cassettes* (New York: Encyclopedia Americana/CBS News Audio Resource Library), cassette no. 2, 07742.
3. William A. Degregorio, *The Complete Book of U.S. Presidents* (New York: Barricade Books, 1993), 591–598.
4. Ibid., 598.
5. Jordan, "House Judiciary Committee's Impeachment Debate."
6. Arthur M. Schlesinger, Jr., ed., *The Almanac of American History* (New York: Barnes and Noble Books, 1993), 599.
7. Barbara Jordan and Shelby Hearon, *Barbara Jordan: A Self-Portrait* (New York: Doubleday, 1979), 22.
8. Ibid., 13–21.
9. Ibid., 23.
10. Ibid., 61–68.
11. "Debating Team Brings Prestige to Black College," Special: Campus Journal, *New York Times,* June 3, 1992, 7.
12. Ibid.
13. Ibid.
14. Jordan and Hearon, *Self-Portrait,* 78.
15. *New York Times,* June 3, 1992, 7.
16. Jordan and Hearon, *Self-Portrait,* 261.

17. Ibid., 82.
18. Ibid., 96–97.
19. Ibid.
20. Ibid., 107.
21. Ibid., 99–101.
22. William L. Clay, *Just Permanent Interests: Black Americans in Congress, 1870–1992,* updated ed. (New York: Amistad, 1993), 54–73. Clay discusses the political relationships that existed among the political parties and black leaders in the 1940s through the 1960s in Missouri, Illinois, and Ohio.
23. Jordan and Hearon, *Self-Portrait,* 132.
24. Ira Bryant, *Barbara Charline Jordan: From the Ghetto to the Capitol* (Houston: D. Armstrong, 1977), 17.
25. Jordan and Hearon, *Self-Portrait,* 140.
26. Ibid., 140–43.
27. Ibid. 142.
28. Ibid., 143–45.
29. Darlene Clark Hines, Elsa Barkley Brown, and Rosalyn Terborg-Penn, eds., *Black Women in America: An Historical Encyclopedia* (Bloomington: Indiana University Press, 1994), 1:658.
30. Jordan and Hearon, *Self-Portrait,* 171.
31. Ibid., 159.
32. Barbara Jordan, Keynote Address, Democratic National Convention, *Official Proceedings of the Democratic National Convention* (Washington, D.C.: Democratic National Committee, 1976).
33. Barbara Jordan, "Profile of Barbara Jordan, Interviewed by Dan Rather," broadcast June 17, 1979, *Vital History Cassettes* (New York: Encyclopedia Americana/CBS News Audio Resource Library), cassette no. 1, code 06791.
34. Ibid.
35. Associated Press, "Barbara Jordan is Hospitalized," *New York Times,* July 31, 1988, sec. 1, p. 24.
36. Jack Nelson, "Democrats Call for National Renewal, Rip Bush, Perot," *Los Angeles Times,* July 14, 1992, A-1; Sam Fulwood, III, "Feeling Betrayed Some See Ex-Lawmaker's Attack on 'Black Racism' as a Ploy to Boost White Vote," *Los Angeles Times,* July 16, 1992, A-6.
37. Ibid.
38. Gill, "Talented Ten."

Chapter 4   Yvonne Brathwaite Burke

1. Interview with Yvonne Brathwaite Burke by the author, June 5, 1996.
2. Brian Lanker, *I Dream a World: Portraits of Black Women Who Changed America* (New York: Stewart, Tabori and Chang, 1989), 131.
3. Shirelle Phelps, ed., and William C. Matney, Jr., consulting ed., *Who's Who among Black Americans,* 8th ed. (Chicago: Gale, 1994).
4. Clay, *Just Permanent Interests,* 219.
5. Lanker, *I Dream a World,* 131.
6. Interview with Yvonne Brathwaite Burke by the author, June 5, 1996.
7. Clay, *Just Permanent Interests,* 257.
8. Ibid, 331.
9. Lanker, *I Dream a World,* 131.

Chapter 5   Cardiss Robertson Collins

1. U.S. House of Representatives, "Music Lyrics and Commerce," *Hearings before the Subcommittee on Commerce, Consumer Protection and Competitiveness of the Committee on Energy and Commerce,* serial no. 103-112, 103d Cong., 2d sess. (Washington, D.C.: GPO, 1994), 2.
2. Ibid.
3. Ibid.
4. David Smallwood, "The Distinguished Lady from Illinois," *N'Digo Magapaper,* Chicago, Oct. 27–Nov. 9, 1994, 9.
5. Clay, *Just Permanent Interests,* 310.
6. U.S. House of Representatives, *Slow Progress Regarding Affirmative Action in the Airline Industry,* fifty-sixth report by the Committee on Government Operations, July 19, 1988 (Washington, D.C.: GPO, 1988), 23–26.

7. Marjorie Margolies-Mezvinsky with Barbara Feinman, *A Woman's Place: The Freshmen Women Who Changed the Face of Congress* (New York: Crown, 1994), 138.
8. Ibid.
9. Ibid.

Chapter 6   Katie Beatrice Green Hall

1. U.S. House of Representatives, H.R. 3345, *Congressional Record,* 98th Cong., 1st sess., Aug. 2, 1983, 22208–22243.
2. Alan Ehrenhalt, ed., *Politics in America: Members of Congress in Washington and at Home* (Washington, D.C.: Congressional Quarterly Press, 1983), 494–495.
3. Ibid.
4. Ibid., 494.
5. Library of Congress, *Women in Congress, 1917–1990* (Washington, D.C.: GPO, 1991), 61–62.
6. Clay, *Just Permanent Interests,* 100–102.
7. Ibid., 99.
8. Ibid., 101.
9. U.S. House, H.R. 3345, 22218.
10. Ibid., 22211.
11. Mary Cohn, ed., "Martin Luther King Holiday," *Congressional Quarterly Almanac,* 98th Cong., 1st sess. (Washington, D.C.: Congressional Quarterly, 1984), 39:600–602.
12. E. R. Shipp, "Rep. Katie Hall Facing Tough Fight in Indiana," *New York Times,* May 7, 1984, sec. B, p. 8.
13. Ibid.
14. Ibid.
15. Associated Press, "Indiana Recount Finds No Votes Are Changed," *New York Times,* July 12, 1984, 16.

Chapter 7   Delegate Eleanor Holmes Norton

1. Congressional Black Caucus Legislative Weekend, Breakfast Forum, 1993.
2. Lanker, *I Dream a World,* 147.
3. Paula Giddings, *When and Where I Enter: The Impact of Black Women on Race and Sex in America* (New York: Bantam Books, 1984), 293.
4. Phelps and Matney, *Who's Who among Black Americans.*
5. Lanker, *I Dream a World,* 147.
6. John LoDico, "Eleanor Holmes Norton," *Contemporary Black Biography* (Chicago: Gale, 1994), 7:212.
7. Giddings, *When and Where I Enter,* 344.
8. The only black public television station in the nation (WHMM), four major black-owned radio stations (WOL, WKYS, WMMJ, and WHUR), two African American–controlled community radio stations on the FM frequency (WPFW, a Pacifica station, and WDCU, the University of the District of Columbia's radio station), and five major black weeklies (the *Washington Afro-American,* the *Capitol Spotlight,* the *Washington Observer,* the *Washington Informer,* and the *National Chronicle*) were all either black-owned or black-controlled.
9. The District of Columbia is divided for purposes of voting into eight wards. Ward 3 is known as "West of the Park," meaning Rock Creek Park. It has the highest concentration of white voters, who generally vote in a bloc.
10. Sharon Pratt Dixon, married the first year of her term (1993) and became known as Sharon Pratt Kelly.
11. The other four delegates are the representatives from Puerto Rico, Guam, American Samoa, and the Virgin Islands. The Puerto Rican representative is called the resident commissioner.

Chapter 8   Maxine Waters

1. Congressional Black Caucus Legislative Weekend, Breakfast Forum, 1993.
2. Lanker, *I Dream a World,* 36.
3. Ibid.

4. Eleanor Cliff and Tom Brazaitis, *War without Bloodshed: The Art of Politics* (New York: Scribner, 1996), 277.
5. This quote as with others in the sections to follow are from Gill, "Talented Ten."
6. Maxine Waters, "A Letter from Maxine," reprint provided by the office of Congresswoman Maxine Waters.

Chapter 9   Barbara-Rose Collins

1. This quotation, the epigraph above, and others in the sections that follow are from Gill, "Talented Ten."
2. Albert B. Cleage, Jr., *The Black Messiah* (New York: Sheed and Ward, 1968), 7.

Chapter 10   Carol Moseley-Braun

1. Edward Walsh, "Carol Braun's Rocky Road to History: After the Upset, It's Still a Long Way to the Senate," *Washington Post,* Apr. 28, 1992, C1.
2. This quotation, the epigraph above, and others in this chapter are from Gill, "Talented Ten."
3. U.S. Senate, *Congressional Record,* 103d Cong., 1st sess., July 22, 1993, S9257–9286.
4. Ibid.
5. Ibid.
6. Ibid.
7. Ibid.
8. Linda Himelstein, "Confederate Daughters' Insignia Hits Senate Snag," *Legal Times,* Washington, D.C., Apr. 5, 1993, 4.

Chapter 11   Corrine Brown

1. Zora Neale Hurston, *Mules and Men* (New York: HarperPerennial, 1990), 2.
2. Michael Barone and Grant Ujifusa, *The Almanac of American Politics, 1994* (Washington, D.C.: National Journal, 1993), 270.
3. N. Y. Nathiri, *ZORA! Zora Neale Hurston: A Woman and Her Community* (Orlando: Orlando Sentinel Communications, 1991), 120–122.
4. Clay, *Just Permanent Interests,* 28.
5. This quotation, the epigraph above, and others in this chapter are from Gill, "Talented Ten."
6. "Indigo, an Asset of Incalculable Value," *Orlando Sentinel Tribune,* Feb. 27, 1993, A14.
7. Katherine Shaver, "Thurman, Brown Join Freshmen in Capitol Hill Orientation," *States News Service,* Washington, D. C., Dec. 3, 1992.

Chapter 12   Carrie Pittman Meek

1. Congressional Black Caucus Legislative Weekend, September, 1993.
2. Ibid.
3. This quotation, the epigraph above, and others in this chapter are from Gill, "Talented Ten."
4. David A. Bositis, *The Congressional Black Caucus in the 103rd Congress* (Washington, D.C.: Joint Center for Political and Economic Studies, 1994), 137.
5. Copy of the original statement was provided by the office of Congresswoman Meek.

Chapter 13   Cynthia Ann McKinney

1. Congressional Quarterly, *Congressional Districts in the 1990s: A Portrait of America* (Washington, D.C.: Congressional Quarterly Press, 1993), 1.
2. Press conference in the House of Representatives press room, June 29, 1995.
3. Ibid.
4. Ibid.
5. Dorothy Gilliam, "With Rights under Attack, Time to Act," *Washington Post,* July 1, 1995, B-1.

6. Press conference.
7. Gilliam, "With Rights under Attack."
8. This quotation, the epigraph above, and others in this chapter are from Gill, "Talented Ten."
9. Michael Barone and Grant Ujifusa, *The Almanac of American Politics, 1988* (Washington, D.C.: National Journal, 1988), 352.
10. Marjorie Margolies-Mezvinsky with Barbara Feinman, *A Woman's Place: The Freshmen Women Who Changed the Face of Congress* (New York: Crown, 1994), 138.
11. Ibid., xii.

Chapter 14   Eva McPherson Clayton

1. This quotation, the epigraph above, and others in this chapter are from Gill, "Talented Ten."
2. Congressional Quarterly, *Politics in America 1994: The 103rd Congress* (Washington, D.C.: Congressional Quarterly Press, 1993), 118.
3. Marian Burros, "Even Women at Top Still Have Floors to Do," *New York Times,* May 31, 1993, sec. 1, p. 1.
4. Barone and Ujifusa, eds., *Almanac of American Politics, 1994,* 941.
5. *Congressional Record,* 46th Cong., 2d sess., Jan. 29, 1901, 1638; quoted in Clay, *Just Permanent Interests* (New York: Amistad, 1993), 42.
6. Jessica Lee, "Women Build Capitol Clout: Perspective on Issues Now Being Sought," *USA Today,* May 4, 1993, 1-A.
7. Jack Nelson, "The Supreme Court: High Court's Opinion on Racial Gerrymandering," *New York Times,* June 28, 1993, sec. A, p. 12.
8. Ibid.
9. Ibid.

Chapter 15   Eddie Bernice Johnson

1. This quotation, the epigraph above, and others in this chapter are from Gill, "Talented Ten."

Chapter 16   Sheila Jackson-Lee

1. This quotation, as with others in the chapter, are from the author's subsequent interviews with Congresswoman Jackson-Lee.

Bibliography

Anderson, Paul. "Immigration Panel Backs Data Bank." *Miami Herald,* Aug. 4, 1994, A-1.

Associated Press. "Barbara Jordan Is Hospitalized." *New York Times,* July 31, 1988, sec. 1, p. 24.

———. "GAO Urges Action in Chisholm Case." *New York Times,* Nov. 17, 1973, 1.

———. "Indiana Recount Finds No Votes Are Changed." *New York Times,* July 12, 1984, 16.

Barone, Michael, and Grant Ujifusa. *The Almanac of American Politics, 1994.* Washington, D.C.: National Journal, 1993.

Berg, Beatrice. "Brooklyn Freshman." *Washington Post,* Dec. 6, 1968, H1.

Bonmeier, James. "Panel May Hold Key to Consensus on Immigration." *Los Angeles Times,* July 11, 1994, 1.

Bositis, David A. *The Congressional Black Caucus in the 103rd Congress.* Washington, D.C.: Joint Center for Political and Economic Studies, 1994.

Bryant, Ira. *Barbara Charline Jordan: From the Ghetto to the Capitol.* Houston: D. Armstrong, 1977.

Burros, Marian. "Even Women at Top Still Have Floors to Do." *New York Times,* May 31, 1993, sec. 1, p. 1.

Cable News Network. *Both Sides with Jesse Jackson.* July 3, 1993. Transcript no. 78, Washington, D.C.

Chisholm, Shirley. "Representative Shirley Chisholm Declares Her Candidacy for the Democratic Presidential Nomination, Jan. 25, 1972, in Brooklyn, N.Y." *Vital History Cassettes.* New York: Encyclopedia Americana, CBS News Audio Resource Library, cassette no. 2 for February 1972, side A, code 02772, New York.

———. *Shirley Chisholm: Unbought and Unbossed.* Boston: Houghton Mifflin, 1970.

———. *The Good Fight.* New York: Harper & Row, 1973.

Clay, William L. *Just Permanent Interests: Black Americans in Congress, 1870–1992.* Updated ed. New York: Amistad, 1993.

Cleage, Albert B., Jr. *The Black Messiah.* New York: Sheed and Ward, 1968.

Clift, Eleanor, and Tom Brazaitis. *War without Bloodshed: The Art of Politics.* New York: Scribner, 1996.

Cohn, Mary, ed. "Martin Luther King Holiday." *Congressional Quarterly Almanac,* 98th Cong., 1st sess., 1983. Washington, D.C.: Congressional Quarterly, 1984, vol. 39.

Congressional Quarterly. *Congressional Districts in the 1990s: A Portrait of America.* Washington, D.C.: Congressional Quarterly Press, 1993.

———. *Politics in America 1994: The 103rd Congress.* Washington, D.C.: Congressional Quarterly Press, 1993.

Davis, Angela Y. *Women, Race & Class.* New York: Vintage Books, 1983.

"Debating Team Brings Prestige to Black College." Special: Campus Journal. *New York Times,* June 3, 1992, 7.

Degregorio, William A. *The Complete Book of U.S. Presidents.* New York: Barricade Books, 1993.

Ehrenhalt, Alan, ed. *Politics in America: Members of Congress in Washington and at Home.* Washington, D.C.: Congressional Quarterly Press, 1983.

Fulwood, Sam, III. "Feeling Betrayed Some See Ex-Lawmaker's Attack on 'Black Racism' as a Ploy to Boost White Vote." *Los Angeles Times,* July 16, 1992, sec. A, p. 6.

Giddings, Paula. *When and Where I Enter: The Impact of Black Women on Race and Sex in America.* New York: Bantam Books, 1984.

Gilliam, Dorothy. "With Rights under Attack, Time to Act." *Washington Post,* July 1, 1995, B-1.

Githens, Marianne, Pippa Norris, Joni Lovenduski, eds. *Different Roles, Different Voices: Women and Politics in the United States and Europe.* New York: HarperCollins, 1992.

Himelstein, Linda. "Confederate Daughters' Insignia Hits Senate Snag." *Legal Times,* Washington, D.C., Apr. 5, 1993, 4.

Hines, Darlene Clark, Elsa Barkley Brown, Rosalyn Terborg-Penn, eds. *Black Women in America: An Historical Encyclopedia.* Vols. 1 and 2. Bloomington: Indiana University Press, 1994.

Hope, Paul. "Dressing Up the Campaign Trail." *The Evening Star,* Washington, D.C., March 14, 1972, A-l.

Howard, Jane. "A Shaker-Upper Wants to Be Madame President Chisholm." *Life Magazine,* Nov. 5, 1971, 5.

Hurston, Zora Neale. *Mules and Men.* New York: HarperPerennial, 1990.

"Indigo, an Asset of Incalculable Value." *Orlando Sentinel Tribune,* Feb. 27, 1993, A14.

Jacobs, Joanne. "National ID Menace to Rights." *Miami Herald,* Aug. 22, 1994, A-13.

Jordan, Barbara. "The House Judiciary Committee's Impeachment Debate, July 25, 1974, Washington, D.C." *Vital History Cassettes.* New York: Encyclopedia Americana, cassette no. 2, code 07742. CBS News Audio Resource Library, New York.

———. Keynote Address. Democratic National Convention. *Official Proceedings of the Democratic National Convention.* Washington, D.C.: Democratic National Committee, 1976.

———. "Profile of Barbara Jordan, Interviewed by Dan Rather." Broadcast June 17, 1979. *Vital History Cassettes.* New York: Encyclopedia Americana, cassette no. 1, code 06791. CBS News Audio Resource Library, New York.

Jordan, Barbara, and Shelby Hearon. *Barbara Jordan: A Self-Portrait.* New York: Doubleday, 1979.

Lanker, Brian. *I Dream a World: Portraits of Black Women Who Changed America.* New York: Stewart, Tabori and Chang, 1989.

Lee, Jessica. "Women Build Capitol Clout: Perspective on Issues Now Being Sought." *USA Today,* May 4, 1993, 1-A.

Library of Congress. *Biographical Directory of the United States Congress, 1774–1994.* Washington, D.C.: Government Printing Office, 1994.

———. *Women in Congress, 1917–1990.* Washington, D.C.: Government Printing Office, 1991.

LoDico, John. "Eleanor Holmes Norton." *Contemporary Black Biography.* Vol. 7. Chicago: Gale, 1994.

Margolies-Mezvinsky, Marjorie, with Barbara Feinman. *A Woman's Place: The Freshmen Women Who Changed the Face of Congress.* New York: Crown, 1994.

Nathiri, N. Y. *ZORA! Zora Neale Hurston: A Woman and Her Community.* Orlando: Orlando Sentinel Communications, 1991.

Nelson, Jack. "Democrats Call for National Renewal, Rip Bush, Perot." *Los Angeles Times,* July 14, 1992, sec. A, p. 1.

———. "The Supreme Court: High Court's Opinion on Racial Gerrymandering." *New York Times,* June 28, 1993, sec. A, p. 12.

Phelps, Shirelle, ed., and William C. Matney, Jr., consulting ed. *Who's Who among Black Americans.* 8th ed. Chicago: Gale, 1994.

Schlesinger, Arthur M., Jr., ed. *The Almanac of American History.* New York: Barnes & Noble Books, 1993.

Shaver, Katherine. "Thurman, Brown Join Freshmen in Capitol Hill Orientation." *States News Service,* Washington, D.C., Dec. 3, 1992.

Shelton, Elizabeth. "Our Full Share." *Washington Post,* Apr. 28, 1969, B1.

Shipp, E. R. "Rep. Katie Hall Facing Tough Fight in Indiana," *New York Times,* May 7, 1984, sec. B, p. 8.

Smallwood, David. "The Distinguished Lady from Illinois." *N'Digo Magapaper,* Chicago, Oct. 27–Nov. 9, 1994, p. 9.

Tiede, Tom. "Mrs. Chisholm: Political Trailblazer." *Washington Post,* Apr. 28, 1969, B1.

Trescott, Jacqueline. "Shirley Chisholm in Her Season of Transition." *Washington Post,* June 6, 1982, H1.

U.S. House of Representatives. "Conference on Women's Employment." *Hearings before the Special Subcommittee on Education of the Committee on Education and Labor.* 91st Cong., 2d sess. Washington, D.C.: Government Printing Office, 1970.

———. *Congressional Record.* 98th Cong., 1st sess., Aug. 2, 1983.

———. "Music Lyrics and Commerce." *Hearings before the Subcommittee on Commerce, Consumer Protection and Competitiveness of the Committee on Energy and Commerce.* Serial no. 103-112. 103d Cong., 2d sess. Washington, D.C.: Government Printing Office, 1994.

———. *Slow Progress Regarding Affirmative Action in the Airline Industry.* Fifty-sixth report by the Committee on Government Operations, July 19, 1988. Washington, D.C.: Government Printing Office, 1988.

Vobejda, Barbara. "Children Show Congress Scars of Gun Violence: Panel Hears Pleas to Limit Sales of Weapons." *Washington Post,* Mar. 11, 1993, A16.

Walsh, Edward. "Carol Braun's Rocky Road to History: After the Upset, It's Still a Long Way to the Senate." *Washington Post,* Apr. 28, 1992, C1.

Walters, Ronald W. *Black Presidential Politics in America: A Strategy Approach.* New York: State University of New York Press, 1988.

Waters, Maxine. "A Letter from Maxine." Reprint. Congressional Office of Congresswoman Maxine Waters.

Index

Clarke, Joe, 169, 170
classism, 2–4, 8, 28, 54
Clay, William L. (Bill), 32, 64–65, 78, 79, 91, 250
Clayton, Eva McPherson, 7–8, 81, 224, 247, 252; on
  Agriculture Committee, 206; birth, 206;
  congressional data, 206; as congressional freshman
  class president, 213–216; congressional years,
  212–220; early years, 208; education, 206; election
  strategy, 211; family, 206; political odyssey, 208–212;
  professional/political background, 206; religion, 206;
  résumé, 206; selected awards/organizational
  affiliations, 206; and Technical Resources
  International, Ltd. (TRI), 206, 209
Clayton, Theaoseus, 206, 208
Cleage, Albert Jr., 136, 138–141
Clinton, Hillary Rodham, 230
Clinton, William Jefferson (Bill), 83, 119, 154, 155,
  245; denunciation of Carol Moseley-Braun's
  Nigerian trip, 248; and District of Columbia
  statehood, 111–112; Haitian policy of, 178–179;
  Eddie Bernice Johnson and, 229; Barbara Jordan
  and, 38, 53, 54; and North American Free Trade
  Agreement (NAFTA), 77; and 103d Congressional
  legislative agenda, 142, 188, 214–215; nominates
  Shirley Chisholm for Jamaican ambassador, 16, 34;
  political support from Maxine Waters, 127–131;
  and Sister Souljah, 71
Clyburn, James, E., 213, 252
Coalition of 100 Black Women, 56, 68
Collins, Barbara-Rose, 7, 81, 124, 247, 251; alleged
  misuse of scholarship funds, 143, 247; birth, 134;
  campaign financing irregularities, 143;
  congressional bid, 139; congressional data, 134;
  congressional years, 142–144; early years, 136–139;
  education, 134; family, 134; and Federal Elections
  Commission, 144; five-prong legislative program,
  143; on Government Operations Committee
  (renamed Government Reform and Oversight
  under 104th Congress), 134; and House Ethics
  Committee, 144; and nationalist movement, 136;
  and Office of Fair Employment Practices, 143;
  political odyssey, 139–142; on Post Office and Civil
  Service Committee, 134; professional/political
  background, 134; on Public Works and
  Transportation Committee (renamed
  Transportation and Infrastructure), 134; religion,
  134; résumé, 134; selected awards/organizational
  affiliations, 134; and Unremunerated Work Act of
  1993, 142; urban agenda of, 142
Collins, Cardiss Robertson, 3, 6–8, 52, 63, 89, 124, 131,
  142, 149, 202, 246, 250; and airline industry, 77, 80,
  240; birth, 68, 75; congressional data, 68;
  congressional years, 76–83; early years, 75–76;
  education, 68; on Commerce Committee, 68, 77;
  family, 68; and gangster rap music hearings, 70–83;
  on Government Operations Committee, 76, 82;
  legislative record, 74–80; on Manpower and
  Housing Subcommittee of Government Operations,
  80; professional/political background, 68; religion,
  68; résumé, 68; retirement of, 8; selected
  awards/organizational affiliations, 68; on
  Subcommittee on Telecommunications, 70, 72, 80;
  and telecommunications industry, 74, 77–79, 82
Collins, Cynthia, 137
Collins, Gary, 137
Collins, George Washington, 68, 74, 76, 77, 250
Columbia University, 14, 21, 103

communists, 61, 92
Community Development Banking bill, 132
Conference of Black Elected Officials, 33
Congressional Black Caucus (CBC), 75, 105, 123, 133,
  159, 178, 180, 247; Annual Dinner, 1980, 78; Yvonne
  Brathwaite Burke chairs, 64–66; chair of, 65, 78, 79;
  Shirley Anita St. Hill Chisholm and, 18, 26, 28–33;
  Cardiss Robertson Collins chairs, 77–79;
  Foundation, 64, 252; Gary Convention, 61–62;
  Barbara Jordan and, 51–52; leadership, 64;
  Legislative Weekend, 64, 100, 190; and Martin
  Luther King, Jr., Holiday legislation, 90–93; Carrie
  Meek and, 185, 188, 190; and North American Free
  Trade Agreement (NAFTA), 130, 229; and
  redistricting, 193–198, 224; in 103d Congress,
  213–219
Congressional Caucus for Women, 68, 213, 219
Congressional Record, 157, 189
congressional seniority system, 6, 26, 27, 75, 82
Congress of Racial Equality (CORE), 25
Connally, John, 52
conservatives, 72, 77, 81, 82, 118, 154, 178, 193
consumers: advocates for, 215; protection of, 77
contiguous districts, 218. *See also* redistricting
Contract with America, 118–121, 240–241
Conyers, John Jr., 27, 33, 41, 78, 90–93, 250
Cook County, Ill., 76
Cook County Recorder of Deeds, 148, 151
Coppin State College, 14
CORE, *see* Congress of Racial Equality
corporate layoffs, 217, 246
Cosby, Bill, 41
Cox, Archibald, 41
crack cocaine, 74, 107, 114, 129
Crawford, Jack, 93, 94
Crawford, Janie, 169
crime, 3, 119, 126–129
crime bill, *see* omnibus anti-crime bill (1993)
Crockett, George Jr., 141–142, 251
Crown Heights, N.Y., 25
C-SPAN, 107, 158, 224
Cullen, Countee, 184

Dade County Community College, 182, 187
Daley, Richard Sr., 75, 79
Daley machine, 76
Dallas, Tex., 223–227, 229, 230
Dallas Veterans Administration Hospital, 225
Davis, Angela, 4
Davis, Danny, 79
Dawson, William L., 250
day care, *see* child care
Daytona Beach, Fla., 167, 171, 186
Decatur, Ga., 194
Dekalb County, Ga., 192
DeLarge, Robert C., 249
Dellums, Ronald V., 29, 32, 93, 198, 250
DeLoach, George, L., 201
Delta Sigma Theta Sorority, 14, 36, 48, 182
Democratic National Committee (DNC), 40–41, 66
Democratic National Committee chair, 32, 33, 52
Democratic National Convention: (1964), 102–103;
  (1968), 23, 36; (1972), 6, 29, 31–33, 56, 58, 59, 62,
  66; (1976), 53; (1980), 78; (1992), 111, 127
Democratic party, 17, 25, 27, 29, 33, 59, 71, 82, 100,
  112, 178, 196, 234; agenda, 242; Caucus, 123, 153;
  centrists, 53, 54; Committee headquarters, 40, 41;

About the Author

Photo: Oggi Ogburn

LaVerne McCain Gill is the producer and creator of the 1994 public radio special "The Talented Ten: African American Women in the 103rd Congress." As former publisher of a weekly newspaper and news commentator on WETA public television, Ms. Gill held membership in the Congressional Press Gallery from 1987 to 1994. She was also an aide to U.S. Senator Alan Cranston. She has received numerous awards, including the 1992 Capital Area Emmy nomination for her public television special on teen sexuality and a 1992 German Borscht Foundation journalistic study fellowship. Ms. Gill was also selected for inclusion in the 1994 edition of *Who's Who among Black Americans.* She co-anchored the national radio broadcast of the Congressional Black Caucus's "Women in Jazz" program and solo-anchored the national radio address of the historic 1990 speech of Winnie Mandela in Washington, D.C.

Ms. Gill holds an M.B.A. from Rutgers University and a B.A. from Howard University. She has taught on the faculties of Howard University, the University of California at Berkeley extension program, and the University of the District of Columbia. She is currently a candidate for a Master of Divinity at Princeton Theological Seminary in Princeton, New Jersey.